PROOF OF AUTHORITY

AN EVIDENTIAL APPROACH TO A BIBLICALLY CHRISTIAN WORLDVIEW

David Wayne Meeker

PROOF OF AUTHORITY

AN EVIDENTIAL APPROACH TO A BIBLICALLY CHRISTIAN WORLDVIEW

Published by Last Chance Music Ministry

David Wayne Meeker

PROOF OF AUTHORITY
By David Wayne Meeker
Copyright ©2021 David Wayne Meeker
All rights reserved worldwide.

ISBN 979-8-9853834-2-3

1. Main category—[Bible] 2. Other categories—[Apologetics]—[Theology, Doctrine]

Published by Last Chance Music Ministry, Hutto, Texas.
Preliminary and general editing services provided by Laura Meeker. Formatting and production art by Don and Donna Marie Benjamin of *Elevation Press*. General editing by Wayne McKenzie and Rene Janiece of *Bittersweet Highway*.
Front cover photo ©Hriana/dreamstime.com.
Back cover photo courtesy of Laura Meeker.
Puzzle piece designed by Pixel Perfect from Flaticon/Freepik. Vintage roses on Memorial page designed by dgim-studio/Freepik.
All Scriptures are The Holy Bible, Berean Study Bible, BSB.
©2016, 2018, by Bible Hub unless otherwise noted.
Used by permission. All rights reserved worldwide.
Comparative Religion Charts adapted from *So What's the Difference?* by Fritz Ridenour. Published by Regal Books ©1976 by Gospel Light Publications, Glendale, CA 91209. Used by permission. All rights reserved.
Eyewitness Chapter: Chronological order of Jesus' Death, Burial and Resurrection adapted from *Harmony of the Gospels*, By Thomas & Gundry, Published by Moody Press ©1978 and *A Harmony of the Four Gospels* by Orville E. Daniel published by Baker Book House Company, Inc. ©1987. Used by permission. All rights reserved.
50 Biblical Figures, taken from *Bible History Daily* ©2016. Used by permission. All rights reserved.
References and Inferences to Genesis in the New Testament adapted from *The Defender's Study Bible*, ©1995 by Word Publishing, Inc. All rights reserved. Used by permission.
Worldview Creed adapted from CARM Apologetics notebook page 222 by Matthew J. Slick, M. Div, ©2003. Used by permission. All rights reserved.
Internal Consistency Chapter, "Harmony of the Gospels" taken from *Blue Letter Bible* ©2016. Used by permission. All rights reserved.
Scientific Consistency Chapter – Reality Check Chart taken from Ray Comfort at *Living Waters.com/Way of the Master*. Used by permission. All rights reserved.
Majority of images used in this book are public domain and were obtained from www.publicdomainpictures.net.

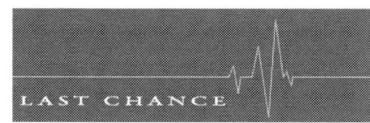

© 2021
Last Chance Music Ministry
lastchancemusic1@aol.com

PRESENTED TO:

Terry + Christy Michaels

Ph.1:21

FROM:

David + Laura Meeker

ON:

Sunday, June 23, 2024

In Loving Memory

Douglas Alan Bender
(1950–2017)

&

Ruth Campbell Satterfield
(1926–2019)

ACKNOWLEDGEMENTS

I have four acknowledgments.

The first and most important acknowledgment I can ever make in this life is to thank the Triune Creator God (Ge. 1:1-2, 26; Mt. 28:19). I thank the Father, the Son and the Holy Spirit. The Son is the one and only true Superhero ever to walk on planet Earth—my Lord and Savior Jesus Christ, who was sent by the Father to save the people of this world from the consequences of their rebellion (Jn. 3:16-18; Col. 1:13), who is literally the Way, the Truth and the Life, and in Him dwells all the fullness of the Godhead bodily (Jn. 14:6; Col. 2:9). And I thank the Holy Spirit, who is the very breath of Scripture (2Ti. 3:16).

Second, I want to thank my wife, Laura, for her preliminary and general editing and all her prayers and encouragement during my seven years of systematic research and investigation to obtain the sources and materials necessary to establish the information presented in *Proof of Authority*. Also, I want to thank both my dad and mom, Doug and Lynn, for their Christian example of Christ's love that they have displayed so clearly in my life.

Third, I acknowledge that I will be making no claims of originality for my book. I have relied heavily upon the works of many of the great defenders of the Christian faith from both the preceding and present generations. In addition to giving credit to each person and organization for the material I have used, I feel a special desire to acknowledge my gratitude to these amazing soldiers for Christ.

- I acknowledge Pastor Chuck Smith[1] who first introduced me to the saving knowledge of Jesus Christ through his book-by-book, chapter-by-chapter and verse-by-verse teaching of the Holy Bible.
- I thank Josh McDowell[2] and Gary R. Habermas[3] for opening my eyes to the evidential truth of Biblical Christianity.

---

1 Founder and Senior Pastor of The Calvary Chapel Movement and the *Word for Today* radio broadcast.
2 *The New Evidence that Demands a Verdict* ©1999 by Josh McDowell. Published by Thomas Nelson, Nashville.
3 *The Verdict of History* ©1988 by Gary R. Habermas, Published by Thomas Nelson, Nashville.

- Thanks to William Lane Craig[4], John Lennox[5] and Norman L. Geisler[6] for their brilliant and compelling apologetics in defense of the Christian faith.
- Last but not least, I acknowledge R. C. Sproul[7], John MacArthur[8] and Paul Washer[9] for their faithful hermeneutic and solid exposition of Scripture and also many others, from whom I have, knowingly or unknowingly, drawn ideas.

Fourth, I acknowledge that this book is being sent out into a lost and dying world with the prayer that it may help many people who search for truth, meaning, and purpose in this life. I write in the fervent hope that this book will ultimately lead to the lost being found and the dead being made alive.

Sincerely,
David Wayne Meeker

---

[4] *Reasonable Faith: Christian Truth and Apologetics* © 1994 by William Lane Craig, Published by Crossway Books.
[5] Lennox is a mathematician and Christian apologist. He is Emeritus of Mathematics at the University of Oxford and an Emeritus Fellow in Mathematics and Philosophy of Science at Green Templeton College, Oxford University.
[6] *Christian Apologetics* ©1976 by Norman L. Geisler, Published by Baker Book House Company.
[7] R. C. Sproul—Theologian and founder of *Ligonier Ministries*.
[8] John MacArthur is pastor-teacher of Grace Community Church in Sun Valley, Calif. He is also president of The Master's University and Seminary.
[9] Paul Washer is founder and missions director of HeartCry Missionary Society.

PROOF OF AUTHORITY
*is lovingly dedicated to
our grandchildren.*

CONTENTS

To the Reader .... page 1
Quotes .... page 10
Introduction .... page 13
Proof One—Archaeological Evidence .... page 41
    a) Chapter Premise
    b) Quotes
    c) 50 Events, Places and Object
    d) 50 Biblical Figures
    e) Maps
    f) Evidence to Evaluate

Proof Two—Predictive Prophecy .... page 61
    a) Chapter Premise
    b) Chronological Dates to the Books of the Bible
    c) Sixty-one Messianic Prophecies in the Old Testament Identifying the Person of Christ
    d) Evidence to Evaluate

Proof Three—Scientific Consistency .... page 77
    a) Quotes
    b) Chapter Premise
    c) Scientific Facts That Agree with the Holy Bible
    d) Intelligent Design, Darwinian Evolution, and Atheism
    e) How Old Are Dinosaur Fossils?
    f) Evidence to Evaluate

Proof Four—Eyewitness Evidence .... page 103
    a) Chapter Premise
    b) Chronological Evidence Found in the Gospels
    c) Early Christian Martyrs Chart
    d) Evidence to Evaluate

Proof Five—Historical Evidence .... page 119
    a) Chapter Premise
    b) Historical Confirmation of Jesus Outside the Holy Bible
    c) Extra-Biblical Historical Evidence for Christ's Life, Teachings, Christianity, Crucifixion and Resurrection
    d) Evidence to Evaluate

Proof Six—Internal Consistency .... page 129
    a) Chapter Premise
    b) Chronological Dates of the Books of the Holy Bible

    c) Jesus: from Genesis to Revelation
    d) Types and Symbols of Christ in the Holy Bible
    e) Old Testament Citations Found in the New Testament
    f) History of Salvation in the Old Testament: Preparing the Way for Christ
    g) The Harmony of the Four Gospels
    h) Christophanies
    i) Evidence to Evaluate

Proof Seven—Manuscript Evidence .... page 157
    a) Chapter Premise
    b) Comparison of Work of Antiquity Chart
    c) Evidence to Evaluate

Proof Eight—Miracles .... page 169
    a) Chapter Premise
    b) Miracles in the Old Testament
    c) Miracles in the New Testament
    d) Evidence to Evaluate

Proof Nine—Mathematical Probability .... page 183
    a) Chapter Premise
    b) Interesting Odds
    c) Just Eight Prophecies
    d) Evidence to Evaluate

World Religions and Cults vs. Biblical Christianity .... page 191
    a) Chapter Premise
    b) Five What-ifs
    c) Religions and Cults vs. Biblical Christianity Charts
    d) Dogmas Declared by the Roman Catholic Church
    e) Evidence to Evaluate

Final Conclusion .... page 219

Rationalizations of Unbelief .... page 255

A Biblical Worldview Creed .... page 261

Examine Yourself Test .... page 263

The Three Steps of Becoming a Christian .... page 271

Terms and Definitions .... page 273

Helpful Resources and Organizations .... page 283

Helpful Websites .... page 285

The Gospel of John .... page 289

TO THE READER

Dear Reader,
Proof of Authority is designed and recommended to be read along with the following:
1. text of the Holy Bible—(Mandatory)
{and}
2. internet capability—(Optional).

The Holy Bible's primary focus is on the Person of Christ. According to the Holy Bible, being right about Jesus Christ is critically important (1Co. 16:22) and those who preach a different Christ are accursed (Ga. 1:8-9). This is why reading, determining, and understanding the Holy Bible correctly is so important. There are two primary requirements necessary with regard to our ability to determine and understand both the meaning and purpose of the Holy Bible. The first requirement is obvious—it must be read (Ro. 10:17). The second requirement is not so obvious, unless you read it!

Once the Holy Bible has been read and its meaning has been generally determined, it can only be understood correctly through its proper interpretation (Ac. 8:30-31), and the proper interpretation can only be obtained through the teaching ministry and work of God the Holy Spirit (Jn. 14:17, 25-26; 16:13; 1Jn. 2:27; Lu. 12:12).

The Holy Bible tells us that it cannot be fully determined or understood without both a Holy Spirit driven desire and submission to first read it, together with the Holy Spirit's Work of Interpretation. It must be taught to us by God the Holy Spirit due to the fact that the Words found within the Holy Bible are not derived by human wisdom but derived by the Wisdom of God the Holy Spirit. Understanding the Holy Bible's spiritual truths can only be interpreted, perceived, and understood correctly by readers who are filled, taught, and guided by the Holy Spirit (Jn.14:15-18; 16:7-8; Ro. 8:9, 26-27; Is. 11:2). According to the Holy Scripture, God the Holy Spirit is our helper (Jn. 14:26), teacher (1Jn. 2:27), and guide (Ps. 25:5). He gives direction and instruction to us in four essential ways:

1. He guides us in all truth (Jn.16:13).
2. He guides us away from sin (Ga. 5:16).
3. He guides us to our purpose (Lu. 4:18).
4. He guides us to the will of God (Ps.143:10).

"The natural and carnal person does not accept the things of the Spirit of God, for they are folly to him, and he is not able to understand them because they can only be spiritually discerned and understood" (1Co. 2:6-16).

The Holy Bible is both a Divinely Inspired and humanly written book that tells us a true story about the world, the way things are, and the way they should be. This is the reason why we must submit and allow the Holy Spirit to help, teach, and guide us through the reading of His Holy Word.

Another reason why it is so important that we determine, perceive, and understand the content of the Holy Bible correctly is so that we can correctly be conformed and transformed through the justification and sanctification process through the work of the Holy Spirit in our life.

The Holy Bible focuses on God's plan and purpose for the world and its occupants. Again it includes both Justification and Sanctification and we must understand that the Holy Bible is not just written to us, but for us. The Holy Bible is God's tool for transforming us as it shows us the Glory of God and the Beauty of Jesus Christ. It could be read through from cover to cover in 90 days at the rate of 12 pages per day. Incidentally, in the time it takes to watch an average two-hour movie at a theater, a person could have read, at an average pace, the following books of the Holy Bible:

Galatians	Philemon
Ephesians	Titus
Philippians	James
Colossians	1st and 2nd Peter
1st and 2nd Thessalonians	2nd and 3rd John
1st and 2nd Timothy	Jude

Another reason why it is so important to read the Holy Bible is because it shows us our sin and our need for a Savior, (i.e. the Gospel message). It also reveals to us the basic patterns and principles that must be applied in the Christian life. The only thing humans are required to provide is submission. If you want to be a true follower of Jesus Christ, you must submit your behavior, including your will, affection, thought, desire, and understanding completely to God.

When you submit all matters of your conscience to Jesus Christ through the work of the Holy Spirit, the result will lead you to repentance and obedience. Even these necessary components for obtaining salvation are a work (Jn. 16:8-11) and gift (Ro. 3:23-24; 6:23) from God as well. That's because Christian submission is not an act of human will, but rather it is a Divine act of God's will. We can only submit to the will and authority of God (Ja. 4:7; Ep. 5:22, 23) through the power of the Holy Spirit (1Co. 2:4, 5; Ro. 15:13). We must submit to God in a similar way, like Christ submitted to the Father on our behalf upon His cross (Mt. 26:39; He. 5:7-8). Christ submitted all to God (Mk. 14:36; Jn. 6:38), even unto death (Mt. 26:38).

We must understand that the Holy Bible is not just a book that exists through the thoughts and ideas of men. It is not like abstract mythological principles and their philosophies, or like world religions that make claims of Divine Origin and Inspiration without having any evidence to substantiate their claims, (i.e. *Proof of Authority*). The Holy Bible is a book based on real-life stories about actual historical events and happenings,[10] and, within its pages, it also reveals to us the greatest story ever told to the human race (Jn. 3:16-18).

It is a story about the One and Only True God and His persistent plan of loving grace and redemption—loving grace and redemption for every race and nation, despite their sin and rebellion against Him—through the greatest and most influential man who has ever lived in all of history, His Son, Jesus Christ. It is a story that has the potential to change your life for both time and eternity.

---

[10] Huston Smith, *The World's Religions*, 1961, Harper, San Francisco, p.317.

God has given us a book of authentic and true stories based on actual historical events because authentic and truthful stories are the way we learn most naturally.

The God of Biblical Christianity is a God of Truth. He originally created humans in His image and likeness to live *for Him*, learn *from Him* and give worship and praise *to Him* in this life through a sincere, loving, and obedient relationship (Jn. 4:24; Ps. 100:4; Pr. 1:5).

This is one of the reasons why Jesus Christ spoke in so many parables.[11] You might be wondering at this point what exactly is a parable and why did Christ use them? Parables are earthly stories with heavenly meaning that illustrate one or more instructive lessons or principles. The reason why Christ spoke in parables while among the crowds is told to us by Matthew. We are told that Jesus spoke in parables because the people did not see, hear or understand. The reason for their inability to comprehend is because of their rejection of Jesus (Mt. 13:10-17). God could have given us an instruction manual or a textbook to teach us about Himself, mankind, and the world. Instead, He chose to give us a collection of real-life experiences of people who heard His voice, experienced His work, and encountered His presence.

This story is incomplete until you read the Holy Bible and discover God's meaning and purpose for your life. I hope and pray that by the time you finish reading *Proof of Authority*, you will come to the realization that the Holy Bible is without a doubt the most amazing and most incredible book ever produced in the history of humanity. It provides us with more than sufficient evidence proving that it is a gift sent to a lost and dying world from the One and Only True God Himself.

Among all the other religious writings in the world today, the Holy Bible is one-of-a-kind, special, and unique. Its teachings, standards, and principles, are accessible to anyone with a desire to discover them. I believe that the desire to seek God is actually a work of the Holy Spirit (Jn. 16:8), and the reason why it's so important for us to read and understand the stories, principles, and teachings found in the Holy Bible is simply because God has revealed

---

[11] Ps. 78:2; Mt. 13:34-36.

certain essential truths about Himself, man, and the world. The essential truths found in the Holy Bible are the following:

1. Who is God?
2. Who is man?
3. Why is man here on earth?
4. What is going wrong with man and the world?
5. Where is man headed?
6. What is the solution for man's problem?

I will be showing you through *Proof of Authority* that the Holy Bible gives people good reasons for God's existence through its proofs of Supernatural Intervention confirming its claims of Divine Origin and Inspiration. Also, I want to point out that the Holy Bible is not just one single book but is actually a collection of 66 individual ancient historical documents divided into two main sections. The Old Testament—*Christ's redemptive work promised (He. 1:1)* and the New Testament—*Christ's redemptive work fulfilled (He. 1:2-4).* The Great Theologian Augustine put it this way: *"The Old [Testament] is the New [Testament] concealed and the New [Testament] is the Old [Testament] revealed."*

> **Overview of the Bible**
>
> **The Old Testament: 39 Books**
> Genesis through Deuteronomy–Law
> Joshua through Esther–History
> Job through Song of Solomon–Poetry and Proverbs
> Isaiah through Daniel–Major Prophets
> Hosea through Malachi–Minor Prophets
>
> Christ's Redemptive Work Promised (Hebrews 1:1)
>
> **The New Testament: 27 Books**
> Matthew, Mark, Luke, John–Gospels
> Book of Acts–Church History
> Romans through Thessalonians–Church Epistles
> Timothy through Philemon–Pastoral/Individual Epistles
> Hebrews through Jude–General Epistles
> Book of Revelation–Future Events
>
> Christ's Redemptive Work Fulfilled (Hebrews 1:2–4)

The 39 Old Testament books deal with the history and faith of the Jewish people in different time periods throughout history. The 27 New Testament books deal with the life of Christ and the history and growth of the 1st-Century Church. These books have the potential to change your life for both time and eternity.

The Holy Bible contains amazing internal unity and cohesiveness within its sixty-six individual historical documents. The Holy Bible can be categorically divided up into two foundational principles and five fundamental principles of truth without creating any conflicts within its many texts. The two foundational categories are as follows:

    A. The first foundational category is the record of the relationship between God and man.

    B. The second foundational category is the redemptive plan of God for man.

The five fundamental principles of truth are as follows:

1. The God of the Holy Bible is the Creator, Sustainer, and Ruler of the Universe and is the Source of all Moral Authority and cannot lie.[12]
2. The Holy Bible is inspired by God and is the infallible, authoritative rule of faith and ethics, and, in its entirety, is Truth.[13]
3. There is only One God Who exists as a Trinity.[14]
4. Mankind was created good and upright. However, man has voluntarily rebelled against God and has incurred judgment, which includes not only physical and spiritual death, but also includes total separation from God in a place of great suffering and torment for all eternity.[15]
5. Jesus Christ is the only solution for the immortal act of man's rebellion against God.[16]

The Holy Bible teaches us many other things, but these two categories and five principles of truth are essential for the correct understanding of the Biblical Christian worldview. They are the most amazing and important truths ever told to the human race.

Whatever else you might gain through the reading of the Holy Bible, it would be a complete tragedy if you missed the heart of its Message to you—mankind's need for God's gracious provision of Jesus Christ as the atonement for mankind's sin.[17]

---

[12] Ex.3:13, 14; 2Ti. 3:16; Tit. 1:2.
[13] Jn. 17:17; 2Ti. 3:16; 2Pe. 3:16; Ps. 119:160.
[14] Is. 42:8; 44:6, 8; 46:9-10; De. 6:4; Ge. 1:26; Mt. 28:19; Mk. 12:29; Lu. 3:21-22; Jn. 15:26; 1Ti. 2:5; Ja. 2:19. Also, see Trinity in *Terms and Definitions*.
[15] Ro. 3:23; 6:23; 1Jn. 1:8-10; 3:4; Ja. 4:17; Ga. 5:19, 20; Is. 59:2; Ge. 3:1-24.
[16] Ac. 2:38; 4:12; Mt. 1:21; Lu. 2:11; Jn. 3:3-8; 5:13; 14:6; 1Jn. 1:9; 2:13; 5:13; Ro. 10:9; 6:23; 5:10; 3:23.
[17] Ro. 5:10, 11; Jn. 3:16-18.

I pray God will speak to your conscience and intellect as you read *Proof of Authority*. By the time you finish reading the information presented in this book, I hope that you will have a better understanding of both the Biblical and evidential aspects of an authentic Christian faith. I hope and pray that you will submit to the work of the Holy Spirit in your life and come to the saving knowledge of Jesus Christ in Whom our only hope resides.

In Christ's Service,
David Wayne Meeker

proof

–noun

1. evidence sufficient to establish a thing as true, or to produce belief in its truth.

—Dictionary.com

"We account the Scriptures of God to be the most sublime philosophy. I find more sure marks of authenticity in the Bible than in any profane history whatsoever." —**Sir Isaac Newton**

"The Bible is worth all other books which were ever printed."
—**Patrick Henry**

"All human discoveries seem to be made only for the purpose of confirming more and more strongly the truths contained in the Sacred Scriptures."
—**Sir William Herschel**

"There came a time in my life when I doubted the divinity of Scripture, and I resolved as a lawyer and a judge I would try the book as I would try anything in the courtroom, taking evidence for and against. It was a long, serious and profound study and using the same principles of evidence in this religious matter as I do in secular matters, I have come to the decision that the Bible is a supernatural Book, that it has come from God, and that the only safety for the human race is to follow its teachings."
—**Salmon P. Chase**

"It is impossible to mentally or socially enslave a Bible reading people. The principles of the Bible are the groundwork of human freedom."
—**Horace Greeley**

"Men do not reject the Bible because it contradicts itself but because it contradicts them." —**E. Paul Hovey**

"The existence of the Bible, as a book for the people, is the greatest benefit which the human race has ever experienced. Every attempt to belittle it is a crime against humanity." —**Immanuel Kant**

"I believe the Bible is the best gift God has ever given to man. All the good of the Savior of the world is communicated to us through the Book. But for it, we could not know right from wrong?" —**Abraham Lincoln**

"Western literature has been more influenced by the Bible than any other book." —**Thomas B. Macaulay**

"The book to read is not the one which thinks for you, but the one that makes you think. No other book in the world equals the Bible for that." —**James McCosh**

"A thorough understanding of the Bible is better than a college education." —**Theodore Roosevelt**

"Even the style of the Scriptures is more than human." —**Sir Richard Steele**

"It is impossible to rightly govern the world without God and the Bible." —**George Washington**

"The New Testament is the very best book that was or ever will be known in the world." —**Charles Dickens**

"Therefore, faithful Christian, seek the truth, listen to the truth, learn the truth, love the truth, tell the truth, defend the truth even to death." —**John Huss**

"Our evaluation of the Bible and other "holy books" is governed by the recognition that the Bible is the inspired Word of God. If God's final Word is found in what we call the Bible, then no other book can be God's Word. To differ with what the Bible says is to differ with God." —**Rick Wade**

"The Bible grows more beautiful as we grow in our understanding of it." —**Johann Wolfgang von Goethe**

"Of the Divine character of the Bible, I think, no man who deals honestly with his own mind and heart can entertain a reasonable doubt, for myself, I must say, that having for many years made the evidences of Christianity the subject of close study, the result has been a firm and increasing conviction of the authenticity and plenary inspiration of the Bible. It is indeed the Word of God." —**Simon Greenleaf**

"A person who rejects Christ may choose to say that I do not accept it, he may not choose to say there is not enough evidence." —**Simon Greenleaf**

"If you're not winning souls, you're not gettin' the job done!"
—**Ruth Satterfield**

"There is a small book one can put in one's pocket, and yet all the libraries of America, numerous as they are, would hardly be large enough to hold all the books which have been inspired by this one little volume. The reader will know what I am speaking of; it is the Bible, as we are used to call it— the Book, the book of mankind, as it has properly been called."
—**Ernest von Dobschutz**

"It is almost impossible to make [people] understand... that I recommend Christianity because I think it is objectively true. But people today are simply not interested in whether a religion is true or false, they only want to know if it will be comforting, inspiring, or socially useful." —**C.S. Lewis**

"There is no body of ancient literature in the world which enjoys such a wealth of good textual attestation as the New Testament." —**F.F. Bruce**

"Christianity is basically a historical religion. That is to say, it is founded not on abstract principles but in concrete events, actual historical happenings."
—**Huston Smith**

"Regardless of what anyone may personally think or believe about him, Jesus of Nazareth has been the dominant figure in the history of Western culture for almost twenty centuries. If it were possible, with some sort of super-magnet, to pull up out of that history every scrap of metal bearing at least a trace of his name, how much would be left?" —**Jaroslav Pelikan**

INTRODUCTION

There is no other historical figure of any other worldview that can come close, even in the slightest degree, to the long list of irrefutable evidence that not only provides proof that Jesus Christ was actually an authentic historical figure, but also that He is exactly Who He claimed to be—God manifested in human flesh.

In *Proof of Authority*, I will be giving an apologetic, or a reasoned defense, for the Supernatural Intervention and Confirmation of the Holy Bible. I will be providing irrefutable evidence that the Biblical Christian faith is not a blind faith or an unreasonable faith, but is actually a rational faith founded on facts, is rationally defensible, and is logical and self-consistent.

This is not to say that Christians themselves are always rational, logical and self-consistent and will on all occasions put God's teachings and standards in perfect practice, even though God has saved them by His grace (Ep. 2:8, 9). According to the Holy Bible, mankind is a fallen creation (Ge. 2:17; Ro. 5:12, 18-21; 6:23; Is. 53.6), and only Jesus Christ is perfect, logical, rational and consistent in all of His teachings (He. 1:1-9). Jesus never told us to follow His people—Jesus said, "Follow Me" (Mt. 4:19; Mk. 8:34).

Although the entire life of Jesus Christ is a Model intended to be emulated by His followers (1Jn. 2:6), due to the effects and consequences of the human transgression and rebellion against God (1Jn. 3:4; Ro. 5:12), primarily the sinful nature (Ro. 8:5-36), they do not always follow perfectly.

Through the sanctification process implemented by God, human beings can be made holy through the merits and justification of Jesus Christ alone (Ro. 3:21-25). That's one of the reasons why the Holy Bible teaches us to abide in Christ (Jn. 15:4-10; Ep. 5:1, 2) and to be like Him.

Unfortunately, as a result of mankind's rebellion against God, we will always struggle with the sinful nature until we receive our resurrected body, soul, and spirit at the end of the age (Ja. 3:2, 17; Re. 20:5, 6). The sinful nature is a particular aspect of humans that causes or compels us to rebel against God (Is. 53:6; 64:6; Ro. 8:3). This refers to the fact that human beings have a natural disposition or tendency to rebel against God. When fallen humans are given a choice to do God's will or their own, they naturally choose to implement their own will.

Proof of the sinful nature is all around us. For example, no one has to teach his or her child to lie or to be selfish—this comes naturally. We as parents have to go through great lengths to teach our children to tell the truth and to put others first. The news media reports are filled with shocking examples of human beings acting badly. The sinful nature of humans comes naturally, and the Holy Bible explains to us that humanity is sinful, not just in theory and practice, but also that we are sinful by our very nature (1Jn. 1:8, 9; Ep. 2:1). Sin is not just what humans do—it's what humans are. Paul talks about this in Romans 7:14-25. We read:

> *[14]We know that the Law is spiritual; but I am unspiritual, sold as a slave to sin. [15]I do not understand what I do. For what I want to do, I do not do. But what I hate, I do. [16]And if I do what I do not desire, I admit that the Law is good. [17]In that case, it is no longer I who do it, but it is sin living in me that does it. [18]I know that nothing good lives in me, that is, in my flesh; for I have the desire to do what is good, but I cannot carry it out. [19]For I do not do the good I want to do. Instead, I keep on doing the evil I do not want to do. [20]And if I do what I do not want, it is no longer I who do it, but it is sin living in me that does it. [21]So this is the principle I have discovered: When I want to do good, evil is right there with me. [22]For in my inner being I delight in God's Law. [23]But I see another law at work in my body, warring against the law of my mind and holding me captive to the law of sin that dwells within me. [24]What a wretched man I am! Who will rescue me from this body of death? [25]Thanks be to God, through Jesus Christ our Lord! So then, with my mind I serve the law of God, but with my flesh I serve the law of sin.*

However, there is Good News! The Holy Bible tells us that those who are re-born through Christ can count themselves dead to sin and alive to Christ (Ro. 6:11). Through Christ's finished work on the cross, Jesus satisfied the wrath of God against our sin. We read in 1Peter 2:24 the following:

²⁴"He Himself bore our sins in His body on the tree, so that we might die to sin and live to righteousness. By His stripes you are healed."

Also in 1Peter 3:18 we read this:

"¹⁸For Christ also suffered for sins once for all, the righteous for the unrighteous, to bring you to God. He was put to death in the body, but made alive in the spirit."

I will also be showing you that the Christian worldview, as articulated in the Holy Bible, is fully logical and reasonable without errors in its teachings, standards, and principles.

Universal Truths

Virtually every person believes in the laws of logic which are these:
- ***The Law of Excluded Middle:*** This law means that something is either true or it is false. There is no middle ground. The following statement abuses the Law of Excluded Middle: *This is neither an apple nor an apple.*
- ***The Law of Identity:*** This law means that something is what it is. The following statement abuses the Law of Identity: *My dog is a gorilla.*
- ***The Law of Non-contradiction:*** This law means that two opposite statements cannot both be true at the same time or in the same way. The following statement abuses the Law of Non-contradiction: *The sun was so hot that I was freezing.*

No Natural Explanation

There are many other universal truths that disregard race, creed, or gender. No matter what culture a person comes from, a number of studies have revealed that everyone incorporates some degree of the same universal characteristic that we can observe in everyday human reality. These characteristics

have no known or natural explanation for their existence but can be found in virtually every person. These particular universal characteristics are as follows (just to name a few):
- The desire for faith, hope, and love
- The desire for acceptance
- The human conscience
- Human emotions
- The ability to think and to logically reason
- The capacity for self-awareness
- The ability for introspection and wonderment
- The sinful nature, birth, reproduction, and death

Have you ever wondered why or thought about why *Truth* is universally the only reason for anyone to believe in anything? The question we should be asking ourselves is, *"Why are these statements true?"* More specifically, *"What is the purpose and reason for these phenomena and why are they universal and transcend all peoples and cultures without any natural explanation?"*

This most certainly would imply that the source of these phenomena must have come from somewhere outside our space-time continuum. Darwinian evolution and atheism have no logical or reasonable explanation for the universal existence of these naturally unexplainable realities, but Biblical Christianity does give us an answer for these phenomena.

The Holy Bible explains to us that man was created in God's image and likeness (Ge.1:26-28). If this is true, as I believe it is, we would expect to see some similarities between the characteristics of God as they are revealed in the Holy Bible and the universal characteristics of human beings as they are revealed in reality—with regard to our mental, moral, social, and creative abilities. This is exactly what we see as explained here:

1. *Mentally*—Humans were created as rational, logical, and volitional agents. In other words, human beings can reason and make choices. This is a reflection of God's intellect and freedom.
2. *Morally*—Humans were created in righteousness and perfect innocence with a conscience, also known as a moral compass. This is a reflection of God's holiness.

3. **Socially**—Humans were created to have a loving relationship with God and others. This reflects the Triune nature of a loving God Who Himself is a Being in relationship.
4. ***Creatively***—Humans were created as spontaneously creative thinkers. In other words, creativity is an integral part of the human experience and has improved human living conditions (airplanes, cars, computers, telephone, television, and light bulbs), just to name a few. This reflects the creative nature of God Who is the Creator of all things.

Other evidence with regard to our mental, moral, social, and creative abilities can also be seen in two other specific areas in this life universally.

1. The fact that there are an estimated 4,200 religions in the world today actually confirms these two Biblical truths with regard to the human condition:
    - There is a ***universal desire*** for a relationship with a higher power in the life of humans.[18]
    - There is a ***universal rebellion*** against the God of Biblical Christianity in the life of humans.
2. The majority of books, movies, and music being sold today are mostly dealing with personal relationships in one way or another and are being sold for multiple billions of dollars annually. Let me ask you a question. Think about your favorite books, movies, and songs. Are they dealing with personal relationships? I think you will be surprised to find out that they are!

This all shows a *universal desire or longing* for a relationship with others in the life of humans and reflects the Triune nature of God Who Himself is a Being in relationship.

Let me explain to you the Biblical evidence for the Triunity argument for God, and you decide its plausibility. First of all, the word "Trinity" is not used in the Holy Bible, but the concept is throughout it. For example: **1)** Who raised Jesus from the dead? Well, it was God the Father (Ga. 1:1; 1Th. 1:10); it was also Jesus Himself (Jn. 2:19; 10:17, 18); and it was the Holy Spirit

---

[18] A 2019 survey conducted by the Pew Research Center, of U.S. adults, 70% view that "God is a person whom people can have a relationship, while 15% believe that "God is an impersonal force. A 2019 survey conducted by the National Opinion Research Center reports that 77.5% of U.S. adults believe in a personal god.

(Ro. 8:11). **2)** Who gave the new covenant? The Father (Je. 31:33, 34); Jesus (He. 8:1-13; 10:29; 12:24; 13:20); the Holy Spirit (He. 10:15-17). **3)** Who sanctifies believers? The Father (1Th. 5:23); Jesus (He. 13:12); the Holy Spirit (1Pe. 1:2). **4)** Who is the Creator? The Father (Ge. 1:1; Is. 44:24; Ac. 17:24; Ep. 3:9); Jesus (Jn. 1:3; Col. 1:16; He. 1, 10); the Holy Spirit (Jb. 33:4). **5)** Who indwells believers? The Father (1Co. 3:16a; 2Co. 6:16; 1Jn. 3:24); Jesus (Jn. 6:56; Ro. 8:10; Ep. 3:17); the Holy Spirit (Jn. 14:16, 17; Ro. 8:9, 11; 1Co. 3:16b). The Holy Bible even describes this in terms of different combinations: Father and Son (Jn. 14:23); Father and Holy Spirit (Ep. 2:21, 22; 1Jn. 3:24); Son and Holy Spirit (Ga. 4:6).

The Image and Likeness of God

The Holy Bible teaches that man is made in the image and likeness of God, which are the unique qualities that allow God to be manifested in the characteristics of human beings. When God created humans, His Will was that they would be filled with His Spirit and walk with His God-given Authority to rule over the world through the influence of His Spirit (Ge. 1:26). Mankind's failure occurred when Adam and Eve handed over that authority to the adversary in the Garden of Eden (Ge. 3:5).

This image and likeness of God, that was present at creation, was partially lost by Adam and Eve at the fall, but the Holy Bible tells us that, despite this partial loss of the Image and Likeness of God, each person fundamentally still has value regardless of class, race, gender, or disability (Jn. 3:16; Ps. 139:13-16; Pr. 22:2).

We must understand that—according to Scripture—Christ is the only perfect image and likeness of God. The author of the book of Hebrews refers to Jesus Christ as the "exact imprint of God" (He. 1:3). The Apostle Paul refers to Jesus as "the visible image of the invisible God and the fullness of God's Deity in bodily form" (2Co. 4:4; Col. 1:15; 2:9) and that "Jesus is God's indescribable gift to us" (2Co. 9:15).

One of the characteristics of being made in the image and likeness of God implies that, just as the Triune Creator is a Being in relationship, so are His creations.

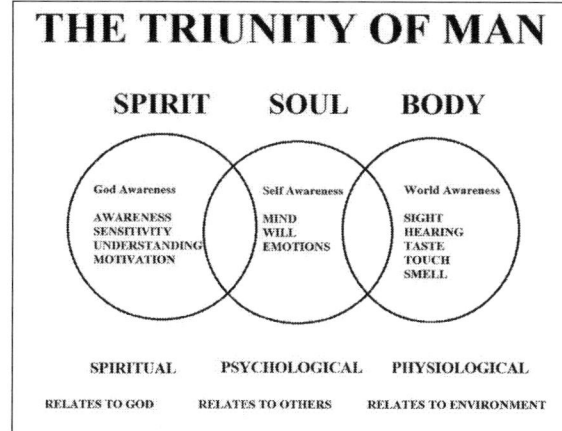

The Holy Bible actually describes human beings with three basic parts: a spirit, a soul, and a body. The human triunity is, as I have already pointed out, a reflection of the Triune Nature of God.

Let me explain. 1Thessalonians 5:23 says, *"Now may the God of peace Himself sanctify you completely, and may your entire spirit, soul, and body be kept blameless at the coming of our Lord Jesus Christ."*

This would reflect the three distinct persons within the One Essence of the Godhead (i.e. the Father, Son, and Holy Spirit).

When the Holy Bible proclaims that God made man in His Own image and likeness, not only does this reflect the Triune Nature and Characteristics of God with regard to the universal, relational aspects of human reality, but this also means that humans are like God in the sense that they are creative, aesthetic, moral, spiritual, and uniquely gifted intellectually. This explains the mental, moral, social, and creative aspects of our human experience. This also reflects and is consistent with the Attributes and Characteristics of God as they are revealed to us in Scripture, and the reason why God did this is so that we can have a meaningful and honest relationship with Him and other people as we live as stewards of this planet He has given us to manage. We are to serve God as we love, trust, and obey Him. Sadly, the harmony of God's originally created order has been hindered significantly due to man's rebellion.

We must understand that because Jesus Christ is the Only Perfect Image and Likeness of God ever to walk on planet Earth, He is the Only One Who was qualified to die for the sins of the world. He was the Only Perfect Unblemished Lamb (1Pe. 1:18-19) being led to the slaughter (Is. 53:7), to give His life as a Ransom for many (Mk. 10:45), in order to present us to His Father holy, blameless, and beyond reproach (Col. 1:22).

Human beings have a universal desire for a relationship with a higher power and fellow humans that transcends all ethnic and cultural groups without any known or natural explanation outside of the Holy Bible. This longing should cause us to revisit the Supernatural Intervention and Confirmation found in the Holy Scriptures; and in the process, you will find that the Holy Bible is consistent and compatible with the human experience and condition like no other worldview in history.

Is Logic Really Necessary?

The accurate use of the laws of logic is a requirement for our ability to understand God's Word and His overall plan for the human race. Unfortunately, when God's Word, the laws of logic, and actual reality become separated from one another within the human conscience, Biblical truth cannot function accurately or correctly in the way God originally intended.

This is obviously the original reason why God has equipped humans with the capacity for clear and sound reasoning in conducting or assessing factually-based information according to strict principles of validity. Therefore, I believe that the universality of the laws of logic themselves are a proof for the existence of God and also provide a reasonable explanation for the rational and logical aspects of the Biblical Christian worldview.

The logical outworking of this presupposition implies that the writings and teachings of non-Biblical and contradictory worldviews, where Supernatural Intervention and Confirmation, as the Holy Bible, are absent, cannot be both rational and logical due to the codification or the absence of the laws, rules, and principles of proof and inference.

All other worldviews without Supernatural Intervention and Confirmation, as the Holy Bible, are without good cause for their explanations and justifications. As a result of this, they do not have good reasons for their beliefs and therefore cannot be relied upon as honest or truthful.

This does not mean, however, that all other contradictory religions without Supernatural Intervention and Confirmation, as the Holy Bible, do not and cannot contain some elements of rationalism, honesty, and truthfulness within their writings. As I have already pointed out, according to the Holy

Bible, all people are created in the image and likeness of God (Ge. 9:6) and can articulate principles that are rational, honest, and truthful. However, Biblical Christianity is the only faith that is internally and externally consistent with science, history, archaeology, the laws of logic, and reason, and also demonstrates an amazing compatibility with the human condition, while at the same time displays evidence of fulfilled predictive prophecy (i.e. Supernatural Intervention and Confirmation).

Three Kinds of Faith

It is true that all worldviews display a type or kind of faith. I have met many people of different beliefs who appear to be just as sincere and enthusiastic as I am in my faith, and I have often thought to myself, "How is this possible?"

If the faith and beliefs found in people of other religions are based on truth claims that are supported by factually-based evidence, then where do these people of other religions get the confidence that supports the sincerity and enthusiasm for their worldview?

Let's examine three possible reasons. There are basically three kinds of faith that we need to look at; and in doing so, we will find a reasonable explanation to this question. There is a faith that is *blind*, a faith that is *unreasonable*, and a faith that is *rational*. Let me explain these types:

1. **Blind faith**—This faith believes in something without having any evidence.
2. **Unreasonable faith**—This faith believes in something in spite of the evidence.
3. **Rational faith**—This faith believes in something because of the evidence.

I will be showing you that Biblical Christianity is a rational faith that is founded on facts and is defensible, logical, and self-consistent. All other faiths without evidence of Supernatural Intervention and Confirmation (i.e. *Proof of Authority*), as the Holy Bible has, are not. Since all other faiths lack the possession of certain relevant information necessary for sound and rational judgment, their belief systems are actually rendered to the status of blind or an unreasonable faith.

What I mean by this statement is that all non-Biblical worldviews lack evidence sufficient to establish them as true, and as a result, there is no logical or reasonable excuse for their beliefs (Ro. 1:20), and this reality is consistent with these two Biblical teachings:

1. Humans are created in the image and likeness of the One True God (Ge. 1:26, 27).
2. Humans are in rebellion against the One True God (Ro. 1:16-26).

I will be arguing in *Proof of Authority* that the faiths of all non-Biblical Judaic/Christian worldviews are *blind* and/or *unreasonable* based on the three definitions of faith identified above.

Because of the irrefutable and undeniable evidence found both internally and externally in the Biblical Christian worldview, the followers of Jesus Christ—as He is revealed in the Holy Bible and in history—have very good reasons for determining the truth claims of their faith (1Pe. 3:15).

Paul the Logician

The God of Biblical Christianity encourages His followers to use their mind (2Ti. 2:15) and to logically reason (Is. 1:18, 19). For example, the Apostle Paul writes in Romans 1:20–22:

> *[20]For since the creation of the world God's invisible qualities, His eternal power and divine nature, have been clearly seen, being understood from His workmanship, so that men are without excuse. [21]For although they knew God, they neither glorified Him as God nor gave thanks to Him, but they became futile in their thinking and darkened in their foolish hearts. [22]Although they claimed to be wise, they became fools.*

Notice that Paul said that we can understand the invisible. The word translated *"understood"* means *"to perceive with the mind."*[19]

Paul is saying that human beings can see the design of the created order of the universe. The elements of a created world can be easily observed. According to Paul, they all testify to a Cause that is Eternal, Intelligent, Powerful, and Divine.

---

19 W.E. Vine, *Expository Dictionary of Old and New Testament Words*, p.173, © 1981 by Fleming H. Revell Company.

The Holy Bible tells us that God is a Divine Being Who is One in Essence and Three in Person—the Father, the Son, and the Holy Spirit. Within One Essence of the Godhead there are Three Distinct "Persons" Who are neither three gods, three parts, nor three modes of God, but are Co-Equally and Co-Eternally God. The first clear indication that God is a Trinity is found in Ge.1:26. Then God said, *"Let Us make man in Our image, after Our likeness, to rule over the fish of the sea and the birds of the air and the livestock, and over all the earth itself and of every creature that crawls upon it."*

Jesus Christ is the only Person of the Godhead Who has a body, and this is why I believe it was the pre-incarnate Christ Himself Who was walking in the garden with Adam (Ge. 3:8). God the Father and the Holy Spirit are a Spiritual Essence, absolutely single and not subject either to division or multiplication (Mk. 12:29, 32; Jn. 17:3); *"and those who worship Him must worship Him in spirit and in truth"* (Jn. 4:23-24). This is the main reason why human beings were created with a spirit as well as a body and soul (1Pe. 1:9; Ro. 12:1, 2), and with the ability to distinguish *truth* from *non-truth*.

This is undoubtedly another reason why God has equipped humans with the capacity for clear and sound reasoning in conducting or assessing factually-based information, according to strict principles of validity (Ep. 4:18; Col. 1:9-14; 2:2; 1Jn. 5:20).

God has revealed Himself through His creation (Ps. 19:1-6; Ro. 1:18-21) and the Person of Jesus Christ Whom Paul said, *"... is the whole fullness of God in bodily form"* (Col. 2:9). That's why Jesus Christ could say, *"Anyone who has seen Me has seen the Father"* (Jn. 14:9) and, *"I and the Father are One"* (Jn. 10:30). Through both the order and complexity that we can observe in the universe and through the life, work, and ministry of Jesus Christ, we can know with absolute certainty that God exists.

Paul is saying that we must use our minds (i.e. logically reason) in considering the evidence of creation, the amazing Supernatural Intervention and Confirmation that is observed through both the Person of Jesus Christ and creation itself. Human beings must come to the only logical conclusion that is derived from the evidence.

Paul is also affirming that we can see the unseen by reasoning from the reality of creation and the reality of the Person of Jesus Christ. Humans who think differently are in an indefensible position (i.e. are without excuse). We also see evidence of logical reasoning in the Apostle Paul's ministry as he debates with philosophers and other people in the synagogues and marketplaces.

Acts 17:1-4

¹When they had passed through Amphipolis and Apollonia, they came to Thessalonica, where there was a Jewish synagogue. ²As was his custom, Paul went into the synagogue, and on three Sabbaths he <u>reasoned</u> with them from the Scriptures, ³<u>explaining and proving</u> that the Christ had to suffer and rise from the dead. "This Jesus I am proclaiming to you is the Christ," he declared. ⁴Some of the Jews were persuaded and joined Paul and Silas, along with a large number of God-fearing Greeks and quite a few leading women.

Acts 17: 17-18

¹⁷So he <u>reasoned</u> in the synagogue with the Jews and God-fearing Gentiles, and in the marketplace with those he met each day. ¹⁸Some Epicurean and Stoic philosophers also began to <u>debate</u> with him. Some of them asked, "What is this babbler trying to say?" while others said, "He seems to be advocating foreign gods." They said this because Paul was proclaiming the good news of Jesus and the resurrection.

We read in 1 Peter 3:15:

¹⁵But in your hearts sanctify Christ as Lord. Always be prepared to <u>articulate a defense</u> to everyone who asks you to <u>give the reason</u> for the hope that you have. But respond with gentleness and respect.

The gifts and abilities that God has given us with regard to understanding and articulating His truth are a necessity for receiving and sharing the saving knowledge of Jesus Christ to a lost and dying world.

The Holy Bible tells us to be imitators of God (Ep. 5:1) and to pattern our thinking after God's revelation (Is. 55:6-8). The Holy Bible also tells us to test everything and hold fast to that which is good (1Th. 5:21) and that we should love God with all our heart, soul, mind, and strength (Mk. 12:30-32).

The Holy Bible also tells us in Proverbs 1:7, *"that the fear of the LORD is the beginning of knowledge; fools despise wisdom and instruction."*

Defining Terms

In *Proof of Authority*, I will be revealing to you the Holy Bible's unique and amazing evidences that prove that the Biblical Christian worldview is the only true and logical worldview in existence today and all competing contradictory worldviews are not.

But first, I want to explain to you what I mean by these four terms: *Logic, Evidence, Faith,* and *Worldview*.

1) **Logic**—could be defined as the Science of Reasoning. According to the *Oxford American College Dictionary*, logic is defined as "reasoning conducted or assessed according to strict principles of validity." Logic is one of the natural laws that God put into place at the creation of the universe. He has created people with a mind that has the ability to logically reason, and when used correctly it will ultimately point us toward the truth about God. Unfortunately, it is easy to misuse this God-given ability. However, when logic is used correctly, we can derive truth through the analysis of facts either directly (deductively), or indirectly (inductively). These two variations of logical reasoning can start either with a complete or an incomplete set of observations and proceed to the likeliest possible explanation for a group of observations.

Logical reasoning involves review, investigation, and analyzing. It will create and test a hypothesis using the best information available. These forms of logic are used by doctors in making a diagnosis based on test results or by jurors who make decisions based on the evidence presented to them.

Logic can take any given presupposition or idea and analyze its relationships and compare them with other known factors and will arrive at a conclusion that identifies a previously unknown phenomena such as the

Supernatural Intervention and Confirmation (i.e. *Proof of Authority*) found in the Holy Bible.

Logic is also used to identify the relationships between fact or fiction, fantasy or reality, truth or deception. It is necessary to derive correct conclusions from factually-based evidence formulated by sound reasoning.

Logic and the reasoning process are very similar to how we solve mathematical equations, but instead of using numbers, logic uses ideas.

2) ***Evidence***—may be defined as that which is sufficient to establish a thing as true or false. *The Random House Dictionary of the English Language* defines evidence as ground for belief; that which tends to prove or disprove.[20] Therefore, Christian evidence would be that which is submitted to prove or disprove the truth claims of the Christian Worldview.

3) ***Faith***—When I think of the word *faith*, I also think of the word *believe* because they are somewhat synonymous. While "faith" surely includes the elements of "belief," they are not exactly one and the same. Faith is a noun and believe is a verb. Faith refers to a person, place, or thing, and believing is putting one's faith into action. For a person to have faith in someone or something they must first believe that someone or something exists. Biblically, true saving faith is described as a gift from God and is defined in Hebrews 11:1 as being sure of what we hope for and certain of what we do not see, and the goal of true saving faith is the salvation of our soul (1Pe. 1:9).

> *[8]For it is by grace you have been saved through faith, and this not from yourselves; it is the gift of God, [9]not by works, so that no one can boast (Ep. 2:8-9).*

With regard to grace, the Holy Bible tells us that human beings:
- Don't deserve it (Ro. 6:23).
- Can't earn it (Ep. 2:8-9).
- And are not worthy of it (Ro. 3:23).

According to the *Oxford American College Dictionary,* faith is defined as:
1. "Complete trust or confidence in someone or something."
2. "A strong belief in God...."

---

[20] The Random House Dictionary of the English Language (New York, 1966). p.495.

For a person to put true saving faith in someone or something means that a person will put their trust, dependence, reliance, and confidence in that someone or something. We also must understand that it is possible to have faith and belief in someone or something while at the same time that someone or something has no ability or power to change anything in one's life. For example, I believe that Antarctica exists; but my belief in Antarctica's existence has no ability or power to effect or change anything in my life, unless I am committed to Antarctica through a job offer, a home purchase, or a business opportunity. Otherwise, my belief in Antarctica would add nothing of value to my life whatsoever! That's because the value of faith is always contingent upon the value of the object in which that faith is placed. The Holy Bible tells us that true saving faith is justifying and transforming and is only found in the Person of Jesus Christ. The difference between saving faith and non-saving faith is this:

- Non-saving faith does not require anyone to put his or her trust, dependence, reliance, and confidence in it.
- True saving faith does.

True saving faith will always consist of putting your trust, dependence, reliance, and confidence toward the object of your faith (Ga. 2:16; Ph. 3:9). Again, the value of faith itself will always be directly contingent upon the value of the object in which that faith is placed. According to the Holy Bible, true saving faith will exhibit conviction for the truth, personal surrender, and a change in your lifestyle that reveals those changes in your actions, thoughts, and priorities (He. 11:1; Jn. 8:24; 1Co. 2:5). That's the reason why the Holy Bible tells us that "without faith it is impossible to please God" (He. 11:6). If we don't have trust, dependence, reliance, and confidence in God, then pleasing Him with our life will become impossible.

To have faith and to believe in Jesus, we must first know something about Him (Ro. 10:14-17). You have to know something about God in order to be able to do His Will, and doing God's Will is how you please Him. Saving faith must affirm our knowledge of Jesus Christ through our actions in the things we say, do, and think. Faith by itself, if it does not have works, is dead (Ja. 2:14, 17). Saving faith will always have these three elements attached to it:

- A strong conviction of the truth.
- A personal surrender.
- A lifestyle that reflects that change.

Millions of people profess to have some understanding about Jesus but they don't really believe that Biblical Christianity is true. Simply to have knowledge or an intellectual understanding of Jesus Christ by itself is not enough for saving faith. The Holy Bible tells us that even the demons believe and tremble (Ja. 2:14-19), which would imply that even knowing the facts and believing them to be true are still not enough in themselves to make us true followers of Jesus Christ. True followers of Christ must entrust themselves first and foremost to God the Son, Jesus Christ who is the only mediator (1Ti. 2:5) and advocate (1Jn. 2:1) between us and God, but also to the work of God the Father, and God the Holy Spirit. Jesus must become the Lord of everything in our life. If Jesus is not Lord ***of all***, then He is not Lord ***at all***.

To the true believer of the Biblical Christian worldview Jesus is:
- Whom they believe.
- Whom they trust.
- Whom they listen to and obey.
- Whom they are commanded to preach.

When you submit to the Work of the Holy Spirit and put your faith in the saving knowledge of Jesus Christ, there will be a change in the desires and priorities in your life.

There are five basic components associated with saving faith:
1. Evidence (Jn. 10:37-38; 20:30-31)
2. Understanding (Ro. 3:23; 6:23; 1Pe. 2:24-25)
3. Acknowledgment (Ac. 2:38)
4. Obedience (Jn. 14:15; 1Pe. 1:14)
5. Trust (Pr. 3:5; Ps. 56:3-4)

Your submission to the Work and Will of God the Holy Spirit (Jn. 16:8) and God the Father (Jn. 6:40) through God the Son (1Pe. 1:2-5) Jesus Christ will become the most important and highest priority in this life.

The value of the Biblical Christian faith is contingent upon the value of the Object in which that faith is placed. In the case of the Biblical Christian worldview, the Person of Jesus Christ is the Object of that faith (Ga. 2:16; Ph. 3:7-10). The value of Christ and His death and Resurrection is incalculable, eternal, and of infinite worth (He. 10:11-15). Let me ask you a question. "Do you think that Jesus Christ is worthy of your commitment and devotion?" Based on the Biblical, historical, and my experiential evidence, I would be forced to answer "Absolutely yes!"

Let me explain. The Holy Bible tells us that Jesus Christ is the Son of God Who went from *the form of God* to *the form of a servant*, and from being *equal to God*, to being in *the likeness of men* (Ph. 2:6-7), and is the One and Only Sacrifice for the people of this world (Jn. 3:16-18)—Who was born of a virgin (Is. 7:14; Mt. 1:23), and became human flesh, (Jn. 1:14) and is the Sinless (1Pe. 2:22; He. 4:15) and Unblemished Lamb (1Pe. 1:19), Who submitted to God's Will and Purpose (Jn. 5:30; 8:29) resulting in the reconciliation and forgiveness for human beings' rebellion against God (Ep. 2:16; Col. 1:20).

God the Son's sacrifice satisfied God the Father's wrath and judgment against mankind (Is. 53:10; 1Th. 1:10) due to our sinful rebellion against Him (Jn. 3:16-18; 36). Christ's sacrificial gift enabled God the Father to justify and sanctify those people who have chosen to believe and abide in Christ (2Jn. 1:9). Justification and sanctification are two graces directly related to the Gospel of Jesus Christ and are always working together in dealing with human sin. Justification and sanctification are necessary components in the process of human conversion and transformation. Justification and sanctification are two theological terms that are used to explain the effects of Christ's saving work upon His cross for sinners (Ro. 5:9; He. 13:12). Because of Christ's sacrificial gift upon the cross, God now considers the followers of Christ to be without sin in a legal sense, yet in a real, practical sense we are still sinners (Ro. 8:3). You might be asking, "Where do we find the legal foundation for justification in Scripture?" Let me explain. God justifies the sinner completely on the basis of the obedience of His Son, Jesus Christ, Who is our Only Advocate and Mediator. Christ's obedient sacrificial gift is the only provision provided by God which declares the transgressor righteous (Ro. 5:18-19; Ga. 3:13; Ep. 1:7; Ph. 2:8).

Justification is a work of the Triune God and does not address by itself the inward restoration and transformation in a person's body, soul, and spirit but is actually a legal declaration in which the Triune God pardons the transgressor of all his or her sin and welcomes and accepts the sinner as righteous in His sight. The Triune God justifies and recognizes the sinner as righteous at the very instant the sinner repents and puts his or her faith and hope in the Person of Jesus Christ (Ro. 3:21-26; 5:16; 2Co. 5:21).

Justification removes the guilt of our transgression and counts the sinner as righteous. Sanctification addresses the domination, authority, and corruption of the transgression in our lives and is the process that God uses to renew and transform the entire person, which includes the things we say, do, and think. When we accept Christ's horrific death and glorious Resurrection on our behalf (He. 5:1-7), His graceful sacrifice covers our sin and removes its consequence (He. 7:27; 10:12, 14).

Thus, because of Christ's righteousness, we now are permitted to have direct access to God because we are now made sinless or clean in a legal sense and because Christ is the Only Legitimate Advocate provided by God to perform this task (1Jn. 2:1; 5:11-12; 1Ti. 2:5). Jesus Christ has secured both justification and sanctification on behalf of those who trust, believe, and abide in Him. Because of this, we now have the ability to receive the free gift of eternal life (Jn. 3:36; 5:24; 20:31). Although every follower of Jesus Christ is once and for all made free from the enslavement of sin, we are not instantly made perfect. We will not be totally and completely made free from sin until we receive our new resurrected body, soul, and spirit at the Last Day.

Also, the Holy Bible describes Jesus with certain characteristics and qualities that can only be collectively ascribed to Him alone and not to any other person, such as: He is loving (Jn. 15:13), forgiving (Lu. 23:34), humble (Mk. 10:45), compassionate (Mt. 9:36), gentle (Mt. 5:9), self-controlled (Jn. 16:33; Ja. 4:7), sinless (1Jn. 3:5), patient (1Ti. 1:16), obedient (Ph. 2:8), honest (Jn. 14:6), prayerful (Lu. 5:16; 18:1), full of Grace and Truth (Jn. 1:14), God (Jn. 1:1; 5:16-18; 10:24-33) and Creator (Jn. 1:1-3). He paid our price while we were still sinners (Ro. 5:8). Jesus is the Living Truth, Wisdom, Knowledge, and Example that God has provided for us in this life (Jn. 14:6, 23; Col. 2:2, 3). Jesus is the Object, as well as the Model, of our faith.

When you have true saving faith in Jesus Christ (Mt. 13:1-13; Ph. 2:13; 1Jn. 3:9), a radical readjustment of your current worldview begins and you start to see the world and its systems in an entirely different way (Ro. 8:5). The Holy Spirit illuminates your understanding from a correct Biblical perspective as to the true nature of things and actually causes you to think differently about your world and reality. You have a desire to love God with all your heart, soul, mind and strength (Mt. 19:19; 22:39; Mk. 12:31; Lu. 10:27; Ro. 13:9; Ga. 5:14; Ja. 2:8).

Faith in Jesus Christ is the only way human beings can obtain a true spiritual transformation in this life. Like Christ, we should be submissive and subordinate to the Father (Jn. 6:38).

I confidently declare to you that Jesus Christ is worthy of our trust, dependence, reliance, confidence, and worship. This is based on my experiential knowledge, including the above-mentioned Biblical texts coupled with Supernatural Intervention and Confirmation Evidence, and well-documented historical evidence.

Here are some additional verses about saving faith: Jn. 3:16; 3:36; 5:24; 6:40; 11:25; 12:46; 20:31; Ac. 8:37; 10:43; 13:39; 16:31; Ro. 9:33; 10:9; 2Ti. 3:15; 1Jn. 5:1.

4) *Worldview*—Due to the importance in understanding this term, I want to explain this definition in a slightly different way in an attempt to help you better understand it. A "worldview" can also be defined as a perspective of reality itself. It can be a view of life, a comprehensive conception of the world from a specific point of view, and is a formal philosophy that explains all the facts of one's life's experiences including the nature of knowledge, reality, and existence.

Every individual has a worldview or a perspective that both interprets and guides his or her life. In this sense, a worldview consciously or subconsciously gives answers to these four questions:

1. Who am I?
2. Where am I?
3. What is wrong?
4. What is the solution?

One of my primary goals for writing *Proof of Authority* is to provide answers to these two very important questions:
1. Is there sufficient evidence to establish the existence of the God of Biblical Christianity?
2. Is there sufficient evidence to establish the Holy Bible as the Word of the God of Biblical Christianity?

By showing you evidence that will positively confirm the answer to the second question, the answer to the first question will also be confirmed; and remember, as you read the information presented in *Proof of Authority,* please keep in mind that, according to the rules of our modern-day legal system, unrefuted evidence equals proof.

The evidence for the Holy Bible's *Proof of Authority* (i.e. Supernatural Intervention and Confirmation) can be proven simply by testing its various truth claims against reality. Putting sound reasoning together with the well-established laws of logic will lead to truthful and reasonable conclusions about the Holy Bible, Biblical Christianity, and God.

I'm also writing *Proof of Authority* to provide people with evidence that will ultimately support the trustworthiness and reliability of the Holy Bible. Because of the well-established universal laws of logic, I am confident that even just nine amazing evidences of Supernatural Intervention and Confirmation (i.e. *Proof of Authority*) will confirm the Holy Bible's claim of Divine Origin and Inspiration within your heart (conscience) and mind (intellect).

Simon Greenleaf, who served as professor of law at Harvard University and was instrumental in organizing the university's law program, said, *"A person who rejects Christ may choose to say that I do not accept it; he may not choose to say there is not enough evidence."*

An Important Observation

Before we get started, I want to share with you a very important observation. Because proof is discovered in the heart (conscience) and mind (intellect), the truth of a particular presupposition or idea can only be applied correctly to that which is actual reality, not to just our perception of it or our feelings towards it.

We must understand that when our perception of reality becomes devoid of its foundation of truth, then our perception of reality is no longer based on reality as it actually exists. When this happens, there is no evidence presented to prove anything that is truthful. Evidence will only convince us of its proof when the heart and the mind are receptive to reality as it actually exists, and it is only then that the evidence can be considered correctly and honestly. To achieve understanding we first need to want understanding (Ep. 4:18). Hence, with an open heart and mind together with a factually-based reality, let's begin our evidentiary adventure with some fascinating facts concerning the Holy Bible.

The Holy Bible is without exception the most amazing and incredible Book on the face of the planet. It's no wonder that it is the best-selling, most-quoted, most-published, most-translated,[21] most-influential, most-circulated, without question the best-documented, most-historically and archaeologically substantiated religious Text in the world.[22] At the same time, it is the most attacked and persecuted Book in the history of mankind.

Beyond all these statistics, the Holy Bible undeniably has the ability to radically transform lives and to bring people from all walks of life to reconciliation with God as we submit to the saving knowledge of His Son, Jesus Christ through the work of the Holy Spirit in our lives. It is also the only religious Book in history that has Supernatural Intervention that confirms and supports its claim of Divine Origin and Inspiration.

As a result of the Supernatural Intervention found in the Holy Bible, it has become the only religious Book on Earth that can cover hundreds of controversial topics without contradicting itself. It remains united in all of its themes, and it is the only worldview in existence today that can predict future events hundreds of years, and, in some cases, thousands of years, into the future with one-hundred-percent accuracy.

I would like you to consider eight other pieces of circumstantial evidence found behind the unique events of the Holy Bible so you will have a more complete comprehension and appreciation with regard to the facts that it reveals to us.

---

21   The Bible is the most-published and most-read book in the world of literature. Carl Jung, *Modern Man In Search of a Soul* (trans. Dell and Bayress; New York: Harcourt Brace, 1933, p. 264.
22   F.F. Bruce, *The New Testament Documents: Are They Reliable?* (Grand Rapids: Eerdman 2003).

Let's take a look at just eight pieces of this circumstantial evidence in question in more detail.

First, the Holy Bible was written over approximately a sixteen-hundred-year time period.

Second, it was written by more than forty different authors from every walk of life who came from different occupations and backgrounds. For example, Solomon was a king, Moses was educated in Egypt, Amos was a shepherd, Luke was a doctor, Peter was a fisherman, and Matthew was a tax collector.

Third, the authors wrote their individual historical documents from many different locations, such as palaces, prisons, the wilderness, and places of exile. It was written in thirteen different countries on three different continents: Asia, Africa, and Europe. For example, Moses wrote in the desert of Sinai, Paul wrote four of his epistles from prison in Rome, Daniel wrote in exile from Babylon, Ezra wrote in the ruined city of Jerusalem, the apostle John wrote while a prisoner banished to the Isle of Patmos in the Mediterranean Sea, and Ezekiel wrote his work while being held captive in Babylon.

Fourth, it was written in three different languages—Hebrew, Aramaic, and Greek—in a wide variety of literary styles without any internal contradictions.

Fifth, the writers had different purposes for writing. Isaiah wrote to warn Israel of God's coming judgment because of their rebellion against Him. Zechariah wrote to encourage a dismayed Israel who had returned from Babylonian exile, and Paul wrote to address problems in different Asian and European churches. Matthew wrote to prove to the Jews that Jesus is the Messiah.

Sixth, it was written under different circumstances. For example, David wrote at a time of war, Jeremiah wrote at a time of deep distress and disappointment at Israel's downfall, Peter wrote while Israel was under Roman occupation and domination, and Joshua wrote while invading the land of Canaan.

Think about bringing forty-plus different people together from different occupations and backgrounds. These people were writing from three different continents, thirteen different countries, speaking in three different languages. Think of them writing sixty-six different documents over a long period of time. These documents are speaking about and giving answers to life's most controversial topics. One would expect to see some major internal inconsistencies and contradictions. I also would expect to see this compilation of sixty-six separate books producing a confusing and incoherent read. In spite of all these different circumstances, the Holy Bible is a perfectly harmonious and consistent account of how God is reconciling sinners like you and me back into a relationship with Himself, through the atoning sacrifice of His One and Only Son, Jesus Christ, upon an old, rugged cross from a hill called Golgotha.[23]

Seventh, it is the only religious Book ever written in the history of man's existence that reveals to us the phenomena of predictive prophecy. God has actually intertwined the predictive prophecy phenomena throughout these sixty-six individual books with such precision and accuracy that it can never be removed from the text. This is amazing, and this one *Proof of Authority* provides enough evidence to prove the Holy Bible's claim of Divine Origin and Inspiration all by itself.

At this point you might be asking, "What exactly is predictive prophecy?" Predictive prophecy is simply God's act of communicating to His people events about the future in advance.

The reason why God did this is that there is no better evidence of His existence than the repeated and constant proof that is derived from the accurate predictions about future events. This demonstrates and confirms that He is the One and Only True God and there is no other,[24] that He is in complete control of the present and future,[25] and it also validates His message and mission.[26]

It is amazing that there are over three-hundred specific and detailed prophecies written in the Old Testament concerning the identity of the coming Messiah that had been fulfilled in the New Testament through the Person of Jesus Christ hundreds of years, and in some cases, thousands of years before Jesus Christ's birth.

---

[23] Mt. 27:33; Mk. 15:22; Lu. 23:33; Jn. 19:17.
[24] Is. 46:8, 9, 11, 21; Hos. 13:4; Joel 2:27; Mk. 12:29.
[25] Is. 14:24; 55:10-11; Ro. 8:28.
[26] Ge. 12:1-3; Mt. 24:14; 28:18-20; Lu. 19:10; 1Pe. 2:9-10.

For example, Zechariah told us that the Messiah would be betrayed for thirty pieces of silver. Isaiah tells us that the Messiah would be born of a virgin and would be called Immanuel, which means in the Hebrew language "God with us"[27] and that the Messiah would be spit upon and beaten, wounded and bruised, and people would cast lots for His garments. David told us the Messiah would be accused falsely, betrayed by a friend, that His hands and feet would be pierced and that He would cry, *"My God, my God, why have you forsaken me?"*[28] Amos told us that on the Day of the Lord there would be darkness (Mk. 15:33) and not light, and gloom with no brightness in it.[29]

Eighth, Archaeology. There is no other ancient book ever written that has as much archaeological evidence to support its accounts than the Holy Bible. Since God is the God of Truth, we should expect His Word to reveal events that are historically accurate, and this is exactly what we see in the Holy Bible. Archaeology presents tangible proof of the historical accuracy of the Holy Bible.

When you put these eight factors together, you begin to understand the astronomical impossibility that the Holy Bible's internal and external accuracy, consistency, coherency, and unity could have been achieved through mere chance, collusion, or common sense. You begin to understand the impossibility that it was achieved through an extremely well-planned conspiracy by forty or more deceitful men, most of whom did not even know each other, and achieved over a sixteen-hundred-year time span. Incidentally, this would be logistically impossible, even with today's modern communication technology.

---

27 Is. 7:14. The Hebrew language has a specific term that emphasizes virginity: "Betula" and occurs many times in the Old Testament, but Isaiah chose the word "Almah" to speak about the mother of Immanuel which literally means: "a young woman of marriageable age." It is clear that the Jewish idea of a marriageable young woman could involve virginity; this can be seen not only in the OT's teaching on adultery but also in the use of "Almah" in Ge. 24:43. The NT settles the implication of "Almah" in Lu. 1:27; 2:36, which uses the Greek word "parthenos" in Mt. 1:25; Lu. 1:27 and "parthenia" in Lu. 2:36 which specifically means "Virgin." Also in Lu. 1:34, Mary confessed to the angel Gabriel that she was a virgin; if she had lied about that, then the angel Gabriel could not have said, "Hail, *thou that art* highly favoured, the Lord *is* with thee: blessed *art* thou among women."

28 Ps. 22:1. "My God, my God"—These are the very words uttered by Christ from the cross; Mt. 27:46; Mk. 15:34.

29 Amos 5:20; Lu. 23:44. Julius Africanus, wrote about AD 221 in speaking of Jesus' crucifixion and the darkness that covered the land during this event. Africanus found a reference in the writings of Thallus in his third book of History, who wrote about AD 52, of an eclipse of the sun without reason. Julius Africanus, *Extant Writings, XVIII* in *The Ante-Nicene Fathers,* ed. by Alexander Roberts and James Donaldson (Grand Rapids: Eerdmans, 1973), vol. VI, p.130, as sited in Gary R. Habermas, *The Historical Jesus: Ancient Evidences for the Life of Christ,* (Joplin Mo: College Press Publishing Company), 1996.

When you see all the evidence presented in this book, you will find a strong and irrefutable case for the Divine Origin and Inspiration of the Holy Bible. What you will discover is that the Holy Bible is the most amazing and most incredible book ever produced on planet Earth. It gives us more than enough good reason to believe that it is the only authentic Word of God in existence today.

We can draw at least three conclusions from these precise and specific Supernatural Interventions found in the Holy Bible:
1. It proves the Divine Origin and Inspiration of the Holy Bible.
2. It provides proof that God exists.
3. It validates God's message and mission.

When the *Proof of Authority* (i.e. Supernatural Intervention and Confirmation) found in the Holy Bible is united with the laws of logic, it will lead us to the logical conclusion that all other contradictory worldviews are false.

This does not mean, however, that other religions do not contain some elements of truth in their writings. I have already pointed out that the Holy Bible declares that all people are created in the image and likeness of God (Ge. 1:26,27; 9:6) and can articulate principles that are true. However, only the Holy Bible can prove its claims of Divine Origin and Inspiration through its *Proof of Authority*. All claims of Divine Origin and Inspiration made by other belief systems, without evidence of *Proof of Authority*, (i.e. Supernatural Intervention and Confirmation) as the Holy Bible, must be viewed as false.

As you take into consideration the *Proof of Authority* found in the Holy Bible, please keep in mind that out of all the other religious books ever written, the Holy Bible is absolutely unique. I have already pointed out that the Holy Bible is actually sixty-six individual ancient historical documents with one amazing unifying message. No other religious writings in the history of the world have ever been compiled by so many authors over such an expanse of time, with such cohesive unity and accuracy.

The Holy Bible displays a flawless internal unity and consistency, even though it was written by forty-plus authors with different social statuses and backgrounds. The authors were shepherds, peasants, philosophers, tax collectors, poets, musicians, a statesman, kings, fishermen, scholars, prophets, a military general, and a priest,[30] all speaking about hundreds of controversial subjects. Yet despite the number of different authors and its miraculous array of topics, its unity and consistency are flawless.

The possibility that the internal and external accuracy, consistency, coherency, and unity found in the Holy Bible could have been achieved through human effort alone, apart from Supernatural Intervention, is unfathomable.

Also, keep in mind that the individual writers of the Holy Bible at the time it was written would have had no idea that their writings would eventually be collected and put together into one Book. Amazingly each individual historical document fits together perfectly into place.

These facts alone make the Holy Bible one-of-a-kind, without any natural explanation. It is inconceivable to me that a book this amazing could be considered anything less than Inspired by God. Although the *Proof of Authority* found in Biblical Christianity is multi-faceted, we will only be looking briefly at nine specific proofs of authority in this book. The nine proofs that we will be discussing are as follows:

1. Archaeological Evidence
2. Predictive Prophecy
3. Scientific Agreement
4. Eyewitness Testimony
5. Historical Evidence
6. Internal Consistency
7. Manuscript Evidence
8. Miracles
9. Mathematical Probability

As you consider Biblical Christianity as a coherent worldview, you will
- see that it is based in reality and consistent with the human experience.
- begin to understand the uniqueness of Biblical Christianity in a vast marketplace of worldviews and ideas.
- start to see a very sophisticated and complex system of evidence emerge that is designed for only one purpose, and that purpose is to give *Proof of Authority* to God's message.

---

30 *The New Evidence that Demands a Verdict*, © 1999 by Josh McDowell. Published by Thomas Nelson, Nashville.

Look at God's Word and the evidence found both internally and externally in Biblical Christianity for *Proof of Authority*. As you discover the evidence for yourself, I hope and pray that the information presented in this book will help you better understand the uniqueness found only in the Biblical Christian worldview.

In Christ's Service,
David Wayne Meeker

PROOF ONE

ar-chae-ol-o-gy

–noun

1. Study of ancient cultures through the excavation and analysis of physical remains.

—The Oxford Dictionary

ARCHAEOLOGY AND THE BIBLE

PREMISE

One of the things I love about the Holy Bible, relative to its archaeological confirmation, is in the precision of what it speaks. It has verified many ancient sites, civilizations, and Biblical people whose existence was in question by the academic world and often dismissed as myths.

Biblical archaeology has silenced many critics as new discoveries continue to support the facts of the Holy Bible. The places, the mountains, the valleys, the cities, and towns like Bethlehem, Jerusalem, Galilee, and so on, are real places. All these locations can still be found today. James D. Agresti said, *"I have yet to encounter archaeological evidence that shows any part of the Bible to be inaccurate."*[31]

Archaeology has proven the internal and external accuracy of the Holy Bible time and time again as it continues to confirm both the Old and New Testament documents to be historically reliable and trustworthy. For example, Luke was accurate in naming 32 countries, 54 cities, and 9 islands.[32] The evidence is there for all to see.

There have been multiple thousands of archaeological discoveries associated with the Old and New Testament periods, excavated in the Bible lands, which confirm the people, places, and objects mentioned in the Bible.

---

31 Agresti, *Rational Conclusions*, p. 88.
32 Sir William Ramsay, *St. Paul The Traveler and Roman Citizen,* Grand Rapids, MI: Baker Book House, 1962, p.36; p. 81; *The Bearing of Recent Discoveries on the Trustworthiness of the New Testament.* Grand Rapids, MI: Baker Book House, 1953, p. 222.

The evidence that supports and validates the reliability and trustworthiness of the Holy Bible and its written accounts is amazing. It is through archaeology that the Old Testament prophets, the New Testament disciples, apostles, and Jesus Christ Himself, have been taken from the realm of invented ideas, religious stories and myths to their rightful place in history by confirming them as legitimate historical figures. James Mann of *U.S. News and World Report* said, *"A wave of archaeology discoveries is altering old ideas about the roots of Christianity and Judaism and affirming that the Bible is more historically accurate than many scholars thought."*[33]

Archaeology does not directly prove the Holy Bible's claim of Divine Origin and Inspiration, but it does directly prove its historical accuracy through observable evidence. This supports and validates the reliability and trustworthiness of the Holy Bible and leaves very little space for the disbelief of a skeptic. Archaeology has not proven so helpful for other religious writings.

Consider the Latter-day Saints Book of Mormon. *"Not one piece of evidence has ever been found to support the Book of Mormon—not a trace of the large cities it names, no ruins, no coins, no letters or documents or monuments, nothing in writing. Not even one of the rivers or mountains or any of the topography it mentions has ever been identified."*[34]

The truth about the Book of Mormon is that there has been no archaeological evidence found that would indicate that it is anything other than an early nineteenth-century composition of American fiction fabricated by Joseph Smith.[35] Due to the many inquiries concerning the alleged use of the Book of Mormon by the LDS Church as a Smithsonian Institute scientific guide, the Department of Anthropology from the Smithsonian Institute issued a response letter entitled "Statement Regarding the Book of Mormon." In this letter they stated that they never used the Book of Mormon in archaeological research and that the Book of Mormon is a religious document and not a scientific guide.[36]

---

33   James Mann, "New Finds Cast Fresh Light on the Bible," *U.S. News and World Report*, August 24, 1981.
34   Dave Hunt, *In Defense of the Faith*, p. 156; also see *The Case for Christ*, p. 107 by Lee Strobel.
35   http://probe.org/examining-the-book-of-mormon
36   You can obtain a copy of the complete "Smithsonian Statement Regarding the Book of Mormon" by corresponding to Anthropology Outreach Office, Department of Anthropology, National Museum of Natural History, MRC 112, Smithsonian Institute, Washington, DC 20560; or go to http://www.utlm.org/onlineresources/smithsonianletter.html

> *Information from the*
> National Museum of Natural History
> SMITHSONIAN INSTITUTION WASHINGTON, D.C. 20560
>
> Your recent inquiry concerning the Smithsonian Institution's alleged use of the Book of Mormon as a scientific guide has been received in the Smithsonian's Department of Anthropology.
>
> The Book of Mormon is a religious document and not a scientific guide. The Smithsonian Institution has never used it in archeological research and any information that you have received to the contrary is incorrect. Accurate information about the Smithsonian's position is contained in the enclosed "Statement Regarding the Book of Mormon," which was prepared to respond to the numerous inquiries that the Smithsonian receives on this topic.

The Institute for Religious Research posted on their website a 1998 letter from National Geographic Society stating that they were unaware of any archaeological evidence that would support the Book of Mormon.[37]

---

[37] National Geographic Society Statement on the Book of Mormon, August 12, 1998. Letter from Julie Crain addressed to Luke Wilson of the Institute for Religious Research.

Here is what other people are saying about the Book of Mormon and its archaeology.

- "With the exception of Latter-day Saint archaeologists, members of the archaeological profession do not, and never have, espoused the Book of Mormon in any sense of which I am aware. Non-Mormon archaeologists do not allow the Book of Mormon any place whatever in their reconstruction of the early history of the New World." – *Ulster Archaeological Society Newsletter*, no.64, Jan.30, 1960, p.3.

- "One cannot fake over 3000 years...of history and have the fake hold water under the scrutiny given the Book of Mormon. The Book of Mormon is either fake or fact. If fake, the cities described in it are non-existent. If fact—as we know it to be—the cities will be there. If the cities exist, and they do, they constitute tangible, physical, enduring, unimpeachable evidence that Joseph Smith was a true prophet of God and that Jesus Christ lives." – *Thomas Ferguson to the First Presidency, March 15, 1958, Ferguson Collection, BYU.*

- "...our testimony of the Book of Mormon remain[s] a matter of faith, and [is] not based upon external proofs found from archaeology." – *Duane R. Aston,* Return to Cumorah, *1998.*

- "It is the personal opinion of the writer that the Lord does not intend that the Book of Mormon, at least at the present time, shall be proved true by any archaeological findings. The day may come when such will be the case, but not now. The Book of Mormon is itself a witness of the truth, and the promise has been given most solemnly that any person who will read it with a prayerful heart may receive the abiding testimony of its truth." – *Prophet Joseph Fielding Smith, Answers to Gospel Questions,* 1998, v,2, p.196.

- "The first myth we need to eliminate is that Book of Mormon archaeology exists... if one is to study Book of Mormon archaeology, then one must have a corpus of data with which to deal. We do not. The Book of Mormon is really there so one can have Book of Mormon studies, and archaeology is really there so one can study archaeology, but the two are not wed. At least they are not wed in reality since no

Book of Mormon location is known with reference to modern topography. Biblical archaeology can be studied because we do know where Jerusalem and Jericho were and are, but we do not know where Zarahemia and Bountiful (nor any other location for that matter) were or are. It would seem then that a concentration on geography should be the first order of business, but we have already seen that twenty years of such an approach has left us empty-handed." – *Dee F. Green, Mormon archaeologist, Dialogue: A Journal of Mormon Thought*, summer 1969, pp. 77-78.

GILBERT M. GROSVENOR
PRESIDENT
OWEN R. ANDERSON
EXECUTIVE VICE PRESIDENT
ALFRED J. HAYRE
VICE PRESIDENT AND TREASURER
EDWIN W. SNIDER
SECRETARY

WILBUR E. GARRETT
EDITOR
ROBERT L. BREEDEN
VICE PRESIDENT, PUBLICATIONS

National Geographic Society
WASHINGTON, D.C. 20036

MELVIN M. PAYNE
CHAIRMAN OF THE BOARD
ROBERT E. DOYLE
VICE CHAIRMAN OF THE BOARD
LLOYD H. ELLIOTT
VICE CHAIRMAN OF THE BOARD
THOMAS W. McKNEW
ADVISORY CHAIRMAN OF THE BOARD

December 23, 1982

Mr. Virgil Jennings
Route 1, Box 105
Shoshone, ID 83352

Dear Mr. Jennings:

We appreciate the interest that prompted you to write the National Geographic Society.

I referred your inquiry to Dr. George Stuart, the staff archaeologist of the National Geographic Society. He informed me that neither the Society nor any other institution of equal prestige has ever used the Book of Mormon in locating archeological sites. Although many Mormon sources claim that the Book of Mormon has been substantiated by archaeological findings, this claim has not been verified scientifically.

I trust this will prove helpful, Mr. Jennings. It was a pleasure to hear from you.

Sincerely yours,

Richard J. Arnold
Research Correspondence

RJA:rd

Here is what the experts are saying about Biblical Archaeology.

BIBLICAL ARCHAEOLOGY QUOTES

"I set out to look for truth on the borderland where Greece and Asia meet, and found it there. You may press the words of Luke in a degree beyond any other historian's and they stand the keenest scrutiny and the hardest treatment." - Sir William Ramsey (eminent archaeologist who changed his mind regarding Luke after extensive study in the field), (1915), The Bearing of Recent Discovery on the Trustworthiness of the New Testament (Grand Rapids, MI: Baker, 1975 reprint), page 89.

"It is therefore legitimate to say that, in respect of that part of the Old Testament against which the disintegrating criticism of the last half of the nineteenth century was chiefly directed, the evidence of archaeology has been to reestablish its authority and likewise to augment its value by rendering it more intelligible through a fuller knowledge of its background and setting. Archaeology has not yet said its last word, but the results already achieved confirm what faith would suggest – that the Bible can do nothing but gain from an increase in knowledge." - Sir Frederic Kenyon, a former director of the British Museum, The Bible and Archaeology (New York: Harper & Brothers, 1940), page 279.

BIBLICAL ARCHAEOLOGY QUOTES

"It may be stated categorically that no archaeological discovery has ever controverted a Biblical reference. Scores of archaeological findings have been made which confirm in clear outline or exact detail historical statements in the Bible. And, by the same token, proper evaluation of Biblical description has often led to amazing discoveries." - Dr. Nelson Glueck, Rivers in the Desert, (New York: Farrar, Strous and Cudahy, 1959), 136.

"Archaeology has confirmed countless passages which have been rejected by critics as unhistorical or contradictory to known facts......Yet archaeological discoveries have shown that these critical charges.....are wrong and that the Bible is trustworthy in the very statements which have been set aside as untrustworthy.....We do not know of any cases where the Bible has been proved wrong." - Dr. Joseph P. Free, Archaeology and Bible History. Scripture Press, Wheaton, IL, 1969, pg. 1.

"The reader may rest assured that nothing has been found [by archaeologists] to disturb a reasonable faith, and nothing has been discovered which can disprove a single theological doctrine. We no longer trouble ourselves with attempts to 'harmonize' religion and science, or to 'prove' the Bible. The Bible can stand for itself." - Dr. William F. Albright, eminent archeologist who confirmed the authenticity of the Dead Sea Scrolls following their discovery

BIBLICAL ARCHAEOLOGY QUOTES

"I know of no finding in archaeology that's properly confirmed which is in opposition to the Scriptures. The Bible is the most accurate history textbook the world has ever seen." - Dr. Clifford Wilson, formerly director of the Australian Institute of Archaeology

"Through the wealth of data uncovered by historical and archaeological research, we are able to measure the Bible's historical accuracy. In every case where its claim can thus be tested, the Bible proves to be accurate and reliable." - Dr. Jack Cottrell, The Authority of the Bible (Grand Rapids: Baker Book House, 1979), pp. 48-49.

"In every instance where the findings of archaeology pertain to the Biblical record, the archaeological evidence confirms, sometimes in detailed fashion, the historical accuracy of Scripture. In those instances where the archaeological findings seem to be at variance with the Bible, the discrepancy lies with the archaeological evidence, i.e., improper interpretation, lack of evidence, etc. -- not with the Bible." - Dr. Bryant C. Wood, archaeologist, Associates for Biblical Research

The Biblical Archaeological Evidence

Go to www.biblearchaeologyreport.com and www.biblearchaeology.org for more details.

50 Events, Places and Objects:

1. The Egypt on Scarab of Khirbet el-Maqatir (2013)
2. The Ophel Pithos (2012)
3. The Seal Impression of the Prophet Isaiah (2018)
4. Discoveries at Khirbet Qeiyafa (2010-2013)
5. The Seal Impression of King Hezekiah (2015)
6. A Roman Ring Inscribed with Pilate's Name (2018)
7. Tel Dan ("David") Stela Inscription (1993)
8. Cyrus Cylinder (1879)
9. Merneptah Stele (1896)
10. Moabite stone (1869)
11. St. Peter's House (2011)
12. The Pool of Siloam (2004)
13. Ashkelon's Arched Gate (1992)
14. The Bulla of a Servant of King Jeroboam II (2020)
15. Reliefs of Assyrian King, Sargon II (2020)
16. Crucifixion Victim (1965)
17. The Nazareth Decree (1878)
18. First-Century Synagogue Discovered Shemesh (2020)
19. Biblical "Yerushalayim' inscription on ancient column (2018)
20. Esarhaddon inscriptions found at the shrine of Jonah (2014)
21. Azaeiah Seal (1970)
22. The Dead Sea Scrolls (1947)
23. Black Obelisk of Shalmaneser (1846)
24. The Pool of Gibeon (1956)
25. The Epic of Gilgamesh (1872)
26. The Rosetta Stone (1798)
27. The Hezekiah's Tunnel (1872)
28. The Pontius Pilate Stone (1961)

29. The Pool of Bethesda (2005)
30. The Silver Ketef Hinnan Scrools (1979-80)
31. The Seal of Megiddo (1904)
32. Lachish letters (1930)
33. Ugaritic Texts (1929)
34. The Jesus Boat (1986)
35. Nazareth (2009)
36. Well-Blundell Prism (1922)
37. King David's Palace (2013)
38. Sennacherib Prism (1830)
39. Gemariah Seal (2018)
40. Jerahimeel Seal (1975)
41. The Walls of Jericho (1952- 1958)
42. The Marble Head of Caesar Augustus (2013)
43. Assyrian Inscriptions (2019)
44. The Magdala Synagogue (2009-2013)
45. Shishak's Invasion Record (2015)
46. The Temple of Arad (1960)
47. The Ostraca of Samaria (1910)
48. Crucified Man found in Italy (2007)
49. Rehoboam's Wall Discovered at Lachish (2019)
50. Statue of Idrimi (1939)

50 Biblical Figures: (Go to: Biblicalarchaeology.org)
EGYPT
1. Shishak (= Shoshenq I), Pharaoh, reigned 945–924, 1Kings 11:40 and 14:25.
2. So (= Osorkon IV), Pharaoh, reigned 730–715, 2Kings 17:4.
3. Tirhakah (= Taharqa), Pharaoh, reigned 690–664, 2Kings 19:9.
4. Necho II (= Neco II), Pharaoh, reigned 610–595, 2Chronicles 35:20.
5. Hophra (= Apries = Wahibre), Pharaoh, reigned 589–570, Jeremiah 44:30.

MOAB
  6. Mesha, king, reigned early to mid-9th century, 2Kings 3:4–27.

ARAM-DAMASCUS
  7. Hadadezer, king, reigned early 9th century to 844/842, 1Kings 22:3.
  8. Ben-hadad, son of Hadadezer, reigned or served as co-regent 844/842, 2Kings 6:24.
  9. Hazael, king, reigned 844/842–ca. 800, 1Kings 19:15, 2Kings 8:8.
  10. Ben-hadad, son of Hazael, king, reigned early 8th century, 2Kings 13:3.

NORTHERN KINGDOM OF ISRAEL
  12. Omri, king, reigned 884–873, 1Kings 16:16.
  13. Ahab, king, reigned 873–852, 1Kings 16:28.
  14. Jehu, king, reigned 842/841–815/814, 1Kings 19:16.
  15. Joash (= Jehoash), king, reigned 805–790, 2Kings 13:9.
  16. Jeroboam II, king, reigned 790–750/749, 2Kings 13:13.
  17. Menahem, king, reigned 749–738, 2Kings 15:14.
  18. Pekah, king, reigned 750(?)–732/731, 2Kings 15:25.
  19. Hoshea, king, reigned 732/731–722, 2Kings 15:30.
  20. Sanballat "I", governor of Samaria under Persian rule, around mid-fifth century, Nehemiah 2:10.

SOUTHERN KINGDOM OF JUDAH
  21. David, king, reigned around 1010–970, 1Samuel 16:13.
  22. Uzziah (= Azariah), king, reigned 788/787–736/735, 2Kings 14:21.
  23. Ahaz (= Jehoahaz), king, reigned 742/741–726, 2Kings 15:38.
  24. Hezekiah, king, reigned 726–697/696, 2Kings 16:20.
  25. Manasseh, king, reigned 697/696–642/641, 2Kings 20:21.
  26. Hilkiah, high priest during Josiah's reign, within 640/639–609, 2Kings 22:4.
  27. Shaphan, scribe during Josiah's reign, within 640/639–609, 2Kings 22:3.
  28. Azariah, high priest during Josiah's reign, within 640/639–609, 1Chronicles 5:39.

29. Gemariah, official during Jehoiakim's reign, within 609–598, Jeremiah 36:10.
30. Jehoiachin (= Jeconiah = Coniah), king, reigned 598–597, 2Kings 24:5.
31. Shelemiah, father of Jehucal the official, late 7th century, Jeremiah 37:3; 38:1.
32. Jehucal (= Jucal), official during Zedekiah's reign, flourished. within 597–586, Jeremiah 37:3; 38:1.
33. Pashhur, father of Gedaliah the official, late 7th century, Jeremiah 38:1.
34. Gedaliah, official during Zedekiah's reign, flourished. within 597–586, Jeremiah 38:1.

ASSYRIA
35. Tiglath-pileser III (= Pul), king, reigned 744–727, 2Kings 15:19.
36. Shalmaneser V (= Ululaya), king, reigned 726–722, 2Kings 17:2.
37. Sargon II, king, reigned 721–705, Isaiah 20:1.
38. Sennacherib, king, reigned 704–681, 2Kings 18:13.
39. Adrammelech (= Ardamullissu = Arad-mullissu), son and assassin of Sennacherib, flourished early 7th century, 2Kings 19:37.
40. Esarhaddon, king, reigned 680–669, 2Kings 19:37.

BABYLONIA
41. Merodach-baladan II (=Marduk-apla-idinna II), king, reigned 721–710 and 703, 2Kings 20:12.
42. Nebuchadnezzar II, king, reigned 604–562, 2Kings 24:1.
43. Nebo-sarsekim, chief official of Nebuchadnezzar II, flourished early 6th century, Jeremiah 39:3.
44. Evil-merodach (= Awel Marduk, = Amel Marduk), king, reigned 561–560, 2Kings 25:27.
45. Belshazzar, son and co-regent of Nabonidus, flourished around 543–540, Daniel 5:1.

PERSIA
46. Cyrus II (=Cyrus the great), king, reigned 559–530, 2Chronicles 36:22.

47. Darius I (=Darius the Great), king, reigned 520–486, Ezra 4:5.
48. Xerxes I (= Ahasuerus), king, reigned 486–465, Esther 1:1.
49. Artaxerxes I Longimanus, king, reigned 465-425/424, Ezra 4:6, 7.
50. Darius II Nothus, king, reigned 425/424-405/404, Nehemiah 12:22.

On the following pages I have added maps of the places, the mountains, the valleys, the cities, and towns like Bethlehem, Jerusalem, Galilee, and so on, to show you that they are real places. All these locations can still be found today (www.bibleatlas.org). Archaeology has proven the internal accuracy of the Holy Bible time and time again as it continues to confirm both the Old and New Testament documents to be historically reliable and trustworthy. The study, research, and science of archaeology have been devastating for the Latter-day Saints, and this is the reason why the Book of Mormon has no maps supporting its topography. "Mormonism does not have one piece of evidence to support the Book of Mormon. Not any of its large cities, not one ruin, coins, letters, documents or monuments, nothing in writing. Not even one of the rivers or mountains or any of the topography it mentions has ever been identified."[38] The Bible, on the other hand, has proven its trustworthiness and reliability through its archaeology.

---

38 Dave Hunt, *In Defense of the Faith*, p. 156; also see *The Case for Christ*, p. 107 by Lee Strobel.

Jesus' Journey to Jerusalem

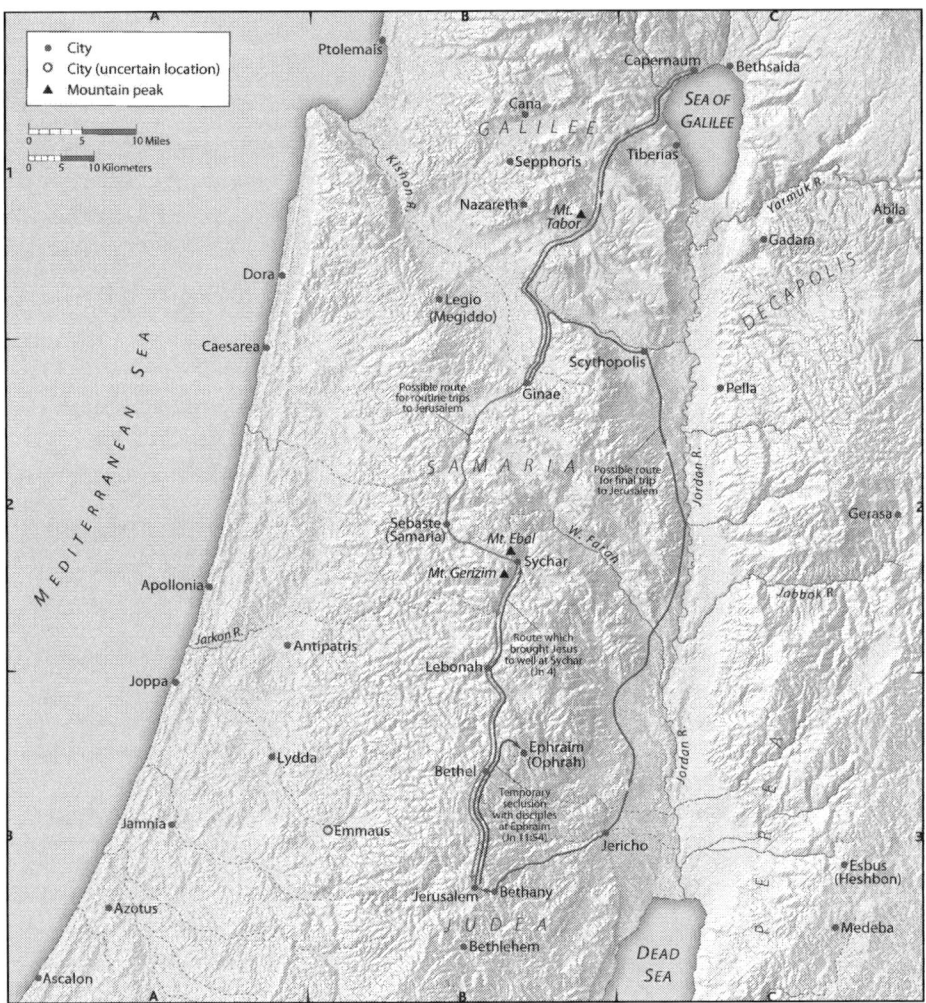

The Ministry of Peter and Philip

The Early Travels of the Apostle Paul

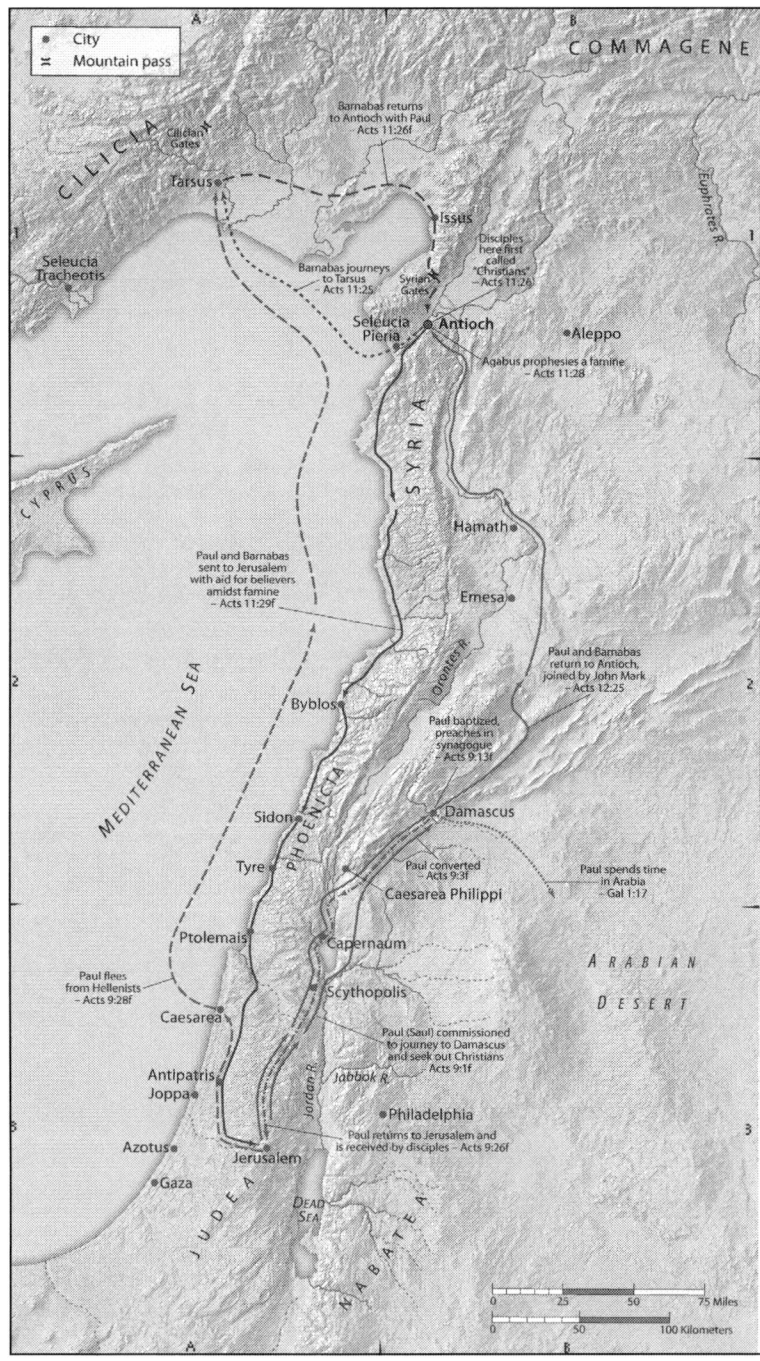

Evidence to Evaluate

- The Holy Bible is without question the best-documented and most-historically and archaeologically-substantiated religious text in the world.
- There is no other ancient book written that has as much archaeological evidence to support its accounts than the Holy Bible.
- Archaeology has proven the accuracy of the Holy Bible in confirming both the Old and New Testament documents to be historically reliable and trustworthy.

Notes

PROOF TWO

proph-e-cy

–noun

1. a prediction of what will happen in the future; the faculty, function, or practice of prophesying.

—*The Oxford American College Dictionary*

PROPHECY AND THE BIBLE

PREMISE

If you found an ancient historical document that could accurately and repeatedly predict the future, would you think that this document would be special, perhaps maybe even Supernatural in its Origin?

Would you agree that fulfilled prophecy is perhaps the most powerful and most amazing evidence of Supernatural Intervention that has ever been discovered on planet Earth? Would you be surprised to find out that the phenomenon of predictive prophecy only occurs in the Holy Bible and no other place? The questions we should be asking ourselves are as follows:

1. *Why* is the phenomenon of Supernatural Intervention and Confirmation found only in the Holy Bible and not anywhere else?
2. *What* is the purpose of the Holy Bible's Supernatural Intervention and Confirmation phenomena?
3. *Where* did the Holy Bible's phenomena of Supernatural Intervention and Confirmation come from?
4. *How* does the evidence of the Holy Bible's Supernatural Intervention and Confirmation phenomena effect the validity of other worldviews?

The answers to these questions are that this incredible and amazing Supernatural Intervention confirms the Holy Bible's claim of Divine Origin and Inspiration and validates the One True God's Message and Mission.

Over two-thousand times the God of Biblical Christianity predicts the future, and there are approximately five-hundred prophecies not yet fulfilled.

To say that this could have happened by common sense, chance, or collusion is an astronomical impossibility.

The Holy Bible explains this phenomenon to us in 2Peter 1:21.

21For no prophecy was ever brought about through human initiative, but men spoke from God as they were carried along by the Holy Spirit.

Incidentally, the studies of psychics show only around 8% of their predictions come true. This means they are wrong 92% of the time. Virtually all of their successes can be attributed to chance and general knowledge of circumstances and usually involve only one person. There is no comparison between Biblical prophecy and the predictions of psychics.

In this chapter I will be focusing on the fact that the Holy Bible is the only religious Book in the world that has 100% accurate predictive prophecy. No other religion in history, apart from Judaism, can compare to the Holy Bible when it comes to the fulfillment of prophecy, whereby proving its claim of Divine Origin and Inspiration.

"When you read the prophecies found in the pages of the Holy Bible you simply have to stand back in awe. It has been said that one fourth of the Bible is predictive prophecy. There are seventeen books and over 1,800 references that appear in the Old Testament about the promises of the Return of Jesus Christ. Out of the 260 chapters in the New Testament, there are 300 references concerning the Second Coming of Christ. That is one out of every 30 verses. Twenty-three of the 27 New Testament books refer to this great event. For every prophecy on the First Coming of Christ, there are eight on Christ's Second Coming."[39]

The prophecies revealed and fulfilled to us in the Holy Bible are proof of God's authority. The reason why God has given us fulfilled prophecies is so that we may know that He exists and is in control of all things present and future (Is. 46:9, 10; 48:3-5).

The God of Biblical Christianity also makes it very clear that He is the only God and there are no greater or lesser gods who exist,[40] and the fact that He can accurately predict the future confirms this truth.

---

[39] Dr. George Sweeting, *Today in the World*, MBI, December ©1989, page 40.
[40] De. 4:35; Is. 45:5; 45:18, 21, 22.

The Old Testament makes various predictions, including many that the modern nation of Israel would be re-gathered after being dispersed globally for 1,900 years.

What amazes me is that the Jewish people have retained their culture and religion after being globally dispersed during that time.

The Holy Bible tells us that, "no one knows the day or the hour of Christ's return" (Mt. 24:36). However, it does tell us about the seasons or events that will occur at the end of human history, and also offers us a global picture regarding the end of history and Christ's Second Coming.

For years critics have made light of the Holy Bible's predictive prophecy about future events. Be that as it may, in recent years, we see that the Holy Bible's global scenario is rapidly coming into focus, just as the Holy Bible predicted. Because of the details described in Scripture, we can conclude that certain events and technologies will need to be in place before Christ's Second Coming at the End of the Age.

The events and technologies that must be in place prior to Christ's return are as follows:

1. A Jewish homeland will be re-established.[41]
2. The Gospel will be preached to all nations.[42]
3. The human race will have the ability to exterminate itself.[43]
4. The human race will have instant worldwide communication capability.[44]
5. The human race will have the ability to globally process and store information, communicate over a network, track, identify, buy, and sell with a digital identification microchip or tattoo that could be implanted under, or applied onto, the skin of human beings.[45]

---

[41] Eze. 34:13; 37:21; Lu. 21:7, 20, 21; Israel's homeland was re-established on May 14, 1948.

[42] Mt. 24:14; 28:18-20; Mk. 16:15, 20; Col. 1:4-6; 1:23; Ro. 10:18.

[43] Mt. 24:21, 22; Countries with nuclear capabilities and powers are as follows: 1.) Russia, 2.) United States, 3.) United Kingdom, 4.) China, 5.) India, 6.) Pakistan, 7.) France, 8.) Israel, 9.) North Korea; https://en.m.wikipedia.org/wiki/List_of_states_with_nuclear_weapons; According to Stockholm International Peace Research Institute (SIPRI), the worldwide total inventory of nuclear weapons as of 2019 stood at 13,865, of which 3,750 were deployed with operational forces.

[44] Mt. 24; Mk. 13; Lu. 21; The 5G network will revolutionize the field of communications, data, and technology.

[45] Re. 13:17; A radio frequency identification device (RFID) Microchip implant (for humans) described at http:// en.m.wikipedia.org/wiki/microchip_implants_(human)#Medical_Records. The Food and Drug Administration (FDA) approved the implanting of microchips in humans for medical purposes Nov. 6, 2004. See: www.ID4Africaevents.com; www.id2020.org (id2020 was joined by the City of Austin, Texas as its newest member and is the first official government partner); See for more details. www.biometricupdate.com; and www.emperortech.com; and id4d.worldbank.org; ID4D directly supports countries to achieve Sustainable

6. There will be a cashless society that operates with digital currency. Cash money as we know it will no longer exist.[46]
7. There will be a global government established.[47]
8. The Uphrates River will dry up.[48]

Most of the events and technologies necessary for the fulfillment of specific prophecy found in Scripture have already been or are in the process of being established on earth today. Plus, we must factor in these other Biblically prophetic events that have also become global realities. 1) Increase in Knowledge and Travel,[49] 2) Ecological Catastrophes,[50] 3) Over-Population and Food Shortages,[51] 4) The Increase of Disease,[52] and 5) Wars and Rumors of Wars.[53]

These fulfilled prophecies are proof of God's authority. This is completely amazing when you start to realize that, apart from Judaism, there are no such fulfilled prophecies in the scriptures of any other religious writings in the world like the Holy Bible. Not one.

Development Target 16.9: "By 2030, providing legal identity for all and to help countries realize the transformational potential of digital identification; see www.earthnow.com EarthNow will deliver real-time surveillance videos of almost anywhere in the world via a large constellation of satellites. 5G technology is 100 times faster than the current 4G with more clarity for the user, followed by reduced latency and immense device connectivity. 5G technology is revolutionary in the field of communications, data, and technology. The 5G video surveillance and Monitoring industry will be profoundly impacted by 5G technologies (www.ifsecglobal.com/video-surveillance-and-the-wider-physical-security-industry/).

46 Re. 13:16-18; The World's digital currency (i.e. cashless society) agenda is currently in progress (www.digitaldollarproject.org); (www.pymnts.com). Federal Reserve Chairman Powell talks about digital currency at IMF. See Brian Brooks digital currency comments @: www.coingeek.com > digital currency). CBDC -Central Bank Digital Currency (http://en.m.wikipedia.org/wiki/Central_bank_digital_currency). The New World Monetary System is on its way, (i.e. the Reset). According to www.blockchain-council.org and the certified crypto currency experts say, that the 5G bandwidth, speed, and power consumption is necessary for the success of the crypto currency system. 5G can result in 100 times faster crypto transactions and more clarity for the user, followed by reduced latency, immense device connectivity. 5G technologies is a revolution in communications, data, and technology.

47 Re. 13:7-8; The United Nations was established Oct. 24, 1945 after World War II. The U.N. is an intergovernmental organization tasked to promote international cooperation and to create and maintain international order. See www.un.org/esa/dsd/agenda21; www.agenda21.com; also see: www.america2050.org : An Infrastructure Vision for the 21st Century (PDF). The U.N. agenda 21 is currently referred to as agenda 2030 for obvious reasons.

48 Re. 9:14; 16:12

49 Knowledge has increased in all directions and includes areas of science, medicine, travel and technology. It is said that 90% of all of the world's knowledge has been brought forth in the last century.

50 http://en.m.wikipedia.org/wiki/list_of_environmental_disasters; http://en.m.wikipedia.org/wiki/2019-20_east_Africa_locust_infestation.

51 www.ifpri.org; *The Global Report on Food Crisis 2019* at www.fsinplatform.org; Julian Cribb, *The Coming Famine*.

52 http://www.sciencedaily.com/releases/2014/10/141028214049.htm; http://www.bcm.edu/departments/molecular-virology-and-microbiology/emerging-infection-and-biodefense/emerging-infectious-diseases.

53 See www.crisisgroup.org; https://revisesociology.com/2021/03/03/ongoing-wars-and-conflicts-in-the-world-today/.

For example, Joseph Smith,[54] Brigham Young,[55] Charles Taze Russell,[56] and the Watch Tower Society[57] have made a myriad of false prophecies that have been conveniently overlooked or explained away by Mormons and Jehovah's Witnesses.[58]

The writings of Buddha are totally lacking in any sort of specific predictive prophecy about the things of the future. In the writings of Confucius, there is absolutely nothing with regard to any predictive prophecies.

In the case of the Quran, the scripture of the Muslims, there are no specific fulfilled predictive prophecies found; we find only the prophecy of Mohammed who said that he would return to Mecca, a self-fulfilling prophecy which he himself did in fact fulfill.

This is quite different from the thousands of specific prophecies that occur in the Holy Bible which confirm its claim of Divine Origin and Inspiration. Only God, Who is outside of our space-time existence and finite knowledge and is all-powerful, could have accurately and consistently known about and guided events thousands of years in the future. The Bible says this about prophecy in 2Peter 1:19-21:

> *19We also have the message of the prophets, which has been confirmed beyond doubt. And you will do well to pay attention to this message, as to a lamp shining in a dark place, until the day dawns and the morning star rises in your hearts. 20Above all, you must understand that no prophecy of Scripture comes from the prophet's own interpretation. 21For no prophecy was ever brought about through human initiative, but men spoke from God as they were carried along by the Holy Spirit.*

Predictive prophecy is simply God's act of telling us events before they occur, through godly men, as a proof of His authority. He gives us predictions that are not vague like Jean Dixon or abstract like Nostradamus but are specific in nature and cannot be accounted for by common sense, chance, or collusion.

---

54 Joseph Smith, *History of the Church of Jesus Christ of Latter-day Saints* (Salt Lake City, UT: Deseret Book Company 1973), 5:394.
55 Brigham Young, *Journal of Discourses* (London: Latter-day Saints Book Depot, 1854-56) 10:250.
56 *Studies in the Scriptures*, Vol. 2 (Brooklyn: Watchtower Bible and Tract Society, 1888), pp. 98-99. Ibid, Vol. 3 (Brooklyn: Watchtower Bible and Tract Society, 1891), pp. 126.
57 Richard Packham, "Joseph Smith As a Prophet," www.exmormon.org/prophet.html.
58 https://en.m.wikipedia.org/wiki/Watch_Tower_Society_unfulfilled_predictions.

There are five rules that apply to Biblical Prophecy which are as follows:
1. The prophecy must be given before the fulfillment takes place.
2. The prophecy must be explicit.
3. The prophecy must potentially be able to be falsified.
4. The prophet cannot have any part in fulfillment.
5. The fulfillment must correspond exactly to the prediction.

We read in the book of Deuteronomy what God says to Moses about a false prophet:

Deuteronomy 18:22

22When a prophet speaks in the name of the LORD and the message does not come to pass or come true, that is a message the LORD has not spoken. The prophet has spoken presumptuously. Do not be afraid of him.

What this means is that a true prophet of God will be 100% accurate all of the time, and a false prophet will not be and should not be acknowledged or recognized as a representative of the One True God.

One of the characteristics of a false prophet is the failure of their predictions. A true prophet of God will make predictions that will always come true— and that is precisely what we see in the Holy Bible.

The Holy Bible tells us in the Gospel of Luke, on the day of Jesus Christ's resurrection, His disciples were going to a village called Emmaus. While on their journey,-Jesus began walking with them on the road, but they did not recognize Him at first. Then Jesus, beginning with Moses and all the Prophets, explained to them all the passages of Scripture concerning Himself (Lu. 24:13-27).

I want to show you some of those passages found in the Old Testament that Christ most likely expounded on that day. We must understand that there were over 300 specific and detailed prophecies that Jesus could have referred to on that day.

Here are 61 predictive prophecies found in the Old Testament that were fulfilled in the New Testament by Christ. We need to understand that the Old Testament prophecies concerning the identity of the coming Messiah were written by men. They were written as they were moved by the Holy

Spirit, (2Pe. 1:21) through the person of Jesus Christ, hundreds of years, and in some cases over a thousand years before there fulfillment in the New Testament.

This is one of the most amazing proofs of authority found in the Holy Bible. Please understand that no other religious writings in the world, except for Judaism, contain fulfilled predictive prophecy like the Holy Bible.

- Not the Islamic Quran or the Hadith.
- Not the Hindu Vedas or the Bhagavad Gita.
- Not Confucianism's Five Classics or the Analects.
- Not the Chinese Taoism's, Tao-Te-Ching, or Daozang.
- Not the Arabic Druze Rasail al-hikmah (Epistles of Wisdom).
- Not the Japanese Shinto Kojiki or the Nihon Shoki.

The Old Testament was written between, 1445 B.C. through 400 B.C. and the New Testament was written between 44 A.D. through 96 A.D. (see the chart on the following page). As you read the evidence, please remember that no Biblical prophecy has ever failed, whereby confirming the Bible's claim of Divine Origin and Inspiration.

Chronological Dates to the Books of the Bible

OLD TESTAMENT			NEW TESTAMENT		
Book	Date	Author	Book	Date	Author
1. Job	Unknown	Anonymous	1. James	A.D. 44-49	James
2. Genesis	1445-1405 B.C.	Moses	2. Galatians	A.D. 49-50	Paul
3. Exodus	1445-1405 B.C.	Moses	3. Matthew	A.D. 50-60	Matthew
4. Leviticus	1445-1405 B.C.	Moses	4. Mark	A.D. 50-60	Mark
5. Numbers	1445-1405 B.C.	Moses	5. 1 Thessalonians	A.D. 51	Paul
6. Deuteronomy	1445-1405 B.C.	Moses	6. 2 Thessalonians	A.D. 51-52	Paul
7. Psalms	1410-450 B.C.	Multiple Authors	7. 1 Corinthians	A.D. 55	Paul
8. Joshua	1405-1385 B.C.	Joshua	8. 2 Corinthians	A.D. 55-56	Paul
9. Judges	about 1043 B.C.	Samuel	9. Romans	A.D. 56	Paul
10. Ruth	about 1030-1010 B.C.	Samuel(?)	10. Luke	A.D. 60-61	Luke
11. Song of Solomon	971-965 B.C.	Solomon	11. Ephesians	A.D. 60-62	Paul
12 Proverbs	971-686 B.C.	Solomon Primarily	12 Philipians	A.D. 60-62	Paul
13 Ecclesiastes	940-931 B.C.	Solomon	13 Colossians	A.D. 60-62	Paul
14. 1 Samuel	931-722 B.C.	Anonymous	14. Philemon	A.D. 60-62	Paul
15. 2 Samuel	931-722 B.C.	Anonymous	15. Acts	A.D. 62	Luke
16. Obadiah	850-840 B.C.	Obadiah	16. 1 Timothy	A.D. 62-64	Paul
17. Joel	835-796 B.C.	Joel	17. Titus	A.D. 62-64	Paul
18. Jonah	about 775 B.C.	Jonah	18. 1 Peter	A.D. 64-65	Peter
19. Amos	about 750 B.C.	Amos	19. 2 Timothy	A.D. 66-67	Paul
20. Micah	735-710 B.C.	Micah	20. 2 Peter	A.D. 67-68	Peter
21. Hosea	750-710 B.C.	Hosea	21. Hebrews	A.D. 67-69	Unknown
22. Isaiah	700-681 B.C.	Isaiah	22. Jude	A.D. 68-70	Jude
23. Nahum	about 650 B.C.	Nahum	23 John	A.D. 80-90	John
24. Zephaniah	635-625 B.C.	Zephaniah	24. 1 John	A.D. 90-95	John
25. Habakkuk	615-605 B.C.	Habakkuk	25. 2 John	A.D. 90-95	John
26. Ezekiel	590-570 B.C.	Ezekiel	26. 3 John	A.D. 90-95	John
27. Lamentations	586 B.C.	Jeremiah	27. Revelation	A.D. 94-96	John
28. Jeremiah	586-570 B.C.	Jeremiah			
29. 1 Kings	561-538 B.C.	Anonymous			
30. 2 Kings	561-538 B.C.	Anonymous			
31. Daniel	538-530 B.C.	Daniel			
32. Haggai	about 520 B.C.	Haggai			
33. Zechariah	480-470 B.C.	Zechariah			
34. Ezra	457-444 B.C.	Ezra			
35. 1 Chronicles	450-430 B.C.	Ezra (?)			
36. 2 Chronicles	450-430 B.C.	Ezra (?)			
37. Esther	450-331 B.C.	Anonymous			
38. Malachi	433-424 B.C.	Malachi			
39. Nehemiah	424-400 B.C.	Ezra			

Jesus Christ fulfilled over 300 Old Testament prophecies that were foretold before He was born. Here are 61 of these prophecies found in Scripture.

CONCERNING HIS BIRTH

1. **Messiah to be born of the seed of a woman.** Found in Genesis 3:15; fulfilled in Luke 2:5-7 and Galatians 4:4.
2. **Messiah to be born of a virgin.** Found in Isaiah 7:14; fulfilled in Matthew 1:18-25, Luke 1:26-38.
3. **Messiah to be of the seed of Abraham.** Found in Genesis 12:2-3; 18:18; fulfilled in Matthew 1:1-2, Luke 3:34, Acts 3:25, Galatians 3:16.
4. **Messiah to be of the seed of Isaac.** Found in Genesis 21:12; fulfilled in Luke 3:23, 34.
5. **Messiah to be of the seed of Jacob.** Found in Numbers 24:17; fulfilled in Luke 3:34.
6. **Messiah to be of the seed of David.** Found in Jeremiah 23:5; fulfilled in Luke 3:31.
7. **Messiah to be of the Tribe of Judah.** Found in Genesis 49:10; fulfilled in Revelation 5:5.
8. **Messiah to be of the family line of Jesse.** Found in Isaiah 11:1; fulfilled in Luke 3:32.
9. **Messiah to be born in Bethlehem.** Found in Micah 5:2; fulfilled in Matthew 2:1-6.
10. **Herod kills children in an attempt to kill the Messiah.** Found in Jeremiah 31:15; fulfilled in Matthew 2:16-18.

CONCERNING HIS NATURE

11. **He would be the Son of God.** Found in Psalm 2:2,7; fulfilled in Matthew 3:17 and Luke 1:32, 33.
12. **He pre-existed creation.** Found in Micah 5:2; fulfilled in 1Peter 1:20.
13. **He shall be called Lord.** Found in Psalm 110:1; fulfilled in Acts 2:36.
14. **Called Immanuel (God with us).** Found in Isaiah 7:14; fulfilled in Matthew 1:22-23.

15. **He will be a Prophet.** Found in Deuteronomy 18:18; fulfilled in Acts 3:18-25.
16. **He will be a Priest.** Found in Psalm 110:4; fulfilled in Hebrews 5:5, 6.
17. **He will be a Judge.** Found in Isaiah 33:22; fulfilled in John 5:22, 23.
18. **He will be a King.** Found in Psalm 2:6; fulfilled in John 18:33-37.
19. **He will be anointed by the Spirit.** Found in Isaiah 11:2; fulfilled in Matthew 3:16, 17.
20. **He will have a zeal for God.** Found in Psalm 69:9; fulfilled in John 2:15-17.

CONCERNING HIS MINISTRY

21. **Preceded by a messenger.** Found in Isaiah 40:3; fulfilled in Matthew 3:1-3.
22. **To begin in Galilee.** Found in Isaiah 9:1, 2, Fulfilled in Matthew 4:12-17.
23. **He would have a ministry of miracles.** Found in Isaiah 35:5-6; fulfilled in Matthew 9:35; 11:4, 5.
24. **He would teach in parables.** Found in Psalm 78:1-4; fulfilled in Matthew 13:34,35.
25. **He was to enter the Temple.** Found in Malachi 3:1; found in Matthew 21:10-12.
26. **He would enter Jerusalem on a donkey.** Found in Zechariah 9:9; fulfilled in Matthew 21:1-7.
27. **He would be a stone of stumbling to Jews.** Found in Isaiah 28:16; Psalm 118:22; fulfilled in 1Peter 2:6-8.
28. **He would be a light to Gentiles.** Found in Isaiah 49:6; fulfilled in Acts 13:46-48.

THE DAY JESUS WAS CRUCIFIED

29. **He would be betrayed by a friend.** Found in Psalm 41:9; fulfilled in John 13:18-27.
30. **He would be sold for 30 pieces of silver.** Found in Zechariah 11:12; fulfilled in Matthew 26:14, 15.
31. **Thirty pieces of silver thrown in the Temple.** Found in Zechariah 11:13; fulfilled in Matthew 27:3-5.

32. **Thirty pieces of silver buys Potters field.** Found in Zechariah 11:13; fulfilled in Matthew 27:6-10.
33. **He would be forsaken by His disciples.** Found in Zechariah 13:7; fulfilled in Mark 14:27,50.
34. **He would be accused by false witness.** Found in Psalm 35:11, 20, 21; fulfilled in Matthew 26:59-61.
35. **He would be silent before accusers.** Found in Isaiah 53:7; fulfilled in Matthew 27:12-14.
36. **He would be like a lamb going to the slaughter.** Found in Isaiah 53:7; fulfilled in Acts 8: 26-35.
37. **He would be wounded and bruised.** Found in Isaiah 53:4-6; fulfilled in 1Peter 2:21-25.
38. **He would be beaten and spit upon.** Found in Isaiah 50:6; fulfilled in Matthew 26:67, 68.
39. **He would be mocked.** Found in Psalm 22:6-8; fulfilled in Matthew 27:27-31.
40. **He would be nailed to a tree.** Deuteronomy 21:22, 23; Psalm 22:16, John 19:18, 20:25; 1Peter 2:24; Galatians 3:13.
41. **His hands and feet would be pierced.** Found in Psalm 22:16; fulfilled in John 20:24-28.
42. **He would be crucified with thieves.** Found in Isaiah 53:12; fulfilled in Matthew 27:38.
43. **He prayed for His enemies.** Found in Isaiah 53:12; fulfilled in Luke 23:34.
44. **He was rejected by His own people.** Found in Isaiah 53:3; fulfilled in John 19:14, 15.
45. **He was hated without a cause.** Found in Psalm 69:4; fulfilled in John 15:25.
46. **His clothes were divided and gambled for.** Found in Psalm 22:18; fulfilled in John 19:23, 24.
47. **He became very thirsty.** Found in Psalm 22:15; fulfilled in John 19:28.
48. **He was offered gall and vinegar.** Found in Psalm 69:21; fulfilled in Matthew 27:34.

49. **His forsaken cry.** Found in Psalm 22:1; fulfilled in Matthew 27:46.
50. **He committed Himself to God.** Found in Psalm 31:5; fulfilled in Luke 23:46.
51. **His bones will not be broken.** Found in Psalm 34:20; fulfilled in John 19:32-36.
52. **His heart would be broken.** Found in Psalm 69:20; 22:14; fulfilled in John 19:34.
53. **His side would be pierced.** Found in Zechariah 12:10; fulfilled in John 19:34, 37.
54. **There would be darkness over the land.** Found in Amos 8:9; fulfilled in Luke 23:44, 45.
55. **He would be buried in a rich man's tomb.** Found in Isaiah 53:9; fulfilled in Matthew 27:57-60.
56. **He would not decay.** Found in Psalm 16:10; fulfilled in Acts 2:31.

HIS DEATH, BURIAL, RESURRECTION, AND ASCENSION

57. **He was begotten as Son of God.** Found in Psalm 2:7; fulfilled in Acts 13:32-35.
58. **He would die.** Found in Isaiah 53:12; fulfilled in Matthew 27:50.
59. **He was raised from the dead.** Found in Psalm 16:8-11; fulfilled in Acts 2:24-31.Matthew 12:40.
60. **He ascended to heaven.** Found in Psalm 68:18; fulfilled in Ephesians 4:8-10; John 3:13.
61. **He is seated at the right hand of God.** Found in Psalm 110:1; fulfilled in Hebrews 1:3, 13.

Evidence to Evaluate

- There is no better evidence of the existence of God than the repeated and constant proof that is derived from the accurate predictions about future events. This demonstrates and confirms that God is in complete control of the present and future while validating His message and mission.

- Biblical Christianity is the only worldview in existence today that can predict events hundreds of years, and in some cases thousands of years, in the future with one-hundred percent accuracy, whereby, proving its claims of Divine Origin and Inspiration.
- The Holy Bible is unique in its content and teachings. No other religious book has ever been compiled by so many writers over such an expanse of time, with such cohesive unity and accuracy.
- The Holy Bible speaks on thousands of different topics and subjects without contradicting itself theologically, morally, ethically, doctrinally, scientifically, historically, or in any other way. With its one central theme, it is clearly one Book with perfect unity and consistency throughout.
- Biblical Christianity is unique and consistent with our everyday issues in life with regard to the human mind, laws of science, laws of logic, ethical and moral values, justice, love, the meaning of life, the problem of evil, suffering, and truth. It corresponds with the reality of our present condition unlike any other worldview on Earth.
- Jesus Christ fulfilled over 300 Old Testament prophecies that were foretold about Him before He was born.
- As a result of the Supernatural Intervention found in the Holy Bible, it has become the only religious Book ever to exist that can cover hundreds of controversial topics without contradicting itself and still remain united in all of its themes.

Notes

PROOF THREE

sci-ence

–noun

1. branch of knowledge involving systematized observation and experimentation.

   —*Oxford Pocket Dictionary and Thesaurus*

"The more I study science the more I believe in God." – **Albert Einstein**

"The visible order of the universe proclaims a supreme intelligence."
– **Jean- Jacques Rousseau**

"Instead of complaining that God had hidden himself, give Him thanks for having revealed so much of himself." – **Blaise Pascal**

"The visible marks of extraordinary wisdom and power appear so plainly in all the works of the creation that a rational creature, who will but seriously reflect on them, cannot miss the discovery of a Deity." – **John Locke**

"As a house implies a builder, and a garment a weaver, and a door a carpenter, so does the existence of the Universe imply a Creator."
– **Marquis de Vauvenargues**

"It is impossible to account for the creation of the universe without the agency of a Supreme Being." – **George Washington**

"The mathematical precision of the universe reveals the mathematical mind of God." – **Albert Einstein**

"I shall allways be convinced that a watch proves a watch-maker and the universe proves a God." – **Voltaire**

"Science without religion is lame, religion without science is blind."
– **Albert Einstein**

"When the Bible touches on scientific subjects, it is entirely accurate."
– **Dr. Donald DeYoung**

SCIENCE AND THE BIBLE

PREMISE

It is difficult to know for sure how many stories are found in the Holy Bible because it is difficult to determine where one story begins and one story ends. It is estimated that there are at least seven hundred stories found in the Holy Bible, perhaps as many as eight hundred. Although 75 percent of the Holy Bible is written in story format, no other ancient stories have captivated the mind of human beings than the story of "Jonah and the Whale" and "Noah and the Great Flood." However, very few people understand that the story of Noah's Ark has been passed down throughout history and has been told by many other cultures around the world. There are over 250 versions of this story found with remarkable similarities to the Biblical account. The majority of these stories talk about a wicked population, one righteous man, a universal destruction of the population on

Examples of Noah's Great Flood Stories from Around the World			
[1] **The Ark Gumana**—Australian Aborigin myth	[2] **Coxcox**—Aztec myth	[3] **Nuh**—from the Islamic Quran	
[4] **Manu**—from the Hindu Puranas	[5] **Tale of the Merchants at Sea**—from the Buddhist Samudda-Vanija Jataka 454	[6] **Ziusudra**—from a Sumerian tablet	
[7] **Nuu and the Flood**—Hawaiian myth	[8] **The Flood of Ife**—Yoruba-Nigerian myth	[9] **The Fuhi Family**—Chinese Flood myth	
[10] **The Blood Flood of Ymir**—Norse mythology from *Prose Edda* by Snorri Sturluson	[11] **Deucalion and Pyrrha**—Greek mythology	[12] **Egyptian Flood Myth**—from *Egyptian Book of the Dead, the Book of Going Forth by Day*, translated by Raymon Faulkner	
[13] **Atrahasis**—from various Akkadian tablets	[14] **Utnapishtim**—from several Babylonian tablets		
China		**Greece**	
One of the Chinese legends explains that the flood was caused by an argument between a crab and a bird. Fuhi, his wife, three sons, and three daughters escaped a great flood and were the only people alive on Earth. After the great flood, they repopulated the world.		There is more than one Greek flood myth, but the one that most likely corresponds to Noah's flood is about Deucalion who is told to build a chest to survive a flood.	

earth by water, and a boat that is created for the sole purpose for their survival. The story has been told in the countries of Assyria, China, Babylonia, and Egypt, as well as the state of Hawaii.[59]

Epic of Gilgamesh discovered in 1853. It is an ancient Babylonian poem-story about a righteous man who was saved from a flood by a huge boat.

Incidentally, Jesus Christ believed in Noah and the Ark and the Great Flood and Jonah and the whale. We read in Matthew 24:38-39, *"For in the days before the flood, people were eating and drinking, marrying and giving in marriage, up to the day Noah entered the ark. And they were oblivious, until the flood came and swept them all away. So will be the coming of the Son of Man."*

And in Luke 11:29-30, 32 we read, *"As the crowds were increasing, Jesus said, 'This is a wicked generation. It demands a sign, but none will be given it except the sign of Jonah. For as Jonah was a sign to the Ninevites, so the Son of Man will be a sign to this generation. The men of Nineveh will stand at the judgment with this generation and condemn it; for they repented at the preaching of Jonah, and now One greater than Jonah is here.'"*

I believe the Jonah story was a miracle implemented by God in achieving His plan and purpose. I believe that Jesus Christ believed these stories to be true and actual historical accounts, not just legendary, allegorical, or mythical (Mt. 12:40-41; 16:4). In this chapter I want to talk about the Holy Bible and its amazing agreement with known scientific facts. First, I want to point out that the Holy Bible is not a science book. It is, however, scientifically accurate in the statements that it makes.[60] The Holy Bible is unlike other religious books that make non-scientific claims. For example, Mormonism's president and prophet, Brigham Young, made a statement in the *Journal of Discourses* July 24, 1870:

---

[59] The Chinese Legend speaks of a man named Fuhi, who, with his wife and three sons, survives a great flood and afterward begins repopulating the earth as the single surviving family. The Hawaiian account speaks of a man called Nu-u, who built a massive canoe, put a house on it, and packed it with animals. Then water covered the earth and only Nu-u and his family was saved.

[60] "When the Bible touches on scientific subjects, it is entirely accurate."– Dr. Donald De Young, Ph. D (Physics)

"Who can tell us of the inhabitants of this little planet that shines of an evening, called the moon? When you inquire about the inhabitants of that sphere you find that the most learned are as ignorant in regard to them as the most ignorant of their fellows. So it is with regard to the inhabitants of the sun. Do you think it is inhabited? I rather think it is. Do you think there is any life there? No question of it; it was not made in vain."

We also see unscientific claims made in the Muslim scriptures as well. For example, in the Quran we find the claims that Jesus was speaking in the cradle (19:29-30), that the sun sets in a pool of murky water (18:86), that King Solomon learned the speech of birds (27:16), a boy and his dog fell asleep in a cave for 309 years (18:19, 25), ants can speak (27:18), and Allah made seven heavens and seven earths (65:12). In the Hadith, the second most authoritative book in Islam, there are the following claims: that angels stop asking Allah to forgive people when they pass wind (Vol. 1, Book 8, number 436: Narrated Abu Huraira), angels don't enter houses with dogs (Vol. 4, Book 54, Number 539, Narrated Abu Taiha), the moon was cut into two pieces (Vol. 6, Book 60, Number 387-388, Narrated Ibn Masud and Abdullah) [see also 389-391], and Muhammad had some people drink camel urine as medicine (Vol. 8, Book 82, Number 794, Narrated Anas). I think the above quotes speak for themselves.

The Scripture verses listed below are consistent with known scientific facts. Many of the references were written in the Holy Bible hundreds, or even in some cases, thousands of years before being recorded anywhere else. Because the Bible was written during the time of the prescientific era, the writers of the Bible could not have themselves known about the scientific accuracy mentioned in their writings.

The fact that there is such agreement with the Holy Bible and with modern science, the Bible once again has proven its claim of Divine Origin and Inspiration. Below is a brief list of scientific facts found in the Holy Bible that would have been impossible for the authors of the Holy Bible to have known. This is evidence of Supernatural Intervention which positively confirms the Holy Bible's claim of Divine Origin and Inspiration.

Look at the available body of information found in the Holy Bible that would indicate whether or not the *"scientific agreement proposition"* is true or false. You be the judge.

Dinosaurs are mentioned in the Bible.

The book of Job describes two dinosaurs—one is called *Behemoth*, and the other is called *Leviathan*. One is described in chapter 40 starting at verse 15 and the other in chapter 41 starting at verse 1. Most people don't know that there are one and a half chapters in the Holy Bible that talk about dinosaurs. Here are these texts in their entirety:

Job 40

*[15]Look at **Behemoth**, which I made along with you. He feeds on grass like an ox. [16]See the strength of his loins and the power in the muscles of his belly. [17]His tail sways like a cedar; the sinews of his thighs are tightly knit. [18]His bones are tubes of bronze; his limbs are rods of iron. [19]He is the foremost of God's works; only his Maker can draw the sword against him. [20]The hills yield him their produce, while all the beasts of the field play nearby. [21]He lies under the lotus plants, hidden among the reeds of the marsh. [22]The lotus plants conceal him in their shade; the willows of the brook surround him. [23]Though the river rages, Behemoth is unafraid; he remains secure, though the Jordan surges to his mouth. [24]Can anyone capture him as he looks on, or pierce his nose with a snare?*

Job 41

*[1]Can you pull in **Leviathan** with a hook or tie down his tongue with a rope? [2]Can you put a cord through his nose or pierce his jaw with a hook? [3]Will he beg you for mercy or speak to you softly? [4]Will he make a covenant with you to take him as a slave for life?*

[5]Can you pet him like a bird or put him on a leash for your maidens? [6]Will traders barter for him or divide him among the merchants? [7]Can you fill his hide with harpoons or his head with fishing spears? [8]If you lay a hand on him, you will remember the battle and never repeat it! [9]Surely hope of overcoming him is false. Is not the sight of him overwhelming? [10]No one is ferocious enough to rouse Leviathan. Then who is able to stand against Me? [11]Who has given to Me that I should repay him? Everything under heaven is Mine.

12 I cannot keep silent about his limbs, his power and his graceful form. 13 Who can strip off his outer coat? Who can approach him with a bridle? 14 Who can open his jaws, ringed by his fearsome teeth? 15 His rows of scales are his pride, tightly sealed together. 16 One scale is so near to another that no air can pass between them. 17 They are joined to one another; they clasp and cannot be separated.

18 His snorting flashes with light, and his eyes are like the rays of dawn. 19 Firebrands stream from his mouth; fiery sparks shoot forth! 20 Smoke billows from his nostrils as from a boiling pot over burning reeds. 21 His breath sets coals ablaze, and flames pour out of his mouth. 22 Strength resides in his neck, and dismay leaps before him. 23 The folds of his flesh are tightly joined; they are firm and immovable. 24 His chest is as hard as a rock, as hard as a lower millstone!

25 When Leviathan rises up, the mighty are terrified; they withdraw before his thrashing. 26 The sword that reaches him has no effect, nor does the spear or dart or arrow. 27 He regards iron as straw and bronze as rotten wood. 28 No arrow can make him flee; slingstones become like chaff to him. 29 A club is regarded as straw, and he laughs at the sound of the lance. 30 His undersides are jagged potsherds, spreading out the mud like a threshing sledge. 31 He makes the depths seethe like a cauldron; he makes the sea like a jar of ointment. 32 He leaves a glistening wake behind him; one would think the deep had white hair! 33 Nothing on earth is his equal—a creature devoid of fear! 34 He looks down on all the haughty; he is king over all the proud.

The Bible says the stars cannot be numbered.

Even today scientists admit that they don't know how many stars there are. Only about 3,000 can be seen with the naked eye. The scientists estimate the number of stars to be about 10^{21} which is amazing because they estimate the number of grains of sand on the earth to be 10^{25}. The Bible refers many times to the great numbers of stars in the heavens. Here are some examples.

Genesis 22

17 I will surely bless you and make your descendants as numerous as the stars in the sky and as the sand on the seashore. Your descendants will possess the gates of their enemies.

Jeremiah 33

22 "As the hosts of heaven cannot be counted and the sand of the sea cannot be measured, so too will I multiply the descendants of My servant David and the Levites who minister before Me."

The Bible says that each star is unique.

1Corintians 15

41 "The sun has one degree of splendor, the moon another, and the stars another; and star differs from star in splendor."

The Bible describes the precision of movement in the universe.[61]

Jeremiah 31

35 "Thus says the LORD, who gives the sun for light by day and orders the moon and stars for light by night, who stirs up the sea so that its waves roar—the LORD of Hosts is His name."
36 "Only if this fixed order departed from My presence, declares the LORD, would Israel's descendants ever cease to be a nation before Me."

The Bible describes the suspension of the earth in space on nothing.

Job 26

7 "He stretches out the north over empty space; He hangs the earth upon nothing."

The Bible describes the spherical shape of the earth.

Isaiah 40

22 "He sits enthroned above the circle of the earth; its dwellers are like grasshoppers."

---

[61] www.bethlehemstar.net

The Bible describes biogenesis (the development of living organisms from other living organisms) and the stability of each kind of living organism.

Genesis 1

11"Then God said, 'Let the earth bring forth vegetation, seed-bearing plants and fruit trees, each bearing fruit with seed according to its kind.' And it was so. 12The earth produced vegetation, seed-bearing plants according to their kinds and trees bearing fruit with seed according to their kinds. And God saw that it was good."

21"So God created the great sea creatures and every living thing that moves, with which the waters teemed according to their kinds, and every bird of flight after its kind. And God saw that it was good."

25And God made the beasts of the earth according to their kinds, the livestock according to their kinds, and everything that crawls upon the earth according to its kind. And God saw that it was good."

The phrase "according to its kind" occurs repeatedly, stressing the reproductive integrity of each kind of animal and plant. Today we know this occurs because all of these reproductive systems are programmed by their genetic codes.

The Bible describes the Hydrologic Cycle.

Job 36

27"For He draws up drops of water which distill the rain from the mist, 28which the clouds pour out and shower abundantly on mankind."

Psalms 135

7"He causes the clouds to rise from the ends of the earth. He sends lightning with the rain and brings the wind from His storehouses."

Jeremiah 10

13"When He thunders, the waters in the heavens roar, and He causes the clouds to rise from the ends of the earth. He sends lightning with the rain and brings the wind from His storehouses."

The Bible describes the recirculation of water on the earth.
Ecclesiastes 1

7"All the rivers flow into the sea, yet the sea is never full; to the place from which the streams come, there again they flow."

The Bible describes the circulation of air currents.
Ecclesiastes 1

6"Blowing southward, then turning northward, round and round the wind swirls, ever returning on its course."

Modern science has proved that the quantity of water on earth is just enough.
Isaiah 40

12"Who has measured the waters in the hollow of his hand, or marked off the heavens with the span of his hand? Who has held the dust of the earth in a basket, or weighed the mountains on a scale and the hills with a balance?"

The Bible describes paths in the sea.
Psalms 8:4-8

4"What is man that You are mindful of him, the son of man that You care for him? 5You made him a little lower than the angels and crowned him with glory and honor. 6You made him ruler of the works of Your hands; You put everything under his feet: 7all sheep and oxen, and even the beasts of the field, 8the birds of the air, and the fish of the sea, all that swim the paths of the seas."

The Bible describes mountains in the sea.
Jonah 2:5, 6

5"The waters engulfed me up to the neck; the watery depths overcame me; the seaweed wrapped around my head. 6To the roots of the mountains I descended; the earth beneath me barred me in forever!"

The Bible describes springs under the sea.

Job 38

16 "Have you journeyed to the vents of the sea or walked in the trenches of the deep?"

The Bible explains why every element in man can be found in the soil.

Genesis 2

7 "Then the LORD God formed man from the dust of the ground and breathed the breath of life into his nostrils, and the man became a living being."

Researchers from NASA's Ames Research Center confirmed that every element in man can be found in soil, prompting one of the scientists to say... "The Biblical scenario for the creation of life turns out to be not far off the mark." Fred Williams. Advance Scientific Knowledge.[62]

The Bible describes the concept of Entropy.

Psalm 102

25 "In the beginning You laid the foundations of the earth, and the heavens are the work of Your hands. 26 They will perish, but You remain; they will all wear out like a garment. Like clothing You will change them, and they will be passed on. 27 But You remain the same, and Your years will never end. 28 The children of Your servants will dwell securely, and their descendants will be established before You."

The Bible Describes the nature of Health, Sanitation, and Sickness.

Leviticus chapter 12 through 14.

The Bible says that the life of the flesh is in the blood and its blood is its life.

Leviticus 17

11 "For the life of the flesh is in the blood, and I have given it for you on the altar to make atonement for your souls, for it is the blood that makes atonement by the life."

14 "For the life of every creature is its blood: its blood is its life."

---

[62] Readers Digest, November 1982

The Bible reveals advanced medical knowledge with regard to sanitary practices.
- Wash in running water (Nu. 19, 31; Le. 15).
- Purify items through fire (Nu. 31)
- Bury human waste outside of camp (De. 23:12).
- Burn animal waste (Le. 4:11, 12).
- Don't eat animals that died of natural causes (Le. 7:24).
- Laws of quarantine (Le. 13, 14, 22; Nu. 19, 20).
- The first antiseptic—hyssop oil (Nu. 19:18; Ps. 51:7).

The Bible speaks about how to deal with contagious bacteria.
Leviticus 13
51 "Then he shall examine the disease on the seventh day. If the disease has spread in the garment, in the warp or the woof, or in the skin, whatever be the use of the skin, the disease is a persistent leprous disease; it is unclean.

52 "And he shall burn the garment, or the warp or the woof, the wool or the linen, or any article made of skin that is diseased, for it is a persistent leprous disease. It shall be burned in the fire."

What the Bible tells us about circumcision and blood clotting (Ge. 17:12; 21:14; Le. 12:3; Lu. 2:21).
God has given His law of circumcision and the procedure is required to be performed on the eighth day after birth. The reason is utterly amazing. Medical researchers recently discovered that the two main blood clotting factors, Vitamin K and Prothrombin, reach there their highest level in life, about 110% of normal, on the eighth day. These blood clotting agents facilitate rapid healing and greatly reduces the chance of infection. You can verify with any obstetrician that the eighth day of life is the ideal time for circumcision.

The Bible talks about dietary guidelines (Ge. 1:29; Da. 1:12-15).
By the 1980s, all the health organizations of the United States had adopted low-fat, high-fiber dietary guidelines. This was the culmination of numerous scientific studies that demonstrated that diets high in vegetables,

fruit, and grains reduced the risk of heart disease, cancer, and many other diseases. Secular physicians generally agree that these dietary guidelines which were producing longer life spans were first developed by religious movements founded in the 1800s. Where did these religious movements get their guidelines? These guidelines are from a meticulous and careful study of the Holy Bible. It appears that man has finally caught up to the dietary recommendations given by God to the Israelites some 3,500 years ago!

Intelligent Design, Darwinian Evolution, and Atheism

Everyone reading this book would have to agree that we exist and did not create ourselves. Since both of these facts are true, we are forced to come to the conclusion that something or someone is responsible for our existence. This line of reasoning would also apply to our universe as well. How did the universe come into existence? After researching this topic, I have come to the realization that there are only three possibilities for how the universe could have come into existence. The three possibilities are as follows:

1. The universe created itself.
2. The universe has always existed and therefore had no need for a creator.
3. The universe was created by something or someone else outside of itself.

Look again at each of these possible explanations in more detail.

1. **The universe created itself.** This can be easily dismissed because it violates the basic law of logic known as the Law of Non-contradiction.

As I have previously pointed out, the Law of Non-contradiction states that a proposition cannot be both true and not true at the same time when using the same context.

Let me explain. For the universe to have created itself, it must have both existed and not existed at the same time. If I could put it another way, in order for the universe to have created itself, it would have had to exist prior to itself, which means that in order for the universe to have created itself, it must have already been in existence. According to this first explanation, the universe existed and did not exist at the same time. Since this explanation contradicts itself and is self-defeating, we will move on to our second possible explanation for the existence of the universe.

2. The universe has always existed and, therefore, had no creator.
This view in years past had respectability, but it has since been scientifically disproved. Most scientists today agree with theists that the universe had a specific beginning. In the past twenty-five years discoveries in the field of astronomy and cosmology have produced an amazing amount of evidence that the universe came into existence quickly or suddenly (i.e. the Big Bang Theory).

This theory is supported by the scientific discovery that the galaxies are moving away from one other at an extremely high rate of speed. By tracing the speed of the galaxies backward, scientists believe that at some point in the past, a tremendous explosion occurred that projected all matter outward from a central point of high-density compression. Scientists are telling us that this was the point in time that marks the birth of our universe.

Also, scientists are now saying that the universe had a beginning because there is evidence that the universe is growing old or is aging.

The second law of thermodynamics, which is one of the most important laws of physics with no known exceptions, states that the amount of usable energy in the universe is decreasing due to a continued loss of heat.

The universe is running out of usable fuel—it is slowly dying a heat death. Logically we would have to conclude that if the universe is winding down, then there must have been a point in the beginning in which the universe was wound up with a maximum amount of energy. Again, scientific evidence is in agreement with the Holy Bible in that the universe is not eternal but had a beginning. Another piece of scientific evidence that can't be passed by without notice is called the *principle of contingency*, which states that everything in the physical universe is dependent upon something else for its existence. Thus, for the universe itself to exist there must be a cause for its existence.

Logically, the universe cannot be eternal if something else caused it to come into existence. Many theists disagree with the modern scientist on the age of the universe and its original cause, but theists and atheistic scientists do agree that the universe had a beginning.

Although most scientists now agree with what the Holy Bible has proclaimed for over 4,000 years, this conclusion still has come as quite a shock to some scientists. Robert Jastrow, an internationally known astronomer and founder and director of NASA's Goddard Institute for Space Studies, has written in his book *God and the Astronomers* these comments with regard to this unexpected and difficult conclusion: *"For the scientist who has lived by his faith in the power of reason, the story ends like a bad dream. He has scaled the mountains of ignorance; he is about to conquer the highest peak; as he pulls himself over the final rock, he is greeted by a band of theologians who have been sitting there for centuries."*[63]

3. The universe was created by something or someone else outside of itself. The Holy Bible is in agreement with this third explanation. Creation out of nothing is the only plausible explanation for the universe's existence. Only an uncaused God Who is eternal, and all-powerful could be, by definition, the Creator of the Universe. Logically, it makes no sense to argue that the universe brought itself into existence out of nothing, because out of nothing will always come to nothing. It would be unscientific and logically contradictory for us to conclude that nothing created everything, which means it would also be logically contradictory to argue that the universe is self-caused because it could not create itself without existing prior to itself; this would be impossible. The Holy Bible affirms that God created the universe and everything in it. The Holy Bible tells us that God spoke, and the universe came into existence.[64]

The case for God's existence is valid, sound, and is the only rational conclusion of the three explanations. It satisfies the law of contingency, the second law of thermodynamics, and the law of causality. It does not violate the Law of Non-contradiction and also provides evidence for the big bang theory.

Look at some of the inconsistent statements made by atheists today—specifically, their false accusations and conclusions that science contradicts Biblical Christianity and that it is an obstacle to science.

Let me take two false statements and reveal to you their complete disregard for the facts on this topic. First, if science contradicted Biblical Chris-

---

[63] Robert Jastrow, *God and the Astronomers* (New York, NY: W.W. Norton & Company, 1978, p. 116.
[64] Ge.1; *The Case for A Creator* by Lee Strobel, published by Zondervan Publishing; *The Privileged Planet: How Our Place in the Cosmos is Designed for Discovery*, by Guillermo Gonzalez & Jay W. Richards. 2004, published by Regnery Publishing.

tianity, then how do atheists explain the indisputable fact that most of the great scientists of the past believed in God and took the Holy Bible seriously? The Institute of Creation Research (USA), for example, lists 31 such scientists together with the scientific disciplines they helped to establish.

They include the following scientists:
- Kepler (astronomy)
- Pascal (hydrostatics)
- Boyle (chemistry)
- Newton (calculus)
- Limnaeus (systematic biology)
- Faraday (electromagnetics)
- Cuvier (comparative anatomy)
- Kelvin (thermodynamics)
- Lister (antiseptic surgery)
- Mendel (genetics)

They also list 21 other equally famous names.

Second, atheists say that Biblical Christianity is an obstacle to science. How do they get around the fact that empirical science first started in Christian Europe, three centuries before the existence of Darwinism? The reason why it did is because of the almost universal belief in a Creator God. This gave the founders of modern science the confidence they needed that the natural world was orderly and therefore capable of systematic investigation.

The reason why the *Founding Fathers of Modern Science* believed in God was simply because the natural world bears all the signs of an Intelligent Designer. Although Albert Einstein never came to a belief in a personal God, he did recognize the impossibility of a non-created universe. The *Encyclopedia Britannica* says that Einstein firmly denied atheism. He expressed a belief in "Spinoza's God Who reveals Himself in the harmony of what exists." This actually motivated his interest in science. We must also take into consideration the views of most of the great philosophers and thinkers of the past like Plato, Socrates, Aristotle, Cicero, Aquinas, Bacon, Newton, and others. Even the famous skeptics like David Hume who lived in the 18th century and John Stuart Mills who lived in the 19th century recognized the credibility of the design argument for God's existence. Another who recognized this credibility is Immanuel Kant (18th century), despite his dismissal of all the traditional arguments for God's existence, except for the moral argument.

The progress made in science over the last fifty years has revealed to us powerful new evidence that life and the universe are the result of Intelligent Design.

I want to again remind you about the many things the atheistic philosophers and Darwinist scientists can't explain. They can't explain the phenomena of the human conscience. They can't explain human emotion, our ability to think, our ability to logically reason, and our capacity for self-awareness and introspection. They can't explain DNA or mutations of DNA, including helpful mutations. They can't explain progress from simple to complex organisms, or the natural selection of new "kinds" or pro-creation and reproduction. They can't explain the complexity of our planet and solar system, the complexity of the human brain and the human eye, the complexity of the DNA code,[65] and the existence and complexity of water and its characteristics.[66] If we want to be honest, they don't even know what gravity is in any fundamental way—but only explain how it behaves.

How could these complex characteristics and attributes occur in human beings and in nature if they are just material things produced in a universe through a random, chance process? How could they occur in a process that is mindless, undirected, and purposeless, through a process unsupported by scientific evidence and logical reasoning called Darwinian evolution? In contrast, the Holy Bible does give answers to these questions. The Holy Bible tells us that God created the universe and everything in it,[67] and that man was created in the image and likeness of God.

If I could choose just one example in creation that refutes the Darwinian theory of evolution, one out of the multiple thousands of examples available, it would have to be the Bombardier Beetle. This beetle would have had to be created with all its systems working. In 1982, authors C.L. Metcalf and R.L.

---

[65] Recommended reading: William A. Dembski, *Mere Creation; Intelligent Design*, Dembski; *Evidence for God*, by Dembski and Licona; John Warwick Montgomery, *Evidence for Faith*; J.P.Moreland (editor) *The Creation Hypothesis*; Lawrence Richards, *It Couldn't Just Happen*.

[66] *The Wonders of God's Creation*, Moody Institute of Science (Chicago, IL); Hugh Davson, *Physiology of the Eye*, 5th ed. (New York: McGraw Hill, 1991).

[67] Ge. 1; Is. 42:5; 45:18; Ep. 3:9; He. 11:3; Re. 4:11.

Flint wrote: *"The bombardier beetle, Brachinus, ejects an acrid fluid which is discharged with a distinct popping sound and a small cloud of vapor that looks like smoke from a miniature cannon."*[68]

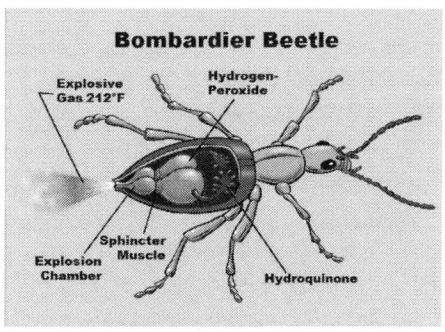

When the beetle senses danger, it internally mixes enzymes contained in one body chamber with concentrated solutions of two harmless compounds confined to a second chamber. These two compounds are known as hydrogen peroxide and hydroquinone. This generates a noxious spray of caustic benzoquinones, which explodes from its body at 212°F. This little beetle blows the Darwinian evolutionary theory to smithereens.

Dr. John Baumgardner, is a 1997 graduate from UCLA with a PhD in Geophysics and Space Physics. He was described by *US News & World Report* as the world's preeminent expert in the design of computer models for geophysical convection. This is the process by which the earth creates volcanoes, earthquakes, and the movement of continental plates. Dr. Baumgardner said, *"Science has flowed from a Christian understanding of reality, a Christian understanding of God, and a Christian understanding of the natural world. In general, I believe that science is legitimate, that it does reveal the glory of God, that it does confirm what the scripture says is valid and true."*[69]

Charles Robert Darwin (Feb. 12, 1809–April 19, 1882) In 1859 Charles Darwin said in his book *The Origin of Species by Means of Natural Selection* on page 158, *"If it could be demonstrated that any complex organ existed, which could not possibly have been formed by numerous, successive, slight modifications, my theory would absolutely break down. But I can find no such case."* Darwinian theory is not just in conflict between evolutionists and creationists anymore, but now has become a conflict between evolutionists themselves.

---

68   Metcalf and Flint, *Destructive and Useful Insects*, 4th ed. (New York: McGraw-Hill, 1962) p. 24.
69   *Rational Conclusions* by John D. Agresti, p. 51.

Although some Darwinists continue to claim that no serious scientists doubt the theory, what are scientists really saying about Darwinian evolution? Currently, there are over 1,000 PhD scientists worldwide who are willing to make public their skepticism about the Darwinian theory and have signed a statement publicly expressing their skepticism about the contemporary theory of Darwinian evolution.

The Scientific Dissent from Darwinism[70] statement reads: *"We are skeptical of claims for the ability of random mutations and natural selection to account for the complexity of life. Careful examination of the evidence for Darwinian theory should be encouraged."* The list of over 1,000 signatories includes member scientists from the Tokyo University of Science and Russian National Academy of Sciences.

REALITY CHECK	
Unproven Theory	Actual Reality
non-life ↓	impossible
life ↓	impossible
male and female ↓	impossible
reproduction ↓	impossible
helpful mutations ↓	impossible
DNA increase ↓	impossible
natural selection to new "kinds" ↓	impossible
progress from simple to complex	impossible

Signers hold doctorates in physics, chemistry, mathematics, medicine, computer science, and biological sciences—the largest single scientific discipline represented on the list and other related disciplines.

Many of the signers are professors or researchers at major universities and research institutions such as MIT, The Smithsonian, Cambridge University, UCLA, UC Berkeley, Princeton, the University of Pennsylvania, Ohio State University, the University of Georgia, and the University of Washington.

"Darwin's theory of evolution is the great white elephant of contemporary thought." – Dr. David Berlinski

Dr. W. H. Thorpe, a Professor of Animal Ethnology from Cambridge, said this: *"The likelihood of life occurring by chance is fantastically improbable. The spontaneous formation of life violates the second Thermodynamic Law, which states that all closed physical systems (such as the earth) tend toward a state of maximum disorder."*

Other prominent signatories include U.S. National Academy of Sciences member Philip Skell, American Association for the Advancement of Science

---

70   www.dissentfromdarwin.org.

Fellow Lyle Jensen, evolutionary biologist and textbook author Stanley Salthe, Smithsonian Institution evolutionary biologist and a researcher at the National Institutes of Health's National Center for Biotechnology Information Richard von Sternberg, Editor of *Rivista di Biologia/Biology Forum*— the oldest still-published biology journal in the world—Giuseppe Sermonti, and Russian Academy of Natural Sciences embryologist Lev Beloussov.

Ronald West, professor of paleontology at Kansas State University, said this: *"Contrary to what most scientists write, the fossil record does not support the Darwinian theory of evolution because it is this theory (there are several) which we use to interpret the fossil record. By doing so, we are guilty of circular reasoning if we then say the fossil record supports this theory."*[71]

Colin Patterson, senior paleontologist at the British Museum of Natural History in London, confessed in a radio interview with the British Broadcasting Corporation on March 4, 1982 the following: *"No one has ever produced a species by mechanisms of natural selection. No one has ever gotten near it, and most of the current argument in neo-Darwinism is about this question."*[72]

Dr. Austin H. Clark, a scientist for many years connected with the Smithsonian Institute in Washington, stated this: *"No matter how far back we go in the fossil records of previous animal life upon the earth we find no trace of any animal forms which are intermediate between the various major groups of phyla. ...The greatest groups of animal life do not merge into one another. They are and have been fixed from the beginning...No animals are known even from the earliest rocks which cannot at once be assigned to their proper phylum or major group. ...There can be only one interpretation of this entire lack of any intermediates between the major groups of animals. ...If we are willing to accept the facts at their face value, we must believe that there were never such intermediates, or that these major groups from the very first bore the same relation to each other that they do at the present day."*[73]

Dr. Clark has also talked about the inadequacy of the fossil record: *"So we see that the fossil record, the actual history of the animal life on the earth, bears us out in the assumption that at its very first appearance animal life in its*

---

71 Ronald West. *Compass*, (May, 1968) p. 216.
72 Patterson Colin. *Cladistics*, interview on British Broadcasting Corporation, March 4, 1982.
73 *The New Evolution, Zoogenesis* (Baltimore: Williams and Wilkins, 1930), p. 129ff.

broader features was in essentially the same form as that in which we now know it. ...Thus, so far as what concerns the major groups of animals, the creationists seem to have the better of the argument. There is not the slightest evidence that any one of the major groups arose from any other."[74]

Norman Macbeth, a Harvard-trained lawyer, authored a book entitled *Darwin Retried* in which he bluntly announced that "classical Darwinism is dead." He declared that while many evolutionists still act confident in public, "the inner circles are full of doubt" (Forward). On page 46 of this book, he also wrote, *"My studies of natural selection had begun with no forebodings, but by this time, I was becoming puzzled and skeptical. A process that operates invisibly, with an intensity that cannot be observed and with no ability to explain specific problems, an impersonal process that is continually given per sonal qualities—this sets my teeth on edge."*

Here is a quote from Professor Colin Reeves from the Department of Mathematical Science at Coventry University: *"Darwinism was an interesting idea in the 19th century, when hand-waving explanations gave a plausible, if not properly scientific framework into which we could fit biological facts. However, what we have learned since the days of Darwin throws doubt on natural selection's ability to create complex biological systems—and we still have little more than hand-waving as an argument in its favour."*[75]

Evolutionist Robert Jastrow, considered by many people to be one of the greatest science writers of our generation, said, *"For a greatly improved eye or brain to appear suddenly, a thousand such changes must occur at once in a single animal, all accidental, and yet in a favorable direction. That would be as unlikely as to toss a coin in the air and have it come up heads a thousand times in a row."*[76]

Princeton professor Edwin Carlston said, *"The probability of life originating from accident is comparable to the probability of the unabridged dictionary resulting from an explosion in a print shop."*[77]

Sir Fred Hoyle, the eminent astrophysicist of Great Britain, wrote this: *"The chance that higher life forms have emerged in this way is comparable with*

---

[74] Animal Evolution, *The Quarterly Review of Biology* (December, p. 539).
[75] Found at *Scientific Dissent from Darwinism* (www.dissentfromdarwin.org).
[76] Robert Jastrow. *Evolution: Selection for Perfection*, Science Digest, 1981, p. 86.
[77] Carlston, Edwin *Reader's Digest* 1963.

the chance that a tornado sweeping through a junkyard might assemble a Boeing 747 from the material therein."[78]

Let no one tell you that all is well in the Darwinian evolution camp and don't be persuaded by the propaganda rhetoric that **"no true scientist"** questions the **"fact"** of evolution.

These statements are contrary to the evidence. In reality, many scientists are critical of the "monkey-to-man" dogma. The fact that the theory of evolution is unsupported by scientific evidence renders Darwinian theory—to be at best—a hypothesis, certainly not a valid theory based on real scientific evidence. We must understand that humans don't come to belief in Darwinian evolution because it presents a compelling argument for its existence. Instead, they believe in Darwinian evolution because of the morally depraved condition of their heart and conscience, and as a result, the righteous and moral God of Biblical Christianity has to be removed from their consciousness and reality. If humans can remove God from their origin story, they don't have to worry about sin, guilt and judgment in their physical life. The theory of evolution actually gives them the feeling that they are free to do whatever it is that they want to do. What this really means is that the debate over origins is really a debate between beliefs or, more specifically, a debate over worldviews.

Could the birth of the evolution hypothesis simply be an attempt by rebellious human beings determined to live a life without any moral responsibility and accountability to a Holy and Righteous God? In his excellent book *The Collapse of Evolution*, Scott Huse, a Christian thinker, has this to say on the topic: *"The conflict of evolutionary theory against the Holy Scriptures is impossible to reconcile."* Huse lists in his book 24 differences between the Bible and evolutionary thinking. He goes on to say, *"The fruit of evolution has been all sorts of anti-Christian systems of belief and practices. It has served as an intellectual basis for Hitler's Nazism and Marx's communism. It has prompted apostasy, atheism, secular humanism and libertinism, as well as establishing a basis for ethical relativism, which has spread through our society like cancer. The mind and general welfare of mankind has suffered greatly as a*

---

[78] Hoyle, Fred. *"Hoyle on Evolution"*, Nature. 1981. Vol. 284, November.

result of this naturalistic philosophy. According to the Bible, man is a responsible creature. One day he will give an account for his life's actions and motives. But when man is viewed as the product of some vague purposeless evolutionary process, he is conveniently freed from all moral obligation and responsibility. After all, he is merely an accident of nature, an intelligent animal at best."[79]

Now, move on to another significant problem for the Darwinian evolutionists.

Are dinosaur fossils really 65 million years old?

In 2005 a group of researchers led by Dr. Mary Schweiter, reported extracting pliable pieces of tissue from a T.rex fossil.[80] Within the tissue they found osteocytes, which are common cells found inside the matrix of bone. What was even more astonishing was when they detected fragments of a common animal protein called collagen.

Follow-up research presented additional support for this discovery.[81] However, the presence of tissue and protein fragments found in 65-million-year-old dinosaur fossils creates a problem for the evolutionist for obvious reasons.

If dinosaurs are 65 million years old, then how did this biological material endure? How could these bones from dinosaurs not be completely fossilized even after millions of years?

The question we should be asking is how accurate are the Darwinian-evolution dating methods? Not surprisingly, this discovery has been widely debated, and attempts have been made to discard these amazing discoveries as fraudulent. However, following studies have found tissue and cells in other dinosaurs and reptile fossils as well.[82]

---

[79] Scott Huse, *The Collapse of Evolution* (Grand Rapids: Baker Book House, 1983), pp. 122-124.
[80] Mary H. Schweitzer et al., *"Soft-Tissue, Vessels and Cellular Preservation in Tyrannosaurus Rex,"* Science 307, no. 5717 (2005): 1952-1955, doi:10.1126/science.1108397.
[81] John M. Asara et al.*"Protein Sequences from Mastodon and Tyrannosaurus Rex Revealed by Mass Spectrometrx,"* Science 316, no. 5822 (2017): 280-285, doi:10.1126/science.1137614; and Mary Higby Schweitzer et al,*"Analyses of Soft Tissue from Tyrannosaurus Rex Suggest the Presence of Protein,"* Science 316, no. 5822 (2007):277-280, doi:10.1126/science.1138709.
[82] *Schweitzer's Dangerous Discovery,* Discovery Magazine 2006: Mary H. Schweitzer et al., *"Biomolecular Characterization and Protein Sequences of the Campanian Hadrosaur B. canadenis,"* Science 324, no. 5927 (2009): 626-631, doi:10.1126/science.1165069; and Mark Armitage and Kevin Anderson, *"Soft Sheets of Fibrillar Bone from a fossil of the Supraorbital Horn of the Dinosaur Triceratops horridus,"* Acta Histochemica 115, no. 6 (2013): 603-608, doi: 10.1016/j.acthis.2013.01.001; and David Surmik et al., *"Spectroscopic Studies on Organic Matter from Triassic Reptile Bone, Upper Silesia,Poland,"* Plo S One 11, no. 3 (2016): e0151143, doi:10.1371, journal. pone.0151143; and Schweiter et.al., *"Molecular Analyses of Dinosaur Osteocytes."*

In addition to collagen, protein such as actin and myosin were also found.[83] These additional discoveries helped verify the authenticity of the dinosaur tissue discovery and undermine the argument of contamination. In fact, dinosaur tissue is now recognized as a "common phenomenon."[84]

Many, many more examples of tissue being extracted from dinosaur fossils could be quoted. Despite the large body of evidence available for the authenticity of the dinosaur fossil tissue discoveries, there still exists a pattern of denial within the evolution camp. This pattern of denial is presumably because of the obvious consequences of these discoveries. However, the Holy Bible explains to us that man and dinosaurs were made on the same day which would be consistent with the soft tissue evidence (Ge. 1:24-31).

Evidence to Evaluate

- There are literally hundreds of scientific statements made in the Holy Bible that are scientifically accurate. Because the Bible was written during the time of the prescientific era, the writers of the Holy Bible could not have naturally known about the accuracy of these scientific details. The fact that there is such agreement in the Holy Bible with modern science has once again proven its claim of Divine Origin and Inspiration.
- The challenge for human beings is whether to believe God and His Word, with its evidence of Supernatural Intervention, or to believe the Darwinian evolution hypothesis. The Darwinian evolution hypothesis is a belief that is scientifically unsupported and logically inconsistent and is in direct opposition to the teachings found within the Holy Bible.
- Despite the large body of evidence available for the authenticity of the dinosaur fossil tissue discoveries, there still remains a pattern of denial within the evolution society for obvious reasons. Many evolutionists find it easier to dismiss the soft tissue evidence rather than try to understand it or explain it.

---

[83] James D. San Antonio et al., *"Dinosaur Peptides Suggest Mechanisms of Protein Survival,"* Plo S One 6, (2011): e20381, doi: 10.1371/journal.pone.0020381; and Schweiter et al., *"Molecular Analyses of Dinosaur Osteocytes."*

[84] Sergio Bertazzo et al., *"Fibres and Cellular Structures Preserved in 75-Million-Year-Old Dinosaur Specimens,"* Nature Communications 6 (2015): 6, doi: 10.1038/n comm8352; Timothy P. Cleland et al., *"Mass Spectrometry and Antibody-Based Characterization of Blood Vessels from Brachylophosaurus canadenis,"* Journal of Proteome Research 14, no. 12 (2915): 5252-5262, doi: 10.1021/acs.jproeome.5600675; *The Journal Bone*, Jan. 2013, Vol. 53, Issue 1, pp. 414-423.

Notes

PROOF FOUR

eye-wit-ness

–noun

1. a person who actually sees some act, occurrence, or thing and can give a firsthand account of it.

—Dictionary.com

EYEWITNESS TESTIMONY

PREMISE

Sir Lionel Luckhoo is widely recognized as the best trial attorney in history. With 245 straight acquittals, he has been listed 14 years as the "World's Most Successful Advocate" in the Guinness Book of World Records. After spending several years examining the evidence for the resurrection of Jesus Christ from a trial-lawyer point of view, he wrote the following: *"I humbly add I have spent more than 42 years as a defense trial lawyer appearing in many parts of the world and am still in active practice. I have been fortunate to secure a number of successes in jury trials, and I say unequivocally the evidence for the Resurrection of Jesus Christ is so overwhelming that it compels acceptance by proof which leaves absolutely no room for doubt."*[85]

Lionel Luckhoo (1968)

Simon Greenleaf

Simon Greenleaf served as professor of law at Harvard University and was instrumental in organizing the university's law program. He said, *"The foundation of our belief is a basis of fact—the fact of the birth, ministry, miracles, death, resurrection by the Evangelists as having actually occurred, within their own personal knowledge it was therefore impossible that they could have persisted*

---

[85] Sir Lionel Luckhoo, *The Question Answered: Did Jesus Rise from the Dead?* Luckhoo Booklets, back page. http://www.hawaiichristiansonline.com/sirlionel.html.

in affirming the truths they have narrated, had not Jesus actually rose from the dead, and had they not known this fact as certainly as they knew any other fact".[86]

The resurrection of Jesus is the very foundation of the Christian faith. Paul writes in 1Corinthians 15:14 -17:

> *[14]"And if Christ has not been raised, our preaching is worthless, and so is your faith. [15]In that case, we are also exposed as false witnesses about God. For we have testified about God that He raised Christ from the dead, but He did not raise Him if in fact the dead are not raised. [16]For if the dead are not raised, then not even Christ has been raised. [17]And if Christ has not been raised, your faith is futile; you are still in your sins."*

What is truly amazing to me is that there is no legitimate scholar of any world religion today that denies that Jesus was a Historical Figure that walked on the earth approximately two-thousand years ago. He was a Good Teacher and Miracle Worker Who died on a cross for the crime of blasphemy. *(Note: Islam does not teach that Christ died on a cross but that Judas did.)* Therefore, the only dispute we have with legitimate scholarship is whether Jesus was the Son of God and resurrected from the dead after His crucifixion.

Look at the evidence for the Resurrection. This evidence should be judged like any other historical event, based on standard rules concerning evidence. Consistent eye-witness testimony from multiple credible witnesses would be considered the strongest form of evidence available to our modern-day legal system. Therefore, if we find such testimony present in the historical record of Christ's Resurrection, then we satisfy a major evidentiary challenge under the traditional rule of law. In fact, we do have multiple eye-witness testimonies regarding the Resurrection of Jesus Christ in Scripture. In 1Corinthians 15:3-6, Paul states the following:

> *[3]"For what I received I passed on to you as of first importance: that Christ died for our sins according to the Scriptures, [4]that He was buried, that He was raised on the third day according to the Scriptures, [5]and that He*

---

[86] Simon Greenleaf (1995)."The Testimony of the Evangelists: The Gospels Examined by the Rule of Evidence," p. 12, Kregel Publications.

appeared to Cephas and then to the Twelve. ⁶After that, He appeared to more than five hundred brothers at once, most of whom are still alive, though some have fallen asleep."

The Holy Bible was written by multiple authors who were eyewitness to the events they recorded. The consistency of their testimony confirms that they recorded real history, and archaeology verifies these events as well.

I find it significant that both the Book of Mormon and the Quran endorse the Holy Bible, or at least part of the Holy Bible. What is significant about this is that the Holy Bible itself provides tests by which it may be judged as having Divine Origin rather than human.

One of these tests is that future revelations must be consistent with previous revelations and the Holy Bible passes this test with one-hundred percent accuracy. However, both of these tests are failed by the Quran and the Book of Mormon.

Another detail that we must look at is that Mohammad lived from around the year A.D. 570 to A.D. 632, and although he considered himself a prophet of God, he was not an eyewitness to the events of the Holy Bible. Likewise, Joseph Smith who lived between 1805 and 1844 A. D. was not an eyewitness to the events of the Holy Bible or the Book of Mormon and lived thousands of years after the supposed history contained in the Book of Mormon.

Smith was not an eyewitness to any of the things he wrote about, and there are no other eyewitness accounts to confirm any of the events described in the Book of Mormon. There is no historical evidence that anything described in the Book of Mormon actually happened, and there is no archaeological evidence to verify the stories found in the Book of Mormon. Archaeologists consult the Holy Bible when they want to know where to dig. They do not consult the Book of Mormon.

The internal consistency of the Holy Bible is woven throughout Scripture from Genesis to Revelation. Look at the chronological order of Jesus Christ's arrest, death, burial, and the Resurrection appearances as revealed to us through eyewitness testimony found in the four Gospels.

(The following timelines are approximate and are based on the chronological evidence as they are found in the four Gospels of the Holy Bible.)

Wednesday afternoon on the Mount of Olives
Jesus gives a discourse to the Disciples about the destruction of Jerusalem and the end of the world.
Matthew 24-25; Mark 13:1-37; Luke 21:15-36

Jesus is again warning His Disciples about His impending crucifixion. The religious leaders in Jerusalem plot His death.
Matthew 26:1-5; Mark 14:1-2; Luke 22:1-2

Wednesday evening
Jesus is honored at Bethany. Mary lavishes expression of devotion, and Jesus is anointed for burial.
Matthew 26:6-13; Mark 14:3-9; John 12:2-8

Jesus' betrayal is plotted.
Matthew 26:1-5; Mark 14:1-2; Luke 22:1-2

Wednesday night in Jerusalem
Judas bargains with Jewish leaders to betray Jesus.
Matthew 26:14-16; Mark 14:10-11; Luke 22:3-6

Thursday in Jerusalem
The disciples inquire about and prepare the Passover Meal in the Upper Room.
Matthew 26:17-19; Mark 14:12-16; Luke 22:7-13; John 13:1

Jesus has His last Passover.
Matthew 26:20; Mark 14:17; Luke 22:14-18

Thursday evening in Jerusalem
Jesus washes the Disciples' feet.
Luke 22:24-30; John 13:2-17

During the Passover Meal, Jesus lets Judas know that He is aware of his intentions.
Matthew 26:21-25; Mark 14:18-21; Luke 22:21-23; John 13:21-30

Judas' betrays Jesus.
Matthew 26:21-25; Mark 14:18-21; Luke 22:21-23; John 13:18-32

After the departure of Judas, Jesus institutes the ordinance of the Lord's Supper.
Matthew 26:26-29; Mark 14:22-25; Luke 22:19-20; John 13:31-32; 1Corinthians 11:23-26

Thursday night in Jerusalem
Jesus begins His farewell discourse to the Disciples in the Upper Room and predicts Peter's three denials.
Matthew 26:31-35; Mark 14:27-31; Luke 22:31-34; John 13:33-38

Jesus predicts coming conflict.
Luke 22:35-38

Jesus comforts His Disciples.
John 14:1-14

Jesus answers Thomas, Philip, and Judas (not Iscariot).
John 14:15-31

Jesus and His disciples sing a hymn and leave for the Mount of Olives.
Matthew 26:30; Mark 14:26; Luke 22:39

On the way to Mount of Olives, Jesus explains He is the Vine and His followers are the branches.
John 15:1-17

On the way to Mount of Olives, Jesus warns about persecution.
John 15:18-16:4

On the way to Mount of Olives, Jesus promises the Holy Spirit.
John 16:5-15

On the way to Mount of Olives, Jesus reveals that sorrow will turn to joy.
John 16:16-22

On the way to Mount of Olives, Jesus commands in Jesus' name.
John 16:23-33

On the way to Mount of Olives, Jesus prayers to the Father.
John 17:1-26

Thursday, toward midnight
Jesus and His disciples go to and are at the Garden of Gethsemane.
Matthew 26:36-38; Mark 14:32-34; Luke 22:40; John 18:1

Thursday, about midnight
Jesus prays for three hours in the Garden of Gethsemane.
Matthew 26:39-44; Mark 14:35-40; Luke 22:41-46

Friday, just after Thursday midnight
The betrayal occurs in the Garden of Gethsemane.
Matthew 26:47-56; Mark 14:43-52; Luke 22:47-53; John 18:2-9

Peter cuts off the ear of the High Priest's slave in the Garden of Gethsemane.
Matthew 26:50-55; Mark 14:46-49; Luke 22:49-53; John 18:10-12

Jesus heals the ear of the High Priest's slave in the Garden of Gethsemane.
Luke 22:51

Events in Jerusalem

Friday, Jerusalem, probably before 1 a.m.
Jesus is taken to Annas, a former High Priest, and here is Peter's first denial of Jesus.
Matthew 26:57-58, 69-70; Mark 14:53-54, 66-68; Luke 22:54-57; John 18:13-24

Friday, probably about 1:00 a.m.
Jesus is taken to Caiaphas' residence.
Matthew 26:57,59-68; Mark 14:53,55-65; Luke 22:54,63-65; John 18:24

Peter denies Jesus the second time.
Matthew 26:71-72; Mark 14:69; Luke 22:58; John 18:25

Friday, probably about 2:00-3:00 a.m.
The chief priests condemn Jesus.
Matthew 26:59-66; Mark 14:55-64

The people beat Jesus and spit upon Him.
Matthew 26:67-68; Mark 14:65; 15:19; Luke 22:63-65; John 18:22;19:3

Peter denies Jesus the third time.
Matthew 26:73-75; Mark 14:70-72; Luke 22:59-62; John 18:26-27

Friday, Jerusalem, probably before 5:00 a.m.
The council (Sanhedrin) condemns Jesus.
Matthew 27:1-2; Mark 15:1; Luke 22:66-23:1; John 18:28

Friday, Jerusalem, probably early morning
Judas regrets his actions and hangs himself.
Matthew 27:3-10; Acts 1:15-19

Friday, Jerusalem, probably about 5:00 a.m.
Jesus' first appearance before Pilate
Matthew 27:2, 11-14; Mark 15:1-5; Luke 23:1-5; John 18:28-38

Friday, Jerusalem, probably before 6:00 a.m.
Jesus is sent to King Herod.
Luke 23:6-12

Friday, Jerusalem, probably about 6 a.m.
Jesus' second appearance before Pilate
Matthew 27:15-31; Mark 15:6-20; Luke 23:13-25; John 18:39-19:15

Christ was scourged.
Mark 15:15; John 19:1

Christ receives a crown of thorns, a purple robe and blows to face.
Matthew 27:29; Mark 15:17; John 19:2,3

The Roman soldiers mock Jesus.
Mark 15:16-19; Matthew 27:27-30

Friday, Jerusalem, about 8:00 a.m.
Jesus is lead away to be crucified.
Matthew 27:31-32; Mark 15:20-21; Luke 23:26-32; John 19:17

Friday, Jerusalem, from 9:00 a.m. to 3:00 p.m.
Jesus' crucifixion
Matthew 27:33-44; Mark 15:22-32; Luke 23:33-43; John 19:18-27

The soldiers cast lots for Jesus' garments.
Matthew 27:35-36; Mark 15:24-25; Luke 23:34; John 19:23-24

The people, priests, and robber mock Jesus.
Matthew 27:39-45; Mark 15:29-33; Luke 23:35-44

Jesus makes John responsible for His mother Mary.
John 19:25-27

Three Hours of Darkness (from noon to 3 p.m.)
Mark 15:33-37; Matthew 27:45-50; Luke 23:44-46

Jesus' death
Matthew 27:46-53; Mark 15:34-38; Luke 23:45-46; John 19:28-30

The veil in the temple is torn in half from top to bottom.
Matthew 27:51; Mark 15:38

An earthquake happens at Jesus Christ's death on the cross.
Matthew 27:54

Graves open up and dead saints arise from the dead, go to the Holy City, and appear to many.
Matthew 27:52, 53

Centurion Guard becomes a Believer.
Matthew 27:54

The spear in his side with blood and water
John 19:34

Friday, Jerusalem, before 6:00 p.m.
Jesus' burial
Matthew 27:57-61; Mark 15:42-47; Luke 23:50-55; John 19:31-42

Saturday, Jerusalem
Pilate assigns guards to Jesus' tomb.
Matthew 27:62-66

Saturday, Jerusalem, about 6:00 a.m.
After the "High Day" Sabbath, the women buy spices.
Mark 16:1; Luke 23:56

After resting on weekly Sabbath, the women visit Jesus' tomb.
Matthew 28:1; Luke 23:56

Sunday, probably before dawn
Jesus rises from the dead!
Matthew 12:38-40

An earthquake occurs; an angel rolls back the stone covering the tomb.
Matthew 28:2-4

The Roman seal is broken.
Matthew 27:62-66; Mark 16:4; John 20:1

Sunday, early morning
The women come to the tomb.
Mark 16:2-4; Luke 24:1-2; John 20:1-2

The women enter the tomb.
Matthew 28:5-8; Mark 16:5-8; Luke 24:3-9

The angels testify.
Matthew 28:5; Mark 16:5,6; Luke 24:4-9; John 20:11-17

Sunday, morning
The disciples do not believe the women.
Mark 16:11; Luke 24:9-11; John 20:18

Peter and John run to the tomb.
Luke 24:12; John 20:3-10

The grave clothes are found.
Luke 23:53;24:12; John 20:5, 6

Jesus appears first to Mary Magdalene.
Mark 16:9, 10; John 20:11-17

The other women meet Jesus.
Matthew 28:9, 10

The guards report to the Jewish leaders and accept bribe.
Matthew 28:11-15

Sunday, afternoon
Jesus appears to Peter.
Luke 24:34; 1Corinthians 15:5

Two disciples on the way to Emmaus meet Jesus.
Mark 16:12-13; Luke 24:13-35

Sunday, evening
Jesus appears before His disciples.
Mark 16:14-18; Luke 24:36-45; John 20:19-25

Sunday, Jerusalem
Jesus again appears before His disciples.
John 20:26-29

Probably early in the next month
Appearances

Jesus is at the Sea of Galilee.
John 21:1-23

Christ ate food.
Luke 24:41-43

Christ was touched.
Luke 24:39; John 20:27

About mid-month
Jesus appears other places in Galilee.
The 11 Disciples go to the mountain in Galilee where Jesus told them to meet Him.
Matthew 26:32; 28:7, 10; Mark 16:7

This is probably the place where over 500 brethren see the resurrected Jesus.
1Corinthians 15:6

Finally, Jesus appears to his brother James.
Matthew 28:16-20; 1Corinthians 15:6-7; Galatians 1:19; Jude 1:1

Jesus teaches His Disciples for 40 days after His Resurrection.
Acts 1:1-3

The Disciples are to stay in Jerusalem until they receive the Holy Spirit.
Acts 1:4-5

The Disciples are again told to stay in Jerusalem until they receive the Holy Spirit.
Luke 24:46-49; Acts 1:6-8

About the end of the month
The Mount of Olives, near Jerusalem
Jesus ascends to Heaven.
Mark 16:19, 20; Luke 24:50-53; Acts 1:9-12

The Disciples were transformed after Resurrection.
Luke 24:52, 53; Mark 16:19, 20; Matthew 28:16-20

Most of Christ's Disciples died as martyrs. These witnesses knew the truth and were willing to lay down their lives for it. What could they have possibly gained in dying for a known lie?

The evidence speaks for itself. These were followers of Jesus Christ and they were willing to die for the truth of His message, and that message is that Christ is the Son of God and the Savior of the world. His death and Resurrection were His ultimate *Proof of Authority* and established Him as the Son of God and the Savior of the world.

Early Christian Martyrs	
Stephen was stoned, and some 2,000 other Christians suffered at the time of Stephen's persecution.	**Matthew the Apostle** was killed by a halberd axe in 60 A.D.
	Mark the Apostle was beaten to death.
James the Great, son of Zebedee, was beheaded in 44 A.D.	**Luke the Apostle** was hanged.
Philip the Apostle was crucified in 54 A.D.	**John the Apostle** was cooked in boiling hot oil but survived and died of old age in 110 A.D.
James the Just was beaten to death by a club after being crucified and stoned.	**Simon the Apostle** was crucified.
Mathias was stoned and beheaded.	**Andrew the Apostle**, Peter's brother, was crucified.
Jude was crucified.	
Bartholomew the Apostle was crucified.	**Peter the Apostle** was crucified upside-down.
Thomas the Apostle was speared.	
	Apostle Paul was beheaded in Rome.

Evidence to Evaluate

- The Holy Bible tells us that there were over five-hundred eyewitness accounts of Jesus Christ's Resurrection. It would be considered the strongest form of evidence available in our modern-day legal system and would satisfy the major evidentiary challenges under the traditional rule of law.
- Men and women are willing to die for what they believe to be true, although it may actually be false; but they do not, however, die for what they know is a lie.

Notes

PROOF FIVE

his-tor-i-cal

–adj.

1. of or concerning history (historical evidence). 2. (of the study of a subject) showing its development. 3. belonging to the past, not the present.

—The Oxford Dictionary

HISTORICAL EVIDENCE

PREMISE

In this chapter, we will examine some of the testimony of the historical evidence and ask the question: Does the evidence support or deny the internal claims of the Holy Bible?

You will see that not only is Jesus documented in the eye-witness testimony compiled in the New Testament, but He is also mentioned as a historical Person outside of the New Testament by several non-Christian and even hostile anti-Christian sources.

From these sources outside of the New Testament, we can learn many facts about Jesus Christ. These facts are as follows:

1. He was known to be wise and virtuous.[87]
2. He had a brother named James.[88]
3. He was known to perform miracles.[89]
4. He was crucified under Pontius Pilate.[90]
5. His crucifixion was accompanied by darkness and an earthquake.[91]
6. He had many Jewish and Gentile disciples.[92]

---

[87] Josephus, *Antiquities of the Jews*, 18.3.3; Also see Shlomo Pines, An Arabic Version of the *Testimonium Flavianum and its Implications*, Israel Academy of Sciences and Humanities: Jerusalem, 1971, (Cited in J. Warner Wallace, *Cold Case Christianity*).
[88] Josephus, 20.9.1.
[89] Origen, *Contra Celsum*, 1.28.
[90] Ronald Mellor, *Tacitus' Annals*, p.23; *Tacitus' Annals*, 15.44; Josephus, 18.3.3.
[91] Ante-Nicene Christian Library: *Translations of the Writings of the Fathers Down to A.D. 325*, eds. Alexander Roberts and James Donaldson, vol. 9, Irenaeus, vol. II-Hippolytus, vol. II-Fragments of Third Century (Edinburgh: T&T Clark, 1870. (Cited in J. Warner Wallace, *Cold Case Christianity*).
[92] Josephus, 18.3.3.

7. He lived during the time of Tiberius Caesar.[93]
8. His Disciples believed that He rose from the dead.[94]
9. His Disciples believed He was God and they met regularly to worship Him.[95]
10. His Disciples were willing to suffer and die for their beliefs.[96]

From non-Christian and even hostile anti-Christian sources, we can be sure that Jesus, in fact, existed. He was crucified, was believed to be resurrected from the dead, and His many followers were willing to suffer and die for that belief.

The secular historical evidence has confirmed the reliability and credibility of the Holy Bible by making these references to Christianity, the Disciples, the Apostles and Jesus Christ Himself.

This is one of the ways that the Holy Bible has been taken from the realm of fairy tales and mythology to its rightful place as a credible Historical Document. The next time someone tells you that there is no evidence for Jesus Christ outside of the Holy Bible, you can share with them these ten facts found in the secular non-Christian historical evidence. Here are some of these facts in more detail.

Flavius Josephus
Jewish Historian (AD 37–100)

I will be quoting Josephus' *Antiquities* from the 10th-century Arabic text. This text is more neutral concerning Jesus because it does not contain some of the disputed passages, but it still tells us quite a bit about Jesus. A reading like this is very likely close to the original that Josephus penned.

"At this time there was a wise man called Jesus. And his conduct was good, and [he] was known to be virtuous. And many people from among the Jews and other nations became his disciples. Pilate condemned him to be

---

93 Ante-Nicene Christian Library, eds. Alexander Roberts and James Donaldson, vol. 9, p. 188. (Cited in J. Warner Wallace, *Cold Case Christianity*).
94 Josephus, 18.3.3.
95 *Pliny the Younger*, Book 10, Letter 96; Lucian, *The Death of Peregrine*, 11-12.
96 C. Suetonius, Tranquillus, Divus Claudius, 25.4; Setonius, *The 12 Caesars*, Nero Claudius, XVI; Tacitus, Annals, 15.44.

crucified and to die. And those who had become his disciples did not abandon his discipleship. They reported he had appeared to them three days after his crucifixion and that he was alive. Accordingly, he was perhaps the Messiah concerning whom the prophets have recounted wonders."[97]

Josephus also mentions other Biblical events and people and places which verify the trustworthiness and reliability of Scripture.

- John the Baptist from Matthew 3:1, 2 and Herod from Luke 3:1 are mentioned in *Antiquities*, Book 18, ch. 5, par. 2 and Book 17, ch. 8, par. 1.
- James the brother of Jesus from Galatians 1:19 is mentioned in *Antiquities*, Book 20, ch. 9, par. 1.
- Ananias the High Priest from Acts 23:2 is mentioned in *Antiquities*, Book 20, ch. 9, par. 1.
- Antipas from Revelation 2:13 is mentioned in *Antiquities*, Book 17, ch. 8, par. 1.
- The Galatians from Galatians 1:2 are mentioned in *Antiquities*, Book 17, ch. 8, par. 3 and Book 12, ch. 10, par. 6.
- Jericho from Numbers 22:1 are mention in *Antiquities*, Book 17, ch. 8, par. 2.
- Jerusalem from Matthew 21:10, 11 is mentioned in *Antiquities*, Book 20, ch. 9, par. 2.
- Judea from Matthew 2:1 is mentioned in *Antiquities*, Book 20, ch.9, par. 1.
- Pontius Pilate from Luke 3:1 is mentioned in *Antiquities*, Book 18, ch. 3, par. 1.
- Sadducees from Matthew 16:1 are mentioned in *Antiquities*, Book 20, ch. 9, par. 1.
- Samaritans from Luke 10:33 are mentioned in *Antiquities*, Book 18, ch. 4, par. 1.
- Tiberius Caesar from Luke 3:1 is mentioned in *Antiquities*, Book 18, ch.6, par4.

---

[97] 10th-century Arabic version of *Testimonium Flavianum and its Implications* by Shlomo Pines. ©The Israel Academy of Science and Humanities, 1971.

There are many other Biblical references made by Josephus in his writings. This is amazing because it authenticates the Holy Bible and verifies the trustworthiness and reliability of Scripture. This is why extra-Biblical references are so important.

Cornelius Tacitus
Roman Historian (AD 56–120)
He mentions "Christus" who is Jesus, in his notable work called *Annals*.

"Consequently, to get rid of the report, Nero fastened the guilt and inflicted the most exquisite tortures on a class hated for their abominations, called Christians by the populace. Christus, from whom the name had its origin, suffered the extreme penalty during the reign of Tiberius at the hands of one of our procurators, Pontius Pilatus, and a most mischievous superstition, thus checked for the moment, again broke out not only in Judaea, the first source of the evil, but even in Rome, where all things hideous and shameful from every part of the world find their centre and become popular." [98]

Pliny the Younger
Politician, Judge, and Author (AD 61–113)
Pliny was governor of Bithynia in Asia Minor. He wrote ten books. In the tenth book, written around 112 AD, he speaks about Christianity in the province of Bithynia and also provides some facts about Jesus.

"They (the Christians) were in the habit of meeting on a certain fixed day before it was light, when they sang in alternate verses a hymn to Christ, as to a god, and bound themselves by a solemn oath, not to any wicked deeds, but never to commit any fraud, theft or adultery, never to falsify their word, nor deny a trust when they should be called upon to deliver it up; after which it was their custom to separate,

---

[98] http://classic.mit.edu/Tacitus/annals.mb.txt.

and then reassemble to partake of food—but food of an ordinary and innocent kind.[99]

The Talmud

The Talmud in Hebrew means "Instruction, learning" and is the central text of Rabbinic Judaism and the primary source of Jewish religious law and theology. The Talmud contains passages that some scholars have concluded are references to Christian traditions about Jesus (through mentions of an individual called "Yeshu," a derivative of Jesus' Aramaic name, Yeshua.

"On the eve of the Passover Yeshu was hanged. For forty days before the execution took place, a herald went forth and cried, 'He is going forth to be stoned because he has practiced sorcery and enticed Israel to apostasy. Anyone who can say any thing in his favor, let him come forward and plead on his behalf.' But since nothing was brought forward in his favor he was hanged on the eve of the Passover!"[100]

In the New Testament we read in Luke 22:1, 2:

¹"Now the Feast of Unleavened Bread, called the Passover, was approaching, ²and the chief priests and scribes were looking for a way to put Jesus to death; for they feared the people."

Lucian

Greek Writer/Novelist, Satirist, Rhetorician (AD 125–180)

He was born in Samosata, Roman Empire, which is now modern-day Turkey. Though Lucian opposed Christianity, he acknowledges Jesus—that Jesus was crucified, that Christians worshiped Him, and that this was done by faith.

---

99 Pliny, Letters, transl. by William Melmoth, rev. by W.H.L. Hutchinson (Cambridge: Harvard Univ. Press, 1935) vol. II, X: 96 as cited in Habermas, Gary R., *The Historical Jesus: Ancient Evidence for the Life of Christ* (Joplin, MO: College Press Publishing Company), ©1996.

100 *The Babylonian Talmud*, transl. by I. Epstein (London: Soncino 1935), vol.III, Sanhedrin 43a, p.281 as cited in Habermas, Gary R. *The Historical Jesus: Ancient Evidence for the Life of Christ* (Joplin, MO: College Press Publishing Company), ©1996.º

"The Christians, you know, worship a man to this day—the distinguished personage who introduced their novel rites, and was crucified on that account. ...You see, these misguided creatures start with the general conviction that they are immortal for all time, which explains the contempt of death and voluntary self-devotion which are so common among them: and then it was impressed on them by their original lawgiver that they are all brothers, from the moment that they are converted, and deny the gods of Greece, and worship the crucified sage, and live after his laws. All this they take quite on faith, with the result that they despise all worldly goods alike, regarding them merely as common property."[101]

Extra Biblical Historical Evidence

Early Non-Christian References to Jesus			
Writer	Date	Writing	Relevance
1 Thallus	A.D. 52	Chronicle	Solar eclipse at the crucifixion
2 Josephus	A.D. 93	Antiquities	Reference to John the Baptist, James, and Jesus
3 Pliny the Younger	A.D. 112	Letter to Trajon	Information about early Christianity
4 Cornelius Tacitus	A.D. 116	Annals	Information on the origin and spread of Christianity
5 Serenius Granianus	A.D. 38-117	Letter to Hadrian	Discussion of charges brought against Christians
6 Suetonius	A.D. 120	Life of Nero	Report of punishment inflicted on Christians
7 Phlegon	A.D. 140	Olympiads	Solar eclipse at the crucifixion
8 Lucian of Samosata	A.D. 170	The Death of Peregrine	Hostile testimony about early Christians

---

[101] Lucian, *The Death of Peregrine*, 11-13, in *The Works of Lucian of Samosata*, transl. by A. W. Fowler and F.G. Fowler, 4 vols. (Oxford: Clarendon, 1949), vol. 4, as cited in Habermas, Gary R. *The Historical Jesus: Ancient Evidence for the Life of Christ* (Joplin, MO :College Press Publishing Company), ©1996.

Other secular writers who refer to Christ and Christianity

9	Epictetus	15	Libanius
10	Aristides	16	Ammianus
11	Galenus	17	Marcellinus
12	Lampridius	18	Eunapius
13	Dio Cassius	19	Zosimus
14	Hinnerius	20	Jewish Rabbis

Evidence to Evaluate

- The extra-Biblical historical evidence of non-Christian and secular sources in fact do corroborate and validate the people, places, and events mentioned in the Holy Bible. This evidence includes Christianity, the Disciples, the Apostles and Jesus Christ Himself as being a legitimate institution and historical figures, respectively.

Notes

PROOF SIX

con-sis-tent

–adj.

1. compatible or in harmony.

—*The Oxford Dictionary*

INTERNAL CONSISTENCY

PREMISE

This chapter will be focusing on the fact that the internal consistency, harmony, and unity of the Holy Bible are most incredible. Throughout Scripture—from the first book of the Holy Bible, Genesis, to the last book of the Holy Bible, Revelation,—there is absolute consistency in what it teaches. We must understand that the Holy Bible, from Genesis to Revelation, reads as one Book, and yet it is made up of 66 individual books. Its English translations have about 807,370 words; 31,173 verses; and 1,189 chapters written by 40 plus authors from different backgrounds and social statuses, written in 13 different countries, on 3 different continents. It was originally written in 3 different languages

Chronological Dates to the Books of the Bible

OLD TESTAMENT			NEW TESTAMENT		
Book	Date	Author	Book	Date	Author
1. Job	Unknown	Anonymous	1. James	A.D. 44-49	James
2. Genesis	1445-1405 B.C.	Moses	2. Galatians	A.D. 49-50	Paul
3. Exodus	1445-1405 B.C.	Moses	3. Matthew	A.D. 50-60	Matthew
4. Leviticus	1445-1405 B.C.	Moses	4. Mark	A.D. 50-60	Mark
5. Numbers	1445-1405 B.C.	Moses	5. 1 Thessalonians	A.D. 51	Paul
6. Deuteronomy	1445-1405 B.C.	Moses	6. 2 Thessalonians	A.D. 51-52	Paul
7. Psalms	1410-450 B.C.	Multiple Authors	7. 1 Corinthians	A.D. 55	Paul
8. Joshua	1405-1385 B.C.	Joshua	8. 2 Corinthians	A.D. 55-56	Paul
9. Judges	about 1043 B.C.	Samuel	9. Romans	A.D. 56	Paul
10. Ruth	about 1030-1010 B.C.	Samuel(?)	10. Luke	A.D. 60-61	Luke
11. Song of Solomon	971-965 B.C.	Solomon	11. Ephesians	A.D. 60-62	Paul
12. Proverbs	971-686 B.C.	Solomon Primarily	12. Philipians	A.D. 60-62	Paul
13. Ecclesiastes	940-931 B.C.	Solomon	13. Colossians	A.D. 60-62	Paul
14. 1 Samuel	931-722 B.C.	Anonymous	14. Philemon	A.D. 60-62	Paul
15. 2 Samuel	931-722 B.C.	Anonymous	15. Acts	A.D. 62	Luke
16. Obadiah	850-840 B.C.	Obadiah	16. 1 Timothy	A.D. 62-64	Paul
17. Joel	835-796 B.C.	Joel	17. Titus	A.D. 62-64	Paul
18. Jonah	about 775 B.C.	Jonah	18. 1 Peter	A.D. 64-65	Peter
19. Amos	about 750 B.C.	Amos	19. 2 Timothy	A.D. 66-67	Paul
20. Micah	735-710 B.C.	Micah	20. 2 Peter	A.D. 67-68	Peter
21. Hosea	750-710 B.C.	Hosea	21. Hebrews	A.D. 67-69	Unknown
22. Isaiah	700-681 B.C.	Isaiah	22. Jude	A.D. 68-70	Jude
23. Nahum	about 650 B.C.	Nahum	23. John	A.D. 80-90	John
24. Zephaniah	635-625 B.C.	Zephaniah	24. 1 John	A.D. 90-95	John
25. Habakkuk	615-605 B.C.	Habakkuk	25. 2 John	A.D. 90-95	John
26. Ezekiel	590-570 B.C.	Ezekiel	26. 3 John	A.D. 90-95	John
27. Lamentations	586 B.C.	Jeremiah	27. Revelation	A.D. 94-96	John
28. Jeremiah	586-570 B.C.	Jeremiah			
29. 1 Kings	561-538 B.C.	Anonymous			
30. 2 Kings	561-538 B.C.	Anonymous			
31. Daniel	538-530 B.C.	Daniel			
32. Haggai	about 520 B.C.	Haggai			
33. Zechariah	480-470 B.C.	Zechariah			
34. Ezra	457-444 B.C.	Ezra			
35. 1 Chronicles	450-430 B.C.	Ezra (?)			
36. 2 Chronicles	450-430 B.C.	Ezra (?)			
37. Esther	450-331 B.C.	Anonymous			
38. Malachi	433-424 B.C.	Malachi			
39. Nehemiah	424-400 B.C.	Ezra			

(Hebrew, Aramaic, and Greek) over a 1600-year period,[102] and speaks on thousands of different topics with total unity without contradicting itself theologically, morally, ethically, doctrinally, scientifically, historically, or in any other way. The Holy Bible does this all with one central theme that focuses on the person of Jesus Christ, whereby, supporting its claim of Divine Origin and Inspiration.

Only an all-knowing and all-powerful God Who transcends both time and space could have known about and guided events thousands of years in the future.

Here are five categories in the form of charts to help you better understand the Holy Bible's internal consistency and unity. These charts are as follows: 1) Jesus: from Genesis to Revelation, 2) Types of Christ throughout the Bible, 3) References and Inferences to Genesis in the New Testament, 4) History of Salvation in the Old Testament, and 5) The Harmony of the Four Gospels.

Keep in mind the time frame of the Old Testament writings relative to the New Testament writings. The Old Testament was written between 1445 to 400 B.C., and the New Testament was written between 44 and 96 A.D.

Jesus in All 66 Books of the Holy Bible
Old Testament

- In Genesis: He is The Seed of the Woman
- In Exodus: He is the Passover Lamb That Was Slain
- In Leviticus: He is the High Priest of God
- In Numbers: He is the Cloud by Day and The Fire By Night
- In Deuteronomy: He is the Prophet Like Moses
- In Joshua: He is the Captain of Our Salvation
- In Judges: He is the Judge and Lawgiver
- In Ruth: He is the Kinsman Redeemer
- In 1 & 2 Samuel: He is the Prophet of The Lord
- In 1 & 2 Kings: He is the Reigning King
- In Ezra: He is the Faithful Scribe

---

[102] *Evidence that Demands a Verdict* by Josh McDowell. Copyright ©1999 by Here's Life Publisher's, Inc.

- In Nehemiah: He is The Restorer of Broken People
- In Esther: He is The Savior of the Helpless
- In Job: He is The Sovereign God Over Human Pain
- In Psalms: He is The Lord Who Is Our Shepherd
- In Proverbs and Ecclesiastes: He is Our Wisdom
- In The Song of Solomon: He is The Lover of Our Souls
- In Isaiah: He is The Prince of Peace
- In Jeremiah and Lamentations: He is The Weeping Prophet
- In Ezekiel: He is The Turning Wheel
- In Daniel: He is The 4th Man in the Fiery Furnace
- In Hosea: He is The Forgiving Husband
- In Joel: He is The Baptizer with The Holy Spirit
- In Amos: He is The Burden Bearer
- In Obadiah: He is The Mighty Savior
- In Jonah: He is The Forgiving God
- In Micah: He is The Messenger with Beautiful Feet
- In Nahum: He is The Avenger of God's Elect
- In Habakkuk: He is The Great Evangelist
- In Zephaniah: He is The Fountain for Cleansing
- In Haggai: He is The Cleansing Fountain
- In Zechariah: He is The Merciful Father
- In Malachi: He is The Abundant Gift-Giver

New Testament

- In Matthew: He is The Messiah Who is King
- In Mark: He is The Messiah Who is Servant
- In Luke: He is The Son of Man
- In John: He is The Son of God
- In Acts: He is The Ascended Lord
- In Romans: He is The Justifier
- In 1 & 2 Corinthians: He is The Gift of The Holy Spirit
- In Galatians: He is The One Who Sets Us Free
- In Ephesians: He is The Head of the Church
- In Philippians: He is The Peace of God

- In Colossians: He is The Fullness of The Godhead
- In 1 & 2 Thessalonians: He is The Soon-Coming King
- In 1 & 2 Timothy: He is The Mediator Between God and Man
- In Titus: He is The Faithful Pastor
- In Philemon: He is Our Benefactor
- In Hebrews: He is The Blood That Washes Away My Sins
- In James: He is The Great Physician
- In 1 & 2 Peter: He is The Chief Shepherd
- In 1 & 2 & 3 John: He is The Everlasting Love
- In Jude: He is The Revealer of Apostasy
- In Revelation: He is The Alpha and The Omega

I want to show you some of the typology and symbolism repeatedly found in the Holy Bible revealed to us in the form of **Shadows, Symbols, and Types of Christ.** According to *Wilson's Dictionary of Bible Types*,[103] there are over one-thousand types, shadows, symbols, pictures, portraits, figures, and patterns found in the Holy Bible as a whole. Biblical symbolism in the form of typology is a unique kind of Supernatural Intervention that always represents or portrays something or someone yet future. When working with Biblical symbolism, one must always follow two cardinal rules: First, we must understand that several different symbols may represent the same reality in the Holy Bible; and secondly, allow the Holy Bible to interpret its own symbols. Be sure to check the context in which a symbol appears, and do not try to force a symbol where it does not fit. Context and Biblical interpretation are like timing in music—without timing and context nothing could be understood or recognized correctly. In most cases, the Holy Bible explains itself to those who diligently study it; and, while doing so, we also must implement two hermeneutical rules of Biblical interpretation: 1) *Always interpret Scripture with Scripture*, and 2) *The Holy Bible itself is the Holy Bible's best commentary*. Remember, Biblical typology is—more often than not—a person or event portrayed in the Old Testament which foreshadows a person or event in the New Testament. When we say that someone or something is a "type of Christ," we are saying that someone or something in the Old Testament acts or corresponds to some characteristic or quality of

---

[103] *Wilson's Dictionary of Bible Types* is a resource freely available at www.studylight.org.

Christ as He is portrayed or viewed in the New Testament. For example, the Old Testament identifies several events as types of Christ's redemption which includes the tabernacle, the sacrificial system, and the Passover.[104] Below are topics and their proof texts for this amazing Supernatural Intervention (i.e. *Proof of Authority*). These texts show the amazing level of internal unity, cohesiveness, and harmony found within the Holy Bible as a whole. Also, we will look briefly at the Old Testament passages about Christ's visible appearances before His incarnation, called Christophanies.

Types of Christ

- **Adam**
  Romans 5:14; 1Corinthians 15:45

- **Abel**
  Genesis 4:8, 10; Hebrews 12:24

- **Abraham**
  Genesis 17:5; Ephesians 3:15

- **Aaron**
  Exodus 28:1; Leviticus 16:15; Hebrews 5:4, 5; 9:7, 24

- **Ark**
  Genesis 7:16; 1Peter 3:20, 21

- **Ark of the Covenant**
  Exodus 25:16; Isaiah 42:6; Psalms 40:8

- **Atonement, Sacrifices Offered on the Day of**
  Leviticus 16:15, 16; Hebrews 9:12, 24

- **Brazen Serpent**
  Numbers 21:9; John 3:14, 15

- **Brazen Altar**
  Exodus 27:1, 2; Hebrews 13:10

- **Burnt Offering**
  Leviticus 1:2, 4; Hebrews 10:10

---

[104] He. 9:8, 9; 10:19, 20; 1Co. 5:7.

Types of Christ

- **Cities of Refuge**
  Numbers 35:6; Hebrews 6:18

- **David**
  2Samuel 8:15; Ezekiel 37:24; Psalms 89:19, 20; Philippians 2:9

- **Eliakim**
  Isaiah 22:20-22; Revelation 3:7

- **First-fruits**
  Exodus 22:29; 1Corinthians 15:20

- **Golden Candlestick**
  Exodus 25:31; John 8:12

- **Golden Altar**
  Exodus 40:5, 26, 27; Hebrews 13:15; Revelation 8:3

- **Isaac**
  Genesis 22:1, 2; Hebrews 11:17-19

- **Jacob**
  Genesis 32:28; John 11:42; Hebrews 7:25

- **Jacob's Ladder**
  Genesis 28:12; John 1:51

- **Joseph**
  Genesis 50:19, 20

- **Joshua**
  Joshua 1:5, 6; 11:23; Acts 20:32; Hebrews 4:8, 9

- **Jonah**
  Jonah 1:17; Matthew 12:40

- **Laver of Brass**
  Exodus 30:18-20; Zechariah 13:1; Ephesians 5:26, 27

- **Lepers Offering**
  Leviticus 14:4-7; Romans 4:25

Types of Christ

- **Man**
  Exodus 16:11-15; John 6:32-35

- **Melchizedek**
  Genesis 14:18-20; Hebrews 7:1-17

- **Mercy Seat**
  Exodus 25:17-22; Romans 3:25; Hebrews 4:16

- **Morning and Evening Sacrifices**
  Exodus 29:38-41; John 1:29, 36

- **Moses**
  Numbers 12:7; Deuteronomy 18:15; Acts 3:20-22; Hebrews 3:2

- **Noah**
  Genesis 5:29; 2Corinthians 1:5

- **Paschal Lamb**
  Exodus 12:3-6, 46; John 19:36

- **Peace Offerings**
  Leviticus 3:1; Ephesians 2:14, 16

- **Red Heifer**
  Numbers 19:2-6; Hebrews 9:13, 14

- **Rock of Horeb**
  Exodus 17:6; 1Corinthians 10:4

- **Samson**
  Judges 16:30; Colossians 2:14, 15

- **Scape Goat**
  Leviticus 16, 20-22; Isaiah 53:6, 12

Types of Christ

- **Sin Offering**
  Leviticus 4:2, 3, 12; Hebrews 13:11, 12

- **Solomon**
  2Samuel 7:12, 13; Luke 1:32, 33; 1Peter 2:5

- **Tabernacle**
  Exodus 40:2, 34; Colossians 2:9; Hebrews 9:11

- **Table and Show Bread**
  Exodus 25:23-30; John 1:16; 6:48

- **Temple**
  1Kings 6:1, 38; John 2:19, 21

- **Tree of Life**
  Genesis 2:9; John 1:4; Revelation 22:2

- **Trespass Offering**
  Leviticus 6:1-7; Isaiah 53:10

- **Vail of the Tabernacle and Temple**
  Exodus 40:21; 2Chronicles 3:14; Hebrews 10:20

- **Zerubbabel**
  Zechariah 4:7-9; Hebrews 12:2, 3

In this section I will be showing you the many citations that are found in the New Testament that directly or indirectly allude to Old Testament passages. These passages provide irrefutable evidence for the amazing harmony, unity, and cohesiveness found in the Holy Bible's 66 individual historical documents.

I will also be showing you in detail the quotes from or allusions to Genesis in the New Testament. This is without a doubt one of the most amazing Supernatural Interventions (i.e. *Proof of Authority*) found in the Holy Bible. The unity in Scripture demonstrates it is Supernatural and Inspirational.

As we study the topic of internal consistency, harmony, and unity of the Holy Bible, I want to remind you once again about the amazing circumstantial evidence found in the Holy Bible. This phenomenon has no natural explanation but is consistent with the Holy Bible's claim of Divine Origin and Inspiration (i.e. Supernatural Intervention and Confirmation).

Look concisely at the books of the New Testament and count how many Old Testament citations are found there: Matthew-102; Mark-39; Luke-68; John-49; Acts-96; Romans-75; 1Corinthians-41; 2Corinthians-13; Galatians-16; Ephesians-10; Philippians-3; Colossians-3; 1Thessalonians-2; 2Thessalonians-2; 1Timothy-8; 2Timothy-2; Titus-0; Philemon-0; Hebrews-99; James-17; 1Peter-22; 2Peter-12; 1John-5; 2John-0; 3John-0; Jude-8; Revelation-245. There are a total of 937 Old Testament passages found in the New Testament that are directly, indirectly, or allude to the Old Testament passages. Below I will show you in detail 200 quotes that are direct or indirect references to the Book of Genesis in the New Testament.

References and Inferences to Genesis in the New Testament

	Genesis Reference	Topic	New Testament Reference
1.	1:1	God in the Beginning	John 1:1
2.	1:1	Beginning of the world	2Timothy 1:9
3.	1:1	Beginning of the world	Titus 1:2
4.	1:1	Creation of the Universe	Hebrews 11:3
5.	1:1	Earth and Heaven in the beginning	Hebrews 1:10
6.	1:3-5	Light out of darkness	2Corinthians 4:6
7.	1:5-7	Earth out of water and in water	2 Peter 3:4-5
8.	1:11	Every seed his own body	1Corinthians 15:38-39
9.	1:11-12	Earth bringing forth herbs	Hebrews 6:7
10.	1:26-27	Made male and female	Mark 10:6-7
11.	1:26-27	Made in image of God	Colossians 3:10
12.	1:27	In the image of God	1Corinthians 11:7
13.	1:29-31	All creatures good	1Timothy 4:4
14.	1:31	All things made by God	Acts 17:24
15.	2:1	All that in them yes	Acts 14:15
16.	2:1	All things created in heaven and earth	Revelation 10:6
17.	2:1	First heaven and first earth	Revelation 21:1
18.	2:1-3	All things created	Colossians 1:16
19.	2:1	Work finished	Hebrews 4:3
20.	2:2	Rest on the seventh day	Hebrews 4:4
21.	2:3	Ceased from His works	Hebrews 4:10
22.	2:3	Created all things	Ephesians 2:9
23.	2:3	World made by Him	John 1:10
24.	2:3	Created all things	Revelation 4:1
25.	2:4	Creation which God created	Mark 13:19
26.	2:4	He that made heaven and earth	Revelation 14:7
27.	2:4-6	Things that were made	Romans 1:20
28.	2:7	Adam a living soul	1Corinthians 15:45
29.	2:7	Man formed	1Timothy 2:13
30.	2:9	Tree of life in paradise	Revelation 2:7

31.	2:9	Fruit of tree of life	Revelation 22:14
32.	2:17	Death by sin	Romans 5:12
33.	2:18	Woman for the man	1Corinthians 11:9
34.	2:22	Woman of the man	1Corinthians 11:8
35.	2:23	Bone of his bone	Ephesians 5:30
36.	2:24	Leave father and mother	Ephesians 5:31
37.	2:24	One flesh	1Corinthians 6:16
38.	2:24	Cleave to his wife	Matthew 19:5
39.	2:24	One flesh	Mark 10:8
40.	3:1	That old serpent	Revelation 20:2
41.	3:1	Subtlety of serpent	2Corinthians 11:3
42.	3:4	Father of lies	John 8:44
43.	3:6	Women is deceived	1Timothy 2:14
44.	3:13	Serpent beguiled Eve	2Corinthians 11:3
45.	3:14	Devil sinned from beginning	1 John 3:8
46.	3:15	Made of a woman	Galatians 4:4
47.	3:15	Satan bruised under foot	Romans 16:20
48.	3:15	Enmity with the woman	Revelation 12:13-17
49.	3:15	That old serpent	Revelation 12:9
50.	3:15	Treading on serpents	Luke 12:19
51.	3:16	Saved in childbearing	1Timothy 2:15
52.	3:16	Women under obedience	1Corinthians 14:34
53.	3:16	Sorrow in travail	John 16:20
54.	3:16	Man the head of the woman	1Corinthians 11:3
55.	3:17	No more curse	Revelation 22:3
56.	3:18	Thorns and briers	Hebrews 6:8
57.	3:18-19	Bondage of corruption	Romans 8:21-22
58.	3:18-19	No more death, sorrow, pain	Revelation 21:4
59.	3:19	Work for your own bread	2Thessalonians 3:12
60.	3:19	By man came death	1Corinthians 15:21
61.	3:20	Mother of us all	Galatians 4:26
62.	3:22	Fruit of tree of life	Revelation 22:2
63.	3:23	Man from the earth	1Corinthians 15:47
64.	4:3-5	Abel a more excellent sacrifice	Hebrews 11:4

65.	4:4	Righteous Abel	Matthew 23:35
66.	4:8	Cain slew his brother	1John 3:12
67.	4:10	Blood of Abel	Hebrews 12:24
68.	4:11	Blood of Abel	Luke 11:51
69.	4:16	The way of Cain	Jude 11
70.	4:26	Prophets since the world began	Luke 1:70
71.	5:1	Book of the generations	Matthew 1:1
72.	5:1	Similitude of God	James 3:9
73.	5:2	Created male and female	Matthew 9:4
74.	5:2	Beginning of the creation of God	Revelation 3:14
75.	5:4	Death reigned from Adam	Romans 5:14-19
76.	5:5	In Adam all die	1Corinthians 15:22
77.	5:3-6	Adam to Enosh	Luke 3:38
78.	5:12-21	Canaan to Methuselah	Luke 3:37
79.	5:18	Enoch, seventh from Adam	Jude 14
80.	3:19	By man came death	1Corinthians 15:21
81.	3:20	Mother of us all	Galatians 4:26
82.	3:22	Fruit of tree of life	Revelation 22:2
83.	3:23	Man from the earth	1Corinthians 15:47
84.	4:3-5	Abel a more excellent sacrifice	Hebrews 11:4
85.	4:4	Righteous Abel	Matthew 23:35
86.	4:8	Cain slew his brother	1John 3:12
87.	4:10	Blood of Abel	Hebrews 12:24
88.	4:11	Blood of Abel	Luke 11:51
89.	4:16	The way of Cain	Jude 11
90.	4:26	Prophets since the world began	Luke 1:70
91.	5:1	Book of the generations	Matthew 1:1
92.	5:1	Similitude of God	James 3:9
93.	5:2	Created male and female	Matthew 9:4
94.	5:2	Beginning of the creation of God	Revelation 3:14
95.	5:4	Death reigned from Adam	Romans 5:14-19
96.	5:5	In Adam all die	1Corinthians 15:22
97.	5:3-6	Adam to Enosh	Luke 3:38
98.	5:12-21	Canaan to Methuselah	Luke 3:37

99.	5:18	Enoch, seventh from Adam	Jude 14
100.	9:6	Life for life	Matthew 26:52
101.	10:8-11	Babylon, the mother of abominations	Revelation 17:5
102.	10:32	All nations on face of earth	Acts 17:26
103.	11:4, 5	That great city	Revelation 17:18
104.	11:10-13	Shem to Canaan	Luke 3:36
105.	11:14-20	Salah to Serug	Luke 3:35
106.	11:22-26	Nahor to Abraham	Luke 3:34
107.	11:31	Abraham dwelt in Haran	Acts 7:4
108.	12:1	Abraham to leave his kindred	Acts 7:3
109.	12:3	All families of earth to be blessed	Acts 3:25
110.	12:3	All nations blessed	Galatians 3:8
111.	12:4	Abraham went out	Hebrews 11:8
112.	12:5	From Haran to Canaan	Acts 7:4
113.	12:7	Unborn seed given the land	Acts 7:5
114.	13:15	Promised to the seed	Galatians 3:6
115.	14:18	Melchizedek	Hebrews 7:1
116.	14:19	Abraham blessed of Melchizedek	Hebrews 7:6, 7
117.	14:20	Tithes to Melchizedek	Hebrews 7:4, 5
118.	15:5	So shall thy seed be	Romans 4:18
119.	15:5	Seed as the stars	Hebrews 11:12
120.	15:6	Faith counted for righteousness	Romans 4:5,9,22
121.	15:6	Abraham believed God	Galatians 3:6
122.	15:6	Imputed righteousness	James 2:23
123.	15:13	Afflicted 400 years	Acts 7:6
124.	15:14	Nations to be judges	Acts 7:7
125.	15:16	Iniquities to be filled up	1Thessalonians 2:16
126.	16:1	No children	Acts 7:5
127.	16:15	A son by Hagar	Galatians 4:22
128.	17:5	Father of many nations	Romans 4:17
129.	17:7	With Abram's seed forever	Luke 1:55
130.	17:8	Oath sworn to Abraham	Luke 1:73
131.	17:10	Circumcision of the fathers	John 7:22
132.	17:11	Sign of Circumcision	Romans 4:11

133.	17:13	Covenant of Circumcision	Acts 7:8
134.	17:17	Abraham and Sarah past age	Romans 4:19
135.	18:2	Angels unawares	Hebrews 13:2
136.	18:10, 14	Sarah to bear at appointed time	Romans 9:9
137.	18:12	Sarah called Abraham "lord"	1Peter 3:6
138.	18:20	Sin of Sodom and Gomorrah	Matthew 10:15
139.	19:1-3	Entertaining angels	Hebrews 13:2
140.	19:5	Going after strange flesh	Jude 7
141.	19:9	Lot dwelling among wicked	2Peter 2:7, 8
142.	19:24	Fire and brimstone from heaven	Luke 17:29
143.	19:25	Judgment on Sodom	Luke 10:12
144.	19:26	Lot's wife	Luke 17:32
145.	21:1	Promise fulfillment	Galatians 4:23
146.	21:2	Sarah conceived seed	Hebrews 11:11
147.	21:3	Abraham begot Isaac	Matthew 1:2
148.	21:4	Isaac the son of Abraham	Luke 3:34
149.	21:9	Son of promise persecuted	Galatians 4:29
150.	21:10	Bondwoman cast out	Galatians 4:30
151.	21:12	Isaac the seed of promise	Galatians 4:28
152.	21:13	Seed of Abraham	Romans 9:7
153.	21:13	Isaac the seed called	Hebrews 11:18
154.	21:14	Hagar in the wilderness	Galatians 4:24, 25
155.	22:1-3	Abraham offers up Isaac	Hebrews 11:17
156.	22:5	Accounting God could raise him up	Hebrews 11:19
157.	22:9	Isaac on the altar	James 2:21
158.	22:16	God swearing by Himself	Hebrews 6:13
159.	22:17	Blessing and multiplying	Hebrews 6:14
160.	22:17	As the sand and stars	Hebrews 11:12
161.	22:18	Heir of all nations of earth	Romans 4:13
162.	23:4	Stranger and sojourner	Hebrews 11:9
163.	23:16-20	Sepulcher bought	Acts 7:16
164.	25:21	Rebekah conceived	Romans 9:10
165.	25:23	Elder to serve the younger	Romans 9:12
166.	25:25, 26	Jacob and Esau	Romans 9:13

167.	25:33	Birthright despised	Hebrews 12:16
168.	26:3	Blessings of Abraham	Galatians 3:14
169.	26:4, 5	Covenant confirmed	Galatians 3:17
170.	27:27-29, 39, 40	Isaac blessed Jacob and Esau	Hebrews 11:20
171.	27:34, 38	No place of repentance	Hebrews 12:17
172.	28:12	Angels descending	John 1:51
173.	28:15	Never leave thee	Hebrews 13:5
174.	29:35	Judah, son of Jacob	Luke 3:33
175.	30:13	Called blessed	Luke 1:48
176.	30:23	Reproach taken away	Luke 1:25
177.	31:42	God of Abraham, Isaac and Jacob	Matthew 22:32
178.	32:12	Seed as the sand	Hebrews 11:12
179.	33:19	Jacob's parcel of ground	John 4:5
180.	35:16, 17	Rachel weeping	Matthew 2:18
181.	37:28	Joseph sold into Egypt	Acts 7:9
182.	38:29	Judah begat Pharez	Matthew 1:3
183.	39:2, 23	The Lord with Joseph	Acts 7:9
184.	41:41-44	Joseph exalted	Acts 7:10
185.	41:54	Dearth in Egypt	Acts 7:11
186.	42:1, 2	Corn in Egypt	Acts 7:12
187.	42:5	Famine in Canaan	Acts 7:11
188.	42:13	Twelve brethren	Acts 7:8
189.	45:1-4	Joseph revealed to his brethren	Acts 7:13
190.	45:9-11	Joseph sending for Jacob	Acts 7:14
191.	46:5, 6	Jacob going to Egypt	Acts 7:15
192.	47:26, 27	Seventy-five souls	Acts 7:14
193.	47:9	Strangers and pilgrims	Hebrews 11:13
194.	47:31	Leaning on top of staff	Hebrews 11:21
195.	48:13-20	Jacob blessed sons of Joseph	Hebrews 11:21
196.	49:9-10	Lion of tribe of Judah	Revelation 5:5
197.	49:10	Lord sprang from Judah	Hebrews 7:14
198.	49:11	Washed garments in blood	Revelation 7:14
199.	49:29, 30	Jacob buried in Canaan	Acts 7:16
200.	50:24-26	Death of Joseph	Hebrews 11:21

I now want to talk to you about the History of Salvation in the Holy Bible as it is found in the Old Testament, confirming once again the unity, harmony, and cohesiveness of the Holy Bible. As early as Genesis 3:15, we see the promise of a coming Savior.

Throughout the Old Testament there are hundreds of promises that the Messiah would come and save His people from their sins (Mt. 1:21; Is. 53:5, 6). Job's faith was that he knew that his "Redeemer lives," and that in the end, His Savor would stand upon the earth (Jb. 19:25). It's very clear that the Old Testament saints were aware of the promised Redeemer, and they understood that they were saved by faith in that Savior.

The Gospel is not just an exclusively New Testament message—it was revealed to the saints in the Holy Bible's oldest book, the book of Job. The Old Testament looks forward to the promised Redeemer and the New Testament looks at the fulfillment of that promise through Jesus Christ. In the Old Testament saints looked forward. Today we look back to the life, death, and Resurrection of the Savior and are saved by faith in Jesus Christ's atonement for our sins (Ro.10:9, 10).

For example, Paul directs us to Abraham, who was saved by faith: *"Abraham believed God, and it was credited to him as righteousness"* (Ro. 4:3; Ge. 15:6). Paul also tells us that David was saved by faith (Ro. 4:6-8); he quoted Psalm 32:1, 2.

In other words, salvation has always been a gift of God by grace through faith (Ge. 12:3; Ga. 3:8, 9; 15:6; Hab. 2:4; Ro. 4:1-8; 8:38, 39; Ep. 2:8, 9).

Also see the *Eyewitness Testimony* chapter to show you again the unity and cohesiveness found within the Gospels—Matthew, Mark, Luke, and John.

I now want to show you the harmony, unity, and cohesiveness found within the Gospels themselves using topics relative to Bible passages (*The Harmony of the Gospels*).

Subjects	Matthew	Mark	Luke	John
Pre-Christ Narratives				
St. Luke's preface			1:1–4	
"God the Word"				1:1–14
The Birth and Early Childhood of Christ				
Birth of John the Baptist foretold			1:5–25	
Annunciation of the birth of Jesus			1:26–38	
Mary visits Elizabeth			1:39–56	
Birth of John the Baptist			1:57–80	
The two genealogies	1:1–17		3:23–38	
Birth of Jesus Christ	1:18–25		2:1–7	
The watching shepherds			2:8–20	
The circumcision			2:21	
Presentation of Jesus in the temple			2:22–38	
The wise men from the East	2:1–12			
Flight into Egypt, and return to Nazareth	2:13–23		2:39	
Christ in the temple with the doctors			2:40–52	
The Baptism of Christ				
Ministry of John the Baptist	3:1–12	1:1–8	3:1–18	1:15–31
Baptism of Jesus Christ	3:13–17	1:9–11	3:21–22	1:32–34
The Temptation of Christ				
The temptation	4:1–11	1:12–13	4:1–13	
The Early Ministry of Christ				
Andrew and another disciple and Simon Peter				1:35–42
Philip and Nathanael				1:43–51
The marriage in Cana of Galilee				2:1–11
Passover and cleansing the temple				2:12–25
Nicodemus comes to Jesus by night				3:1–21
Christ and John baptizing				3:22; 4:2
Christ at the well of Sychar				4:3–42
John the Baptist in prison	4:12; 14:3	1:14; 6:17	3:19–20	3:24
Christ returns to Galilee	4:12	1:14–15	4:14–15	4:43–45

Subjects	Matthew	Mark	Luke	John
The synagogue at Nazareth				4:16–30
Andrew and Simon, James and John called	4:13–22	1:16–20	5:1–11	
Miracles of Christ				
The nobleman's son at Capernaum healed				4:46–54
The Demoniac in the synagogue healed		1:21–28	4:31–37	
Simon's mother-in-law healed	8:14–17	1:29–34	4:38–41	
Circuit around Galilee	4:23–25	1:35–39	4:42–44	
Healing a leper	8:1–4	1:40–45	5:12–16	
Christ stills the storm	8:18–27	4:35–41	8:22–25	
Demoniacs in the land of the Gadarenes	8:28–34	5:1–20	8:26–39	
Jairus' daughter; woman healed	9:18–26	5:21–43	8:40–56	
Blind men and demoniac	9:27–34			
Healing the paralytic	9:1–8	2:1–12	5:17–26	
Matthew the publican	9:9–13	2:13–17	5:27–32	
"Thy disciples fast not"	9:14–17	2:18–22	5:33–39	
The Feast and Miracle at Bethsaida				
The feast at Jerusalem				5:1
The pool of Bethsaida				5:2–15
Jesus and the irate Jews				5:16–47
Ministry and Parables				
Plucking ears of corn on Sabbath	12:1–8	2:23–28	6:1–5	
The withered hand healed	12:9–21	3:1–12	6:6–11	
The twelve apostles	10:2–4	3:13–19	6:12–16	
The sermon on the mount	5:1–7:29		6:17–49	
The centurion's servant healed	8:5–13		7:1–10	
The widow's son at Nain			7:11–17	
Messengers from John	11:2–19		7:18–35	
Woe denounced to the cities of Galilee	11:20–24			
Call to the meek and suffering	11:25–30			
Anointing the feet of Jesus			7:36–50	
Second circuit around Galilee			8:1–3	
Parable of the sower	13:1–23	4:1–20	8:4–15	
Parable of the candle under a bushel		4:21–25		
Parable of the seed growing secretly		4:26–29		
Parable of the wheat and tares	13:24–30			
Parable of the grain of mustard seed	13:31–32	4:30–32	13:18–19	
Parable of the leaven	13:33			
On teaching by parables	13:34–35	4:33–34		

Subjects	Matthew	Mark	Luke	John
The wheat and tares explained	13:36–43			
The hidden treasure; the pearl; the net	13:44–52			
His mother and His brethren	12:46–50	3:31–35	8:19–21	
Reception at Nazareth	13:53–58	6:1–6		
Third circuit around Galilee	9:35–38; 11:1	6:6		
Sending forth of the twelve	10:5–42	6:7–13	9:1–6	
Herod's opinion of Jesus	14:1–2	6:14–16	9:7–9	
Death of John the Baptist	14:3–12	6:17–29		
Feeding of the five thousand	14:13–21	6:30–44	9:10–17	6:1–15
Christ walking on the sea	14:22–33	6:45–52		6:16–21
Miracles in Gennesaret	14:34–36	6:53–56		
"The Bread of Life"				6:22–65
The washed hands	15:1–20	7:1–23		
The Syrophoenician woman	15:21–28	7:24–30		
Miracles of healing	15:29–31	7:31–37		
Feeding of the four thousand	15:32–39	8:1–9		
The sign from heaven	16:1–4	8:10–13		
The leaven of the Pharisees	16:5–12	8:14–21		
Blind man healed		8:22–26		
Outside of Galilee				
Peter's profession of faith	16:13–19	8:27–29	9:18–20	6:66–71
The passion foretold	16:20–28	8:30–38; 9:1	9:21–27	
The transfiguration	17:1–9	9:2–10	9:28–36	
The coming of Elias	17:10–13	9:11–13		
The lunatic healed	17:14–21	9:14–29	9:37–42	
Back in Galilee				
The passion again foretold	17:22–23	9:30–32	9:43–45	
The fish caught for the tribute	17:24–27			
The little child	18:1–5	9:33–37	9:46–48	
One casting out devils		9:38–41	9:49–50	
Offenses	18:6–9	9:42–48	17:2	
The lost sheep	18:10–14		15:4–7	
Forgiveness of injuries	18:15–17			
"Binding and loosing"	18:18–20			
Parable of the unmerciful servant	18:21–35			
"Salt with fire"		9:49–50		
Ministry in Jerusalem				
Journey to Jerusalem			9:51	7:1–10
Fire from heaven			9:52–56	
Answers to disciples	8:19-22		9:57–62	
Teaching at the feast of tabernacles				7:11–53
Woman taken in adultery				8:1–11

Subjects	Matthew	Mark	Luke	John
Dispute with the Pharisees				8:12–59
The man born blind				9:1–41
The good shepherd				10:1–21
Feast of the Dedication				10:22–30
Departure beyond Jordan				10:40–42
In Galilee				
Mission of the seventy			10:1–16	
The return of the seventy			10:17–24	
The good Samaritan			10:25–37	
Mary and Martha			10:38–42	
The Lord's prayer	6:9–13		11:1–4	
Prayer effectual	7:7–11		11:5–13	
The blasphemous Pharisees reproved	12:22–37	3:20–30	11:14–23	
The unclean spirit returning	12:43–45		11:24–28	
The sign of Jonah	12:38–42		11:29–32	
The light of the body	5:15; 6:22–23		11:33–36	
The Pharisees	23:1–39		11:37–54	
What to fear	10:26–33		12:1–12	
Covetousness	6:25–33		12:13–31	
Watchfulness			12:32–54	
Galileans that perished			13:1–9	
Woman healed on the Sabbath			13:10–17	
The grain of mustard seed	13:31–32	4:30–32	13:18–19	
The leaven	13:33		13:20–21	
Towards and at Jerusalem				
Journey towards Jerusalem			13:22	
"Are there few that be saved?"			13:23–30	
Warning against Herod			13:31–33	
Prophecy against Jerusalem	23:37–39		13:34–35	
Dropsy healed on the Sabbath			14:1–6	
Choosing the chief rooms			14:7–14	
Parable of the great supper	22:1–14		14:15–24	

Subjects	Matthew	Mark	Luke	John
Following Christ with the cross	10:37–38		14:25–35	
Parables of the lost sheep; piece of money; prodigal son			15:1–32	
Parables of the steward; rich man and Lazarus			16:1–31	
Offenses	18:6–15		17:1–4	
Faith and merit	17:20		17:5–10	
The ten lepers			17:11–19	
How the kingdom cometh			17:20–37	
Parable of the unjust judge			18:1–8	
Parable of the Pharisee and the publican			18:9–14	
Divorce	19:1–12	10:1–12		
Infants brought to Jesus	19:13–15	10:13–16	18:15–17	
The rich man inquiring	19:16–26	10:17–27	18:18–27	
Promises to the disciples	19:27–30	10:28–31	18:28–30	
Laborers in the vineyard	20:1–16			
Death of Christ foretold	20:17–19	10:32–34	18:31–34	
Request of James and John	20:20–28	10:35–45		
Blind men at Jericho	20:29–34	10:46–52	18:35–43	
Zaccheus			19:1–10	
Parable of the ten talents	25:14–30		19:11–28	
Raising of Lazarus			11:1–44	
Meeting of the Sanhedrin			11:45–53	
Christ departs to Ephraim			11:54–57	
The anointing by Mary	26:6–13	14:3–9	7:36–50	12:1–11
Christ enters Jerusalem	21:1–11	11:1–10	19:29–44	12:12–19
Cleansing the temple (second)	21:12–16	11:15–18	19:45–48	
The barren fig tree	21:17–22	11:11–14; 11:19–23		
Exhortation to prayer and forgiveness	6:14–15	11:24–26		
The questioning of the chief priests	21:23–27	11:27–33	20:1–8	
Parable of the two sons	21:28–32			

Subjects	Matthew	Mark	Luke	John
Parable of the wicked husbandmen	21:33–46	12:1–12	20:9–18	
Parable of the wedding garment	22:1–14		14:16–24	
The tribute money	22:15–22	12:13–17	20:20–26	
The Sadducees confuted	22:23–33	12:18–27	20:27–40	
The great commandment	22:34–40	12:28–34		
David's Son and David's Lord	22:41–46	12:35–37	20:41–44	
The hypocrisy and ambition of the Pharisees	23:1–39	12:38–40	20:45–47	
The widow's mite		12:41–44	21:1–4	
Christ's second coming foretold	24:1–51	13:1–37	21:5–36	
Parable of the ten virgins	25:1–13			
Parable of the talents	25:14–30		19:11–27	
The last judgment	25:31–46			
Greeks visit Jesus; voice from heaven				12:20–36
The judgment of unbelief				12:37–50
Last passover; conspiracy of Jews	26:1–5	14:1–2	22:1–2	
Judas Iscariot	26:14–16	14:10–11	22:3–6	
Paschal supper	26:17–30	14:12–26	22:7–23	13:1–35
Contention of the apostles			22:24–30	
Peter's fall foretold	26:31–35	14:27–31	22:31–39	13:36–38
Last discourse; the departure; the Comforter				14:1–31
The vine and the branches; abiding love				15:1–27
Work of the Comforter in the disciples				16:1–33
The prayer of Christ for them				17:1–26
Gethsemane	26:36–46	14:32–42	22:40–46	18:1
The Betrayal and Trial of Christ				
The betrayal	26:47–56	14:43–52	22:47–53	18:2–11
Christ before Annas and Caiaphas; Peter's denial	26:57–58; 26:69–75	14:53–54; 14:66–72	22:54–65	18:12–27
Christ before the Sanhedrin	26:59–68	14:55–56	22:66–71	
Christ before Pilate	27:1–2; 27:11–14	15:1–5	23:1–6	28:33–40
Accusation and condemnation	27:15–26	15:6–15	23:13–25	18:29; 19:16

Subjects	Matthew	Mark	Luke	John
The Crucifixion and Burial of Christ				
Treatment by the soldiers	27:27–31	15:16–20	23:36–37	19:1–3
The crucifixion	27:32–38	15:21–28	23:26–34	19:17–24
The mother of Jesus at the cross				19:25–27
Mockings and railings	27:39–44	15:29–32	23:35–39	
The penitent malefactor			23:40–43	
The death of Christ	27:50	15:37	23:46	19:28–30
Darkness and other portents	27:45–53	15:33–38	23:44–45	
The bystanders	27:54–56	15:39–41	23:47–49	
The side pierced				19:31–37
The burial	27:57–61	15:42–47	23:50–56	19:38–42
The guard of the sepulchre	27:62–66; 28:11–15			
The Resurrection and Ascension of Christ				
The resurrection	28:1–10	16:1–11	24:1–12	20:1–18
Disciples going to Emmaus		16:12–13	24:13–35	
Appearances in Jerusalem; doubts of Thomas		16:14–18	24:36–49	20:19–29
Appearance at the Sea of Tiberias				21:1–23
Appearance on the mount of Galilee	28:16–20			
Unrecorded works				20:30–31; 21:24–25
The ascension		16:19–20	24:50–53	

In this section we will briefly look at the proof text for the visible appearances of Christ in the Old Testament called Christophanies. Some Bible commentators believe that whenever someone receives a visit from "the Angel of the Lord," this was in fact the pre-incarnate Christ.

These appearances can be seen in the following passages found in the Old Testament: Genesis 16:7-14; 22:11-18; Judges 5:23; 2Kings 19:35. Bible commentators also believe that these passages are Christophanies as well: Genesis 12:7-9; 18:1-33; 19:1-38; 32:22-30; Exodus 3:2; Deuteronomy 31:14-15; Job 38-42.

Repeatedly in Scripture we see Christ claiming that He pre-existed before the world began. For example, in John 8:57-59 we read the following:

> *57"Then the Jews said to Him, 'You are not yet fifty years old, and You have seen Abraham?'" 58'Truly, truly, I tell you,' Jesus declared, 'before Abraham was born, I am!' 59 "At this, they picked up stones to throw at Him. But Jesus was hidden and went out of the temple area."*

In John 17:4-5 Jesus said, *"I have glorified You on earth by accomplishing the work You gave Me to do. 5And now, Father, glorify Me in Your presence with the glory I had with You before the world existed."*

Not only did Jesus continually proclaim that He pre-existed before the world began, but His disciples believed it as well. In John 1:1-3 we read this affirmation:

> *"1in the beginning was the Word, and the Word was with God, and the Word was God. 2He was with God in the beginning. 3Through Him all things were made, and without Him nothing was made that has been made."*

In John 20:27-28 we also read that Thomas believed that Jesus was God:

> *27"Then Jesus said to Thomas, 'Put your finger here and look at My hands. Reach out your hand and put it into My side. Stop doubting and believe.' 28Thomas replied, "My Lord and my God!"*

The Holy Bible is consistent with all of its topics—including Christ's pre-existence.

Each of these Christophanies is a study in and of itself. Get your Holy Bible out, start your study today, and you will be amazed.[105]

I also want to show you some inconsistencies found in the Quran, the Muslim holy book, with regard to finding out from *what man was created*. We read in the Quran five different ways:
1. From a clot of congealed blood (Surah 96:2).
2. From mud (Surah 15:26).
3. From dust (Surah 3:59).
4. Out of nothing (Surah 19:67; 52:35).
5. From a sperm-drop (Surah 16:4).

There are also inconsistencies about the number of days required for creation—was it six (Surah 7:54; 11:7; 25:59) or was it 8 days (Surah 41:9, 10, 12)? Also, the Quran is mistaken about what Christians and Jews believe (Surah 5:73, 75; 9:30).

No other religious writings of any other worldview demonstrate the internal consistency and unity like the Holy Bible. None!

Evidence to Evaluate

- The Holy Bible is unique in its content and teachings, and no other religious book has ever been compiled by so many writers over such an expanse of time, with such cohesive unity and accuracy.
- The Holy Bible speaks on thousands of different topics and subjects without contradicting itself theologically, morally, ethically, doctrinally, scientifically, historically, or in any other way. The Holy Bible has one central theme and is clearly one book, with perfect unity and consistency throughout, whereby proving its claim of Divine Origin and Inspiration.
- Biblical Christianity is unique and consistent with our everyday issues in life. It is unique with regard to the human mind, laws of science, laws of logic, ethical and moral values, justice, love, the meaning to life, the problem of evil, suffering, and truth. Biblical Christianity corresponds with the reality of our present condition unlike any other worldview on earth.

---

105 Additional reading: *He Came Down from Heaven* by Douglas McCready. Published by InterVarsity Press, USA, 2005; *Jesus, Divine Messiah: The Old Testament Witness* by Robert L. Reymond, Published by Christian Focus Publications 1990.

Notes

PROOF SEVEN

man-u-script

–noun

1. handwritten or typed text.

—The Oxford Dictionary

THE MANUSCRIPT EVIDENCE

PREMISE

Engineer James Agresti was a jet engine designer, a loyal and committed atheist for many years. For some reason, he doesn't explain to us why, he spent a year to carefully read the Holy Bible and to study the objective evidence for its accuracy. The following comment was his conclusion: *"In summary, the evidence for the textual accuracy of the New Testament books is overwhelming. With the exception of about two paragraphs in the entire New Testament, the manuscript evidence is so strong, there is no rational basis for any kind of uncertainty over the substance of the text."*[106]

It was a study of objective evidence for the Holy Bible's accuracy that played a major role in Mr. Agresti's conversion to Christianity.

The Old Testament Manuscript Evidence

Jewish scholars performed amazing care in copying and preserving Scripture. The Dead Sea Scrolls discovered in 1947 are dated from the third century B.C. to the first century A.D.

These manuscripts predated by 1,000 years the previous oldest manuscripts. They represent every Old Testament book except Esther (as well as non-Biblical writings).

There is word-for-word accuracy in more than 95% of the cases, and the 5% variation consists of slips of the pen and spelling. When the Bible manuscripts are compared to other ancient writings, they stand alone as the best-preserved literary works of all antiquity.

---

106 Agresti, *Rational Conclusion*, p. 129.

There are thousands of existing Old Testament manuscripts and fragments copied throughout the Middle East, Mediterranean, and European regions that agree phenomenally with each other.

In addition, these texts substantially agree with the Septuagint version of the Old Testament, which was translated from the Hebrew to Greek some time during the 3rd Century B.C.

The New Testament Manuscript Evidence

The manuscript evidence for the New Testament is also dramatic, with nearly 25,000 ancient manuscripts discovered and archived so far. At least 5,800 are copies and fragments in the original Greek.

Some manuscript texts date to the early 2nd and 3rd centuries. The time between the original autograph, our earliest existing manuscripts, and fragments is a remarkably short 40–60 years.

There are 10,000 Latin manuscripts and 9,300 manuscripts in various other ancient languages. These languages include Syriac, Slavic, Gothic, Ethiopic, Coptic, and Armenian. The Biblical manuscript evidence surpasses the manuscript reliability of other ancient manuscripts that we trust as authentic today.

The Dead Sea Scrolls in More Detail

In 1947, in the midst of the War for the Independence of the Republic of Israel, came the discovery at Qumran of the first seven Dead Sea Scrolls by a Bedouin shepherd boy looking for his straying goat.

The Bedouin boy of the Ta'amra tribe discovered seven scrolls in a cave now named "Cave 1" Khirbet Qumran on the Northwest shore of the Dead Sea.

Three of these scrolls were then purchased by archaeologist Eliezer Lipa Sukenik for the Hebrew University. Others were bought by Mar Athanasius Samuel for the Metropolitan of the Syrian Orthodox Church in Jerusalem. From 1949-1954, additional fragments of more than 950 different scrolls were found in ten nearby caves by Bedouins and participants of a joint archaeological expedition led by Professor Father Roland de Vaux for the École Biblique et Archéologique Française and the Rockefeller Museum.

The discovery of the Dead Sea Scrolls, most of which dated from 200 B.C. to 68 A.D., drastically increased our assurance that the Old Testament we have today has been faithfully transmitted throughout the centuries. Some even date to 300 B.C. or older, like the Great Isaiah Scroll which was carbon-dated as old as 335 B.C.

The most manuscript fragments were found in Cave 4—over 15,000. The final cave, Cave 11, was discovered in 1956. The first seven scrolls remain in the property of the Israel Museum, while most of the fragments are owned by the Israel Antiquities Authority (IAA). According to the Dead Sea Scrolls Foundation, there are over 100,000 fragments from 800 or 900 original manuscripts, typically dating from the 3rd to 1st Centuries B.C.

The second site, Wadi Al-Murabba'at, 11 miles south of Qumran, contained documents from army fugitives in the Second Jewish Revolt against Rome (A.D. 132-135) and included a well-preserved scroll of the Minor Prophets. The third site south of En Gedi included a Greek translation of the Minor Prophets from the 1st Century A.D. The fourth site, 8.5 miles north of Jericho, contained legal documents from Samaritans massacred by soldiers of Alexander the Great in 331 B.C. The fifth site at Masada contained a copy of Ecclesiastes (75 B.C.) and fragments of Genesis, Leviticus, and Psalms. Among the Hebrew and Aramaic texts discovered at Qumran, there were 25 Greek documents found—six in Cave 4 and nineteen in Cave 7.

Cave 7 represents a variety of Greek material from Exodus (7Q1) and Jeremiah (7Q2) as well as materials (7Q3-19) potentially from the Gospel of Mark, Second Peter, the Book of Jude, and the Book of Enoch.[107] This raises the interesting possibility that Cave 7 may have been a depository for documents stored during the Flight to Pella by the Jerusalem Church. This is the actual community in which the Apostle Jude lived and ministered. Unfortunately, thorough and comprehensive research into this possibility is not

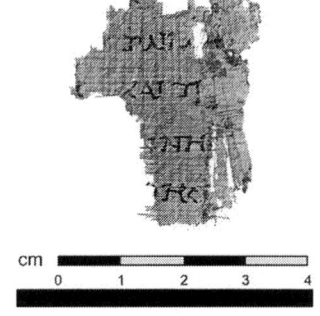

Qumran manuscript fragment 7Q5, identified as lines from St. Mark 6:52-53. *(Courtesy of the Israel Antiquities Authority).*

---

[107] *Eyewitness to Jesus: Amazing New Evidence About the Origin of the Gospels*, Copyright 1996, published by Doubleday. Written by Carsten Peter Thiede and Matthew D'Ancona.

currently possible due to the cave's entrance mysteriously collapsing, and the reluctance of the Israeli Antiquities Authority to re-excavate.

References

1. McDowell, Josh (1977). *More Than a Carpenter*, p. 48. Tyndale House Publishers.
2. *CNN* (2008, October 30). "Archeologist Finds 3,000-Year Old Hebrew Text." Deem, R. (2010, January 12). "10th Century Hebrew Inscription on Pottery from Khirbet Qeiyafa, Israel Confirms Biblical Claims."GodandScience.org.
3. Caesar, S. (2010, January 6). "The Blessing of the Silver Scrolls." BibleArchaeology.org. Published in Bible and Spade, Spring 2006. Barkay, G., Vaughan, A.G., Lundberg, M.J., & Zuckerman, B. (2004). "The Amulets from Ketef Hinnom: A New Edition and Evaluation." The American Schools of Oriental Research.
Bible History Daily, "The Greatest Finds in Biblical Archaeology." Biblical Archaeological Society.
4. *The Digital Dead Sea Scrolls*, "The Great Isaiah Scroll."
5.0 5.1 Bonani, G., Ivy, S., et. al. (1992). "Radiocarbon Dating of Fourteen Dead Sea Scrolls." *Radiocarbon*, Vol. 34, No. 3, pp. 843–849.
5. Burkitt, F.C. "The Hebrew Papyrus of the Ten Commandments." *The Jewish Quarterly Review*, 15(1903), 392–408.
6. Williams, Tyler F. (2009, July 15). "Qumran Psalms Scroll (11Q5/11QPs-a)." BiblicalStudies.ca.
7. P.J. Parsons (1983). P.Oxy.L 3522 LXX Job 42:11–12. "Oxyrhynchus Online." Papyrology Websites.
8. K. Luchner (1998). P.Oxy.LXV 4443 LXX, Esther E16-9.3. "Oxyrhynchus Online." Papyrology Websites.
9. Walch, Stephen (2011, September 28). "Dead Sea Scrolls." *The Way to Yahuweh*.
10. Papyri.info. Oxyrhynchus. *Columbia University*. Accessed July 15, 2012.
11. Rives, Stephen (2011, September 27). Old Testament Manuscripts and 18 Tiqqune Sepherim EastSide Church of the Cross. Also *Looking Under the Hood: Origins of the Bible Slideshow*.

12. Library of Congress. *Scrolls from the Dead Sea: The Ancient Library of Qumran and Modern Scholarship*. www.Loc.gov.
13. John Rylands University Library. Bible Greek or Hebrew. Image Collections.
14. Israel Museum, *The Digital Dead Sea Scrolls*.
15. Papyrology Websites, "Oxyrhynchus Online." Browse By Date.
16. Wikipedia. Dead Sea Scrolls Accessed April 17, 2012.
17. Martinez, F.G. & Tigchelaar, E.J.C. (1998). "The Dea Sea Scrolls Study Edition." Vol. 2. Index (contains listing of Dead Sea Scrolls). *Wm. B. Eerdman's Publishing Company*.
18. Wikipedia. Oxyrhynchus Papyri Accessed July 15, 2012.
19. Sussman, Ayala & Peled, Ruth (1993). "The Dead Sea Scrolls." Jewish Virtual Library.
20. [21.0 21.1] Dead Sea Scrolls Foundation. "About the Scrolls."
21. [22.0 22.1] Boa, Kenneth. "How Accurate is the Bible?" Bible.org.
22. Lawler, Andrew (2010, January). "Who Wrote the Dead Sea Scrolls?," p. 2. *Smithsonian Magazine*.
23. Kent, Donna. "RadioCarbon Dating of Dead Sea Scrolls." Retrieved from David W. Brooks, University of Nebraska website.
24. The Israel Museum. "The Digital Dead Sea Scrolls: Discovery." Jerusalem. Accessed April 17, 2012.
25. Davies, Philip R. (2009). "Dead Sea Scrolls." *Encyclopaedia Britannica, History*.
26. Wallace, Daniel B. (2012, February 10). "Earliest Manuscript of the New Testament Discovered?." The Center for the Study of New Testament Manuscripts.
27. Welte, Michael (2008). "Kurzgefasste Liste der Griechischen Handschriften des NT." Quoted by Wieland Willker in "Update-list of Greek NT Uncials."
28. Wallace, Daniel B. (2007). "Greek New Testament Manuscripts Discovered in Albania." Bible.org.
29. Williams, Jimmy (1995). "Are the Biblical Documents Reliable?" Probe Ministries.

30. Slick, Matt. "Manuscript Evidence for Superior New Testament Readability." *Christian Apologetics and Research Ministry*.
31. Bruce Metzger and Bart Ehrman, *The Text of the New Testament: Its Transmission, Corruption and Restoration* (Oxford University Press, Fourth Edition 2005), p. 50.
32. J. David Thomas. "P.Oxy. LXIV 4404." POxy Papyrus Web. The Center for Study of Ancient Documents. Stelios Ioannou School for Research in Classical and Byzantine Studies, Oxford. *The Center for the Study of New Testament Manuscripts*. "Manuscript P104."
33. *The Center for the Study of New Testament Manuscripts*. "Manuscript P46."
34. J. David Thomas. "P.Oxy. LXIV 4403." POxy Papyrus Web. The Center for Study of Ancient Documents. Stelios Ioannou School for Research in Classical and Byzantine Studies, Oxford. *The Center for the Study of New Testament Manuscripts*. "Manuscript P103."
35. *The Center for the Study of New Testament Manuscripts*. "Manuscript P22."
36. *The Center for the Study of New Testament Manuscripts*. "Manuscript P27."
37. *The Center for the Study of New Testament Manuscripts*. "Manuscript P45."
38. *The Center for the Study of New Testament Manuscripts*. "Manuscript P47."
39. *The Center for the Study of New Testament Manuscripts*. "Manuscript P49."
40. *The Center for the Study of New Testament Manuscripts*. "Manuscript P75."
41. *The Center for the Study of New Testament Manuscripts*. "Manuscript P87."
42. *The Center for the Study of New Testament Manuscripts*. "Manuscript P91."
43. J. David Thomas. "P.Oxy. LXIV 4401." POxy Papyrus Web. The Center for Study of Ancient Documents. Stelios Ioannou School for Research in Classical and Byzantine Studies, Oxford.

The Center for the Study of New Testament Manuscripts. "Manuscript P101."
44. *The Center for the Study of New Testament Manuscripts.* "Manuscript P107."
45. *The Center for the Study of New Testament Manuscripts.* "Manuscript P108."
46. *The Center for the Study of New Testament Manuscripts.* "Manuscript P109."
47. *The Center for the Study of New Testament Manuscripts.* "Manuscript P111."
48. *The Center for the Study of New Testament Manuscripts.* "Manuscript P113."
49. *The Center for the Study of New Testament Manuscripts.* "Manuscript P114."
50. *The Center for the Study of New Testament Manuscripts.* "Manuscript P37."
51. *The Center for the Study of New Testament Manuscripts.* "Manuscript P100."
52. J. David Thomas. "P.Oxy. LXIV 4402." POxy Papyrus Web. The Center for Study of Ancient Documents. Stelios Ioannou School for Research in Classical and Byzantine Studies, Oxford.
    The Center for the Study of New Testament Manuscripts. "Manuscript P102."
53. *The Center for the Study of New Testament Manuscripts.* "Manuscript P115."
54. Palmer, David. Table of NT Greek Manuscripts BibleTranslation.ws
55. The Center for Study of New Testament Manuscripts. "Manuscripts."
56. INTF. "Continuation of the Manuscript List." University of Münster.
57. Baker, Matt (2011, December 15). "Oldest New Testament Manuscripts." UsefulCharts.com.
58. Seid, Timothy. *A Table of Greek Manuscripts: Interpreting Ancient Manuscripts.*
59. Willker, Wieland. "Complete List of Greek NT Papyri."

60. Head, Peter M. "Early Greek Bible Manuscript Project: NT Mss. on Papyrus."
61. Wikipedia. List of New Testament Papyri, accessed April 17, 2012.

Authors/Works	Recorded	Dates of Mss.	Time Span	Copies Survived
Caesar	100–44 B.C.	A.D. 900	1,000 yrs	10
Livy	59 B.C.–A.D. 17	A.D. 300	400 yrs	27
Plato	427–347 B.C.	A.D. 900	1,200 yrs	7
Tacitus (Annals)	A.D. 56–120	A.D. 800	900 yrs	3
Pliney the Younger (History)	A.D. 61_113	A.D. 850	750 yrs	7
Thucydides (History)	460–400 B.C.	A.D. 100	600 yrs	20
Suetonious (De Vita Caesarum)	A.D. 69–140	A.D. 800	900 yrs	200+
Herodotus (History)	484–425 B.C.	A.D. 100	600 yrs	75
Sophocles	496–406 B.C.	A.D. 1000	1,400 yrs	193
Catullus	54 B.C.	A.D. 1550	1,600 yrs	3
Eripides	480–406 B.C.	A.D. 1100	1,500 yrs	9

Authors/Works	Recorded	Dates of Mss.	Time Span	Copies Survived
Demosthenes	383–322 B.C.	A.D. 1100	1,300 yrs	200
Aristotle	384–322 B.C.	A.D. 1100	1,400 yrs	40
Aristophanes	450–385 B.C.	A.D. 900	1,200 yrs	10
Homer	900 B.C.	400 B.C.	500 yrs	643
New Testament	A.D. 35–100	A.D. 100–150	5–30 yrs	5,700

(This chart was adapted from two sources: 1. *Christian Apologetics*, **by Norman Geisler, 1976, p.307, and** 2. *A Ready Defense*, **by Josh McDowell, 1993, p. 45).**

Evidence to Evaluate

- When the Bible manuscripts are compared to other ancient writings, they stand alone as the best-preserved literary works of all antiquity.
- The Biblical manuscripts exhibit a word-for-word accuracy in more than 95% of the cases, and the 5% variation consists of slips of the pen and spelling.
- The manuscript evidence for the New Testament is dramatic, with nearly 25,000 ancient manuscripts discovered and archived so far, at least 5,800 of which are copies and fragments in the original Greek.

Some manuscript texts date to the early 2nd and 3rd Centuries, with the time between the original autograph and our earliest existing manuscripts and fragments being a remarkably short 40–60 years. There are 10,000 Latin manuscripts and 9,300 manuscripts in various other ancient languages including Syriac, Slavic, Gothic, Ethiopic, Coptic, and Armenian. The Biblical manuscript evidence surpasses the manuscript reliability of other ancient manuscripts that we trust as authentic today.

Notes

PROOF EIGHT

mir-a-cle

–noun

1. extraordinary events attributed to some supernatural agency; a remarkable occurrence.

—The Oxford Dictionary

MIRACLES IN THE BIBLE

PREMISE

A "miracle" is defined in most current dictionaries as a phenomena or supernatural event in the physical world that surpasses all known or natural power, incapable of being explained by the laws of nature.

Although God never operates contrary to the laws of nature, which He has established, He has the prerogative to supersede them. God used miracles as proof of His authority in validating His Mission and Message.

There were many miracles of God in the Old Testament: for example, the ten plagues in Egypt, the parting of the Red Sea, the manna from Heaven, the water from the rock, the ground's opening up and swallowing Korah and the rebels, the sun's and the moon's standing still, the three Judeans in Nebuchadnezzar's fiery furnace, Daniel in the lion's den, and many others.

The whole purpose for Jesus' miracles is the same—to give proof of His authority. The Bible tells us in John 7:31 that many people believed in Him because of the miraculous signs that He performed. This was precisely the purpose of miracles in Jesus' ministry. They were signs authenticating His Message and Mission (Lu. 7:20-22).

Jesus performed miracles so that you may believe that He is the Christ, the Son of the Living God and so that you may have eternal life (Jn. 20:31).

God anointed Jesus with the Holy Spirit and with power (Ac. 10:38). As a result, the people were both amazed and astonished beyond measure (Mk. 2:12; Jn. 20:30, 31).

Here is a concise list of the Old and New Testament miracles. There are so many miracles found in the Holy Bible that it is difficult to put an exact number on their total quantity. Although I have identified approximately 83 obvious miracles recorded in the Old Testament and approximately 80 obvious miracles found in the New Testament, we will only be looking at a partial list of these 163 obvious miracles.

Miracles in the Bible—Old Testament

1. Creation of the world
   (Genesis 1)
2. The great flood
   (Genesis 7; 8)
3. The confusion of languages
   (Genesis 11:1-9)
4. The fire on Abraham's sacrifice
   (Genesis 15:17)
5. The conception of Isaac
   (Genesis 17:17; 18:12; 21:2)
6. The destruction of Sodom
   (Genesis 19)
7. Lot's wife turned into a pillar of salt
   (Genesis 19:26)
8. The closing of the wombs of Abimelech's household
   (Genesis 20:17, 18)
9. The opening of Hagar's eyes
   (Genesis 21:19)
10. The conception of Jacob and Esau
    (Genesis 25:21)
11. The opening of Rachel's womb
    (Genesis 30:22)
12. The flaming bush
    (Exodus 3:2)

Miracles in the Bible—Old Testament

13. Moses' leprosy
    (Exodus 4:6, 7, 30)

14. The plagues in Egypt
    (Numbers 16:46-50)

15. The pillar of cloud and fire
    (Exodus 13:21, 22; 14:19, 20)

16. Passage through the Red Sea
    (Exodus 14:22)

17. The destruction of Pharaoh and his army
    (Exodus 14:23-30)

18. Sweetening the waters of Marah
    (Exodus 15:25)

19. Manna
    (Exodus 16:4-31)

20. Quails
    (Exodus 16:13)

21. The defeat of Amalek
    (Exodus 17:9-13)

22. The transfiguration of the face of Moses
    (Exodus 34:29-35)

23. Water from the rock
    (Exodus 17:5, 7)

24. Thundering and lightning on Mount Sinai
    (Exodus 19:16-20; 24:10, 15, 17)

25. Miriam's leprosy
    (Numbers 12:10-15)

26. Judgment by fire
    (Numbers 11:1-3)

27. The destruction of Korah
    (Numbers 16:31-35; Deuteronomy 11:6, 7)

Miracles in the Bible—Old Testament

28. The plague
    (Numbers 16:46-50)

29. Aaron's rod buds
    (Numbers 17:1-9)

30. Water from the rock in Kadesh
    (Numbers 20:8-11)

31. The scourge of serpents
    (Numbers 21:6-9)

32. The destruction of Nadab and Abihu
    (Leviticus 10:1, 2)

33. Balaam's donkey speaks
    (Numbers 22:23-30)

34. The preservation of Moses
    (Deuteronomy 34:7)

35. The Jordan River divided
    (Joshua 3:14-17; 4:16-18)

36. The fall of Jericho
    (Joshua 6:20)

37. The Midianites destroyed
    (Judges 7:16-22)

38. Hailstones on the confederated kings
    (Joshua 10:11)

39. The sun and the moon stand still
    (Joshua 10:12-14)

40. Dew on Gideon's fleece
    (Judges 6:37-40)

41. Samson's strength
    (Judges 14:6; 16:3, 29, 30)

42. Samson supplied with water
    (Judges 15:19)

Miracles in the Bible—Old Testament

43. The falling of the god Dagon
    (1Samuel 5:1-4)

44. Nursing cows return to the ark of the covenant (walking away from their calves)
    (1Samuel 6:7-14)

45. The plague of hemorrhoids on the Philistines
    (1Samuel 5:9-12; 6:1-18)

46. Jeroboam's hand withered
    (1Kings 13:3-6)

47. The appearance of blood
    (2Kings 3:20-22)

48. The panic of the Syrians
    (2 Kings 7:6, 7)

49. Elijah is fed by ravens
    (1Kings 17:6)

50. Is fed by an angel
    (1Kings 19:1-8)

51. Increases the widow's meal and oil
    (1Kings 17:9-16; Luke 4:26)

52. Raises the widow's son
    (1Kings 17:17-24)

53. Rain in answer to Elijah's prayer
    (1Kings 18:41-45)

54. Brings fire down upon Ahaziah's army
    (2Kings 1:10-12)

55. Divides the Jordan River
    (2Kings 2:8)

56. Is transported to the heavens
    (2Kings 2:11)

Miracles in the Bible—Old Testament

57. Elisha divides the Jordan River
    (2Kings 2:14)

58. Sweetens the waters of Jericho
    (2Kings 2:19-22)

59. Increases a widow's supply of oil
    (2Kings 4:1-7)

60. Raises the Shunammite woman's child
    (2Kings 4:18-37)

61. Renders the poisoned stew harmless
    (2Kings 4:38-41)

62. Feeds one hundred men
    (2Kings 4:42-44)

63. Cures Naaman
    (2Kings 5:1-19)

64. Strikes down Gehazi with leprosy
    (2Kings 5:26, 27)

65. Causes the axe to float
    (2Kings 6:6)

66. Reveals the counsel of the king of Syria
    (2Kings 6:12)

67. Causes the eyes of his servant to be opened
    (2Kings 6:17)

68. Strikes the army of the king of Syria with blindness
    (2Kings 6:18)

69. The dead man was restored to life
    (2Kings 13:21)

70. The destruction of Sennacherib's army
    (2Kings 19:35; Isaiah 37:36)

Miracles in the Bible—Old Testament

71. Return of the shadow on the sun dial
    (2Kings 20:9-11)

72. Hezekiah's cure
    (Isaiah 38:21)

73. The deliverance of Shadrach, Meshach, and Abed-nego
    (Daniel 3:23-27)

74. Of Daniel
    (Daniel 6:22)

75. The sea was calmed when Jonah was thrown into it
    (Jonah 1:15))

Miracles in the Bible—New Testament

1. The virgin birth
   (Matthew 1:18-25; Luke 1:26-38)

2. Changing water into wine
   (John 2:1-11)

3. Healing the royal nobleman's son
   (John 4:46-54)

4. Healing of a possessed man
   (Mark 1:21-28; Luke 4:33-37)

5. Healing of Peter's mother-in-law
   (Matthew 8:14-15; Mark 1:29-31; Luke 4:38-39)

6. Healing the sick during the evening
   (Matthew 8:16; Mark 1:32; Luke 4:40-41)

7. Catching a large number of fish
   (Luke 5:3-10)

8. Healing the leper
   (Matthew 8:1-3; Mark 1:40-42)

9. Healing a centurion's servant
   (Matthew 8:5-13; Like 7:1-10)

10. Healing a paralytic
    (Matthew 9:1-6; Mark 2:1-12; Luke 5:18-26)

11. Healing the withered hand
    (Matthew 12:9-14; Mark 3:1-6)

12. Raised a widow's son
    (Luke 7:11-17)

13. Calming the stormy sea
    (Matthew 8:23-27; Mark 4:35-41; Luke 8:22-25)

14. Healing the Gerasene demoniac
    (Matthew 8:28-32; Mark 5:1-13; Luke 8:26-33)

15. Healing the woman with internal bleeding
    (Matthew 9:20-22; Mark 5:25-34; Luke 8:43-48)

Miracles in the Bible—New Testament

16. Raising Jairus' daughter
    (Matthew 9:18-19, 23-25; Mark 5:22-24, 35-43; Luke 8:41-42, 49-58)

17. Healing two blind men
    (Matthew 9:27-31)

18. Healing a mute demoniac
    (Matthew 19:32-33)

19. Feeding 5000 men and their families
    (Matthew 14:16-21, Mark 6:35-44; Luke 9:12-17; John 6:5-14)

20. Walking on water
    (Matthew 14:22-33; Mark 6:45-52; Luke 8:22-25)

21. Miraculous healing of many people of Gennesaret
    (Matthew 14:34-36)

22. Healing a demoniac girl
    (Mark 15:21-28)

23. Healing of a deaf man with a speech impediment
    (Mark 7:31-37)

24. Feeding of 4000 men and their families
    (Matthew 15:29-39; Mark 8:1-10)

25. Healing a blind man
    (Mark 8:22-26)

26. Healing a man born blind
    (John 9:1-41)

27. Healing a demoniac boy
    (Matthew 17:14-21, Mark 9:17-19; Luke 9:37-43)

28. Catching a fish with a coin in its mouth
    (Matthew 17:24-27)

29. Healing a blind and mute demoniac
    (Matthew 12:22; Luke 11:14)

30. Healing a woman with an 18-year infirmity
    (Luke 13:10-13

Miracles in the Bible—New Testament

31. Healing a man with dropsy
    (Luke 14:1-6)

32. Healing ten lepers
    (Luke 17:11-19)

33. Raising Lazarus
    (John 11:1-44)

34. Healing blind Bartimaeus
    (Mark 10:46-52)

35. Jesus curses the fig tree with no fruit
    (Matthew 21:18-22; Mark 11:12-14, 20-25)

36. Restoring severed ear
    (Luke 22:45-54)

37. Resurrection of Jesus
    (Matthew 28; Mark 16; Luke 24; John 20)

38. The ascension of Jesus
    Acts 1:1-11

Evidence to Evaluate

- God used miracles in the Old Testament as proof of His authority in validating His message and mission.
- The purpose of the miracles found in the New Testament in Jesus' ministry are for the same reason as the miracles found in the Old Testament—they were signs authenticating His message and mission. Jesus performed miracles so you may believe that He is the Christ, the Son of the living God, and so you may have eternal life.
- Because God, the Creator of the Universe, wishes to reveal Himself to us in many ways—such as the fine-tuning of creation, predictive prophecy, and through the person of Jesus Christ—we should also understand that miracles are a natural and logical way for God to do this and, by doing so, He provides proof of His authority, whereby validating His message and mission.

Notes

PROOF NINE

Mathematical Probability

prob-a-bil-i-ty

–noun

Mathematics the extent to which an event is likely to occur, measured by the ratio of the favorable cases to the whole number of cases possible.

—The Oxford American College Dictionary

MATHEMATICAL PROBABILITY

PREMISE

The focus of this chapter is to look at the probability of Christ's fulfilling the prophecies of the Old Testament. We will now look at the mathematical probability calculations of Biblical prophecy by Peter Stoner.

Peter Stoner

Peter Stoner was chairman of the department of mathematics and astronomy at Pasadena City College until 1952; chairman of the science division, Westmont College, 1953-1957; professor emeritus of science, Westmont College; professor emeritus of mathematics and astronomy at Pasadena City College. In his book entitled *Science Speaks,* Stoner calculated the mathematical probability or chances that one man could fulfill just eight of the prophecies of the Messiah in His lifetime.

The Bible has over three hundred specific and detailed prophecies concerning the identity of the Jewish Messiah. These prophecies were fulfilled by Jesus Christ and recorded in the New Testament, confirming its claim of Divine Origin and Inspiration. Probability is also known as "odds" and is a branch of mathematics that measures the likelihood that a given event will occur. To begin, look at some interesting "odds."

- Being struck by lightning in a year = 7×10^5.
- Being killed by lightning in a year = $2 \times 2 \times 10^6$.

- Becoming President = 1×10^7.
- A meteorite's landing on your house = 1.8×10^{14}.
- Eventually dying = 1 in 1.

As you can see, the probability of being struck or killed by lightning, becoming President, or having a meteorite land on your house progressively increases given the event. However, someone somewhere will be that person and that person could be you.

The Bible is full of prophecies that are either events that have happened or events that will happen. In 1969, Peter Stoner gave his students eight prophecies that were fulfilled by Jesus Christ in the New Testament and asked the class to figure the probability of all of their being fulfilled by one man. The prophecies he chose stated that the Messiah would...

1. Be born in Bethlehem.
2. Be preceded by a messenger.
3. Ride on a donkey.
4. Be betrayed by a friend.
5. Be betrayed for thirty pieces of silver.
6. Be betrayed for money used to purchase the potter's field.
7. Be silent as a lamb.
8. Have his hands and feet pierced.

The class came up with a staggering number: the combined probability of one person's fulfilling eight of the Old Testament prophecies would be one chance in 10 to the 17th power; that is a 1 followed by 17 zeros.

Peter Stoner submitted his figures for review to a committee of the *American Scientific Affiliation*. Upon examination, they verified that his calculations were dependable and accurate in regard to the scientific material presented.[108]

In *Science Speaks*, Dr. Stoner looks at the probability that Jesus Christ could have fulfilled even just eight of the 300 prophecies that pertained to Him in the Holy Bible. This is one of the most amazing probability studies ever to be conducted.

---

108 Peter Stoner, *Science Speaks*, Chicago: Moody Press, 1969, p. 4; (www.sciencespeaks.dstoner.net).

Here are these eight prophecies from the Old Testament and their fulfillment by Jesus Christ in the New Testament: 1) Jesus Christ's probability of fulfilling each prophecy and 2) Jesus Christ's total mathematical probability of fulfilling all eight prophecies. Keep in mind the time span between the prophecies of the Old Testament and their New Testament fulfillment are hundreds, and in some cases, even thousands of years.

Old Testament Prohecy	New Testament Prohecy	Probability	Old Testament Prohecy	New Testament Prohecy	Probability
Christ to be born in Bethlehem (Mi. 5:2)	And Herod asked where Christ had been born… they answered Bethlehem (Mt. 2:4-6)	2.8×10^5 or 1 in 280,000	30 pieces of silver cast to the potter (Zec. 11:13)	30 pieces of silver used to buy the potter's field (Mt. 27:3-10)	1×10^5 or 1 in 100,000
Forerunner of Christ (Mal. 3:1)	John the Baptist, the forerunner of Christ (Mk. 1:2-8)	1×10^3 or 1 in 1,000	Although innocent, Christ Kept silent when on trial (Is. 53.7)	Jesus kept silent when questioned (Mk. 14:60-61)	1×10^3 or 1 in 1,000
Christ to enter Jerusalem riding on a donkey (Zec. 9:9)	Christ enters Jerusalem riding on a donkey (Mt. 21:4-11)	1×10^2 or 1 in 1,000	Christ crucified (Ps. 22:16)	Jesus was crucified (Jn. 19:17, 18)	1×10^4 or 1 in 10,000
Christ to be betrayed by a friend (Ps. 41:9)	Judas betrayed Jesus (Lu. 22:21)	1×10^3 or 1 in 1,000			
Christ to be betrayed for 30 pieces of silver (Zec. 11:12)	Judas sold out Jesus for 30 pieces of silver (Mt. 26:15)	1×10^3 or 1 in 1,000			

Evidence to Evaluate

- Dr. Peter Stoner's mathematical probability studies provide evidence that the odds of one person's fulfilling eight of the Old Testament prophecies would be one chance in 10 to the 17th power (1×10^{17}); that is a 1 followed by 17 zeros. Dr. Stoner submitted his figures for review to a committee of the American Scientific Affiliation. Upon examination, they verified that his calculations were dependable and accurate in regard to the scientific material presented.
- Let us ask the question, "What is the probability of one man fulfilling just eight prophecies?" When the principles of probability are applied, it would be astronomically impossible and couldn't have been achieved through human effort alone. Fulfilling these prophecies can only be explained as the result of Supernatural Intervention (i.e. *Proof of Authority*).
- When we factor in the time span between the writings of the Old Testament and their fulfillment by Jesus Christ in the New Testament, we would have to conclude at least one of two possibilities:

1. The prophecies were either given to Godly men by God through the work of the Holy Spirit, as Scripture has indicated,

{or}

2. This amazing phenomenon was achieved by 40 or more deceitful men, the majority of whom never knew each other, written over a 1600-year period, in 13 different countries, on three different continents, in three different languages, by men through common sense, chance, or collusion with 100% cohesive unity, harmony, and accuracy without any prophetic failure.

These are the only two possible explanations. What you must do is choose the one explanation that makes more sense while implementing the well-established laws of logic.

Notes

WORLD RELIGIONS AND CULTS VS. BIBLICAL CHRISTIANITY

Before we get started on this chapter, I want to explain my approach with regard to this topic. I will basically be implementing three Biblical passages in this process:

1. 2Timothy 4:2: *"preach the word; be ready in season and out of season; reprove, rebuke, and exhort, with complete patience and teaching."*
2. 1Peter 3:15: *"but in your hearts honor Christ the Lord as holy, always being prepared to make a defense to anyone who asks you for a reason for the hope that is in you; yet do it with gentleness and respect."*
3. 1John 4:1: *"Beloved, do not believe every spirit, but test the spirits to see whether they are from God. For many false prophets have gone out into the world."*

I want to explain the information about world religions and pseudo-Christian organizations with patience, gentleness, and respect without compromising Biblical truth (Tit. 2:1) and the laws of logic in the process. We must start this topic first by identifying the two basic worldview categories as they are revealed to us through the Holy Bible.

According to the Holy Bible, there are only two groups of people on Earth with regard to spiritual truth. There are those who travel on the *Wide Road*, and there are those who travel on the *Narrow Road*. The Holy Bible explains to us that the *Wide Road* is spacious and will lead to eternal destruction, and there are many people that travel on it. The *Narrow Road* is described as difficult but will lead to eternal life, and those who find it are few (Mt. 7:13, 14).

Travelers on the *Narrow Road* are those who trust in Jesus Christ alone in obtaining salvation, and travelers on the *Wide Road* are those who do not and represent all worldviews that exclude the Biblical teaching of salvation by grace through faith in Jesus Christ alone (Ro. 3:24).

As a result of these two Biblical truths, we now understand better why there are so many people who are living on Earth today with a desire to be open-minded with regard to non-Biblical world religions and pseudo-Christian organizations. They have made the assumption that the worldview they choose doesn't really matter; to them, all paths will ultimately lead to the same God (Pr. 14:12; Ac. 4:12).

However, upon a careful examination of the teachings of the world's most popular worldviews, we see some major differences in their beliefs that cannot be overlooked and must be carefully scrutinized.

Christianity, for example, has had a number of people and organizations proclaiming to have special spiritual authority from God. These include Charles Taze Russell (Jehovah's Witnesses), Ellen G. White (Seventh-day Adventist), Mary Baker Eddy (Christian Science), and Joseph Smith (Jesus Christ of Latter-day Saints), and the Roman Catholic Church, along with many others.

Each started their organizations with claims of being the one true Christian Church. They each had a unique teaching, and they appealed to the Holy Bible as the basis for their spiritual authority; yet each of their teachings not only contradict one another, but they also contradict the clear teaching of the Holy Bible. Some of them also have numerous false prophecies and many internal inconsistencies and contradictions documented in their writings. For example, the Roman Catholic Church teaches that Mary's virginity was never-ending-or-changing (perpetual),[109] she was born without sin (Immaculate Conception)[110] and she is a co-redeemer and co-mediator with Jesus Christ.[111] Biblical Christianity teachings are in direct opposition to Roman Catholic theology.

---

109 Joseph kept her a virgin until she gave birth to Jesus: Mt. 1:24-25. Brothers and sisters of Jesus are mentioned in Mt. 12:46-47; Mt. 13:54-56; Mk. 6:2-3; Jn. 2:12; Ac. 1:14; Ga. 1:19. The Bible calls Jesus "the firstborn" of Mary in Luke 2:7, which implies that she had other children.

110 Pope Pius IX proclaimed the dogma of the *Immaculate Conception* of Mary on Dec. 8, 1854; The Catholic Church celebrates the Feast of the Immaculate Conception on Dec. 8; in many Catholic countries, it is a holy day of obligation or patronal feast, and in some a national public holiday. Biblical proof text: Ro. 3:23, 24; 1Jn. 1:8-10.

111 1985, Pope John Paul II recognized Mary as "co-redemptix" during a speech in Guayaquil, Ecuador. In his *Encyclical Redemptoris Mater*, Pope John Paul II referred to Mary as 'Mediatrix' three times, and as 'Advocate' twice. http://www.whidbey.net/-dcloud/fbns/marycoredeemer.html. In Lu. 1:47, Mary referred to the Lord as "my Savior," not merely "a Savior" or "the Savior." No sinless person needs the Savior: 1Ti. 2:5; He. 9:15.

The problem Biblically with Roman Catholicism is that there is absolutely no proof text in Scripture to support their teachings for the papacy, the worship and adoration of Mary, the immaculate conception of Mary, or the perpetual virginity of Mary. There is no proof text supporting the assumption of Mary or Mary as a co-redeemer and co-mediator, petitioning saints in Heaven for their prayers, apostolic succession, the ordinances of the Church functioning as sacraments, infant baptism, confession of sin to a priest, purgatory, indulgences, or the equal authority of the Church tradition and Scripture.

The Biblical support for the teachings of the Roman Catholic Church is not found anywhere in the Holy Bible. There is only opposing proof text found which cannot be attributed to the teachings of Jesus Christ or His apostles.[112]

Mormonism teaches that there are many universes and many gods in existence and that the god of planet Earth was once a man and man may become a god.[113] They teach that Jesus Christ is the spirit brother of Lucifer.[114]

Biblical Christianity teaches there is only one God[115] Who is revealed in Three Persons—the Father, the Son, and the Holy Spirit,[116] that all things were created through Christ,[117] and that man cannot become a god.[118]

Jehovah's Witnesses teach Jesus Christ is not God but God's first created being[119] and that Jesus and Michael the Archangel are the same person.[120] They believe that Jesus was resurrected spiritually from the dead but not physically.

Biblical Christianity teaches that Jesus is God manifested in the flesh[121] and is not a created being or Michael the Archangel,[122] but actually Jesus is the Creator[123] and He physically rose from the dead.[124]

---

[112] Recommended Reading: Reasoning from the Scriptures with Catholics by Ron Rhodes © Copyright 2000.
[113] LDS Apostle Bruce McConkie, Mormon Doctrine p. 237), Lorenzo Snow, 5th LDS president, June 1840 "As man is, God once was; as God is, man may become."
[114] LDS texts-Abraham 3:27; D&C 93:21; Moses 4:1.
[115] Is. 45:5-22; Ex. 34:14; De. 4:35, 39.
[116] Mt. 3:16, 17; Lu. 3:21, 22.
[117] Jn. 1:1-5; Col. 1:16.
[118] 1Ki. 8:60; 1Ti. 2:5; Ja. 2:19.
[119] "You Can Live Forever in Paradise on Earth" [Brooklyn: Watchtower Bible and Tract Society of New York, 1982], p. 58.
[120] "Reasoning from the Scriptures" [Brooklyn: Watchtower Bible and Tract Society of NewYork, 1985] p. 218.
[121] Col. 2:9; Mt. 1:23; Is. 9:6.
[122] Jn. 1:1-3; As famed Greek scholar A.T. Robertson commented: *"Not the first of creatures as the Arians held and Unitarians do now, but the originating source of creation through whom God works"* (Archibald Thomas Robinson, Word Pictures in the New Testament, Grand rapids: Baker Book House, 1933, p.321).
[123] Jn. 1:1-3, 10; Col. 1:16; 1Co. 8:6.
[124] Christ said He was not a spirit, but had a flesh-and-bone body (Lu. 24:39, 42, 43; Jn. 2:19-21; 21:12, 13). His followers physically touched Him, (Mt. 28:9; Jn. 20:17). Christ eats food with them on several occasions, thereby proving that He had a physical body (Lu. 24:30, 42-43; Jn. 21:12-13).

World religions have also proclaimed to have special spiritual authority from God. In the case of Orthodox Judaism they almost got it right, but they do not recognize Jesus Christ as their Messiah, claim that the New Testament is not true, and that Jesus is not God incarnate. Biblical Christianity affirms all three to be true (Jn. 1:1). The reason for this is that Biblical Christianity focuses on the New Covenant as mediated through Jesus Christ, as recorded in the New Testament. Judaism places emphasis on correct conduct focusing on the Mosaic Covenant, as recorded in the Torah and Talmud. Incidentally, there are more Messianic Jews in the world today than at any other time in history. At this point you might be asking, "What is Messianic Judaism?" Messianic Jews believe that Jesus is the Messiah and that the Tanakh (Hebrew Bible) and New Testament are authoritative Scripture. Salvation in Messianic Judaism is achieved only through acceptance of Jesus as one's Savior, and Jewish Law does not contribute to salvation. There are around 20,000 Messianic Jews in Israel. In Jerusalem, there are twelve Messianic congregations. In 2012 the estimated number of Messianic Jews worldwide was about 350,000.[125] We must realize that human civilization owes the Jewish people a debt of gratitude. Let me explain.

The Jewish people:
- Preserved for us the Old Testament and the Ten Commandments.
- Gave us the New Testament which is the advancement and unfolding of the Old Testament.
- Gave us the wonderful Jewish heritage.
- Gave us our blessed Lord Jesus and salvation.

When the first Christian Church was born some 2,000 years ago in Jerusalem, 3,000 people responded to the first Gospel Message preached by Peter (Ac. 2:14-41). It was a 100 percent Jewish Church. Peter and all of Jesus' Apostles were Jewish. All the people who responded to Peter's message were Jewish. The person who emerged as the leader of the Jerusalem Church was the Jewish brother of Jesus named James. This means Christianity was started by Messianic Jews following a Jewish Messiah.

---

[125] www.oneforisrael.org; www.jewsforjesus.org; Messianic Judaism, Wikipedia.

Hinduism is a religion that teaches that all religions are different paths leading to one goal—all religions are different means to one end. Hinduism accepts all religions as valid, but Biblical Christianity teaches that Jesus Christ is the Only Way to God. He is the Only Mediator between God and men (Jn. 14:6; 1Ti. 2:5) and there is no other name under heaven given by which men can be saved (Ac. 4:12). Islam's holy book, the Quran, declares many things about Jesus Christ, and He is spoken of in about 93 verses. He is spoken about more often than any other person in the entire Quran. The Quran teaches that Jesus healed the sick and raised the dead (2:87; 3:49; 5:113), He was born through the virgin Mary (3:45-47; 23:50; 19:16-22), He brought the Gospel to the Jewish people (3:49-51; 13:38), He was an Apostle and Prophet of God (3:49; 6:85-90), He ascended to Heaven (3:55), and that He is beside Allah during the Judgment (4:159).

Although the Quran does get some things right, it gets a lot of things wrong—relative to the well-established historical teachings of the Biblical Christian faith.

Islam is not only the most widely recognized source of persecution for Christians in the world today; it also denies the Deity of Jesus Christ, the Triune nature of God, the Atoning Work of Christ on the cross,[126] and teaches Christ is just one of the many prophets of God.[127] Islam teaches that Jesus Christ is less important than Muhammad who himself was a self-proclaimed sinner,[128] who had people killed,[129] and said there were more women in hell than men and that women lack intelligence.[130] They teach that Christ did not die on a cross[131] but that Judas did.[132] Biblical Christianity teaches that Jesus is God manifested in the flesh,[133] He died on a cross for the sins of the world,[134] and that Christ was without sin.[135] Another difference we see between Islam and Christianity is in the way God is described.

---

126 Quran: 4:116, 168.
127 Quran: 112:3; 19:35.
128 *The Hadith:* Vol. 1, Book 12, Number 711, Narrated Abu Huraira; Vol. 8, Book 75, Number 319, Narrated Abu Huraira.
129 *The Hadith:* Vol. 3, Book 29, Number 72, Narrated Anas bin Malik.
130 *The Hadith:* Vol. 1, Book 6, Number 301, Narrated Abu Said Al-Khudri.
131 Quran: 4:157-158.
132 Quran: 3:169; 4:156-159. 1Co. 15:3, 4.
133 Col. 2:9; Jn. 1:1.
134 Jn. 3:16-18.
135 Lu. 1:35; Mt. 27:24; Jn. 19:4; 2Co. 5:21; He. 4:15; 1Jn. 3:5; 1Pe. 1:18-19; 2:21-22; Is. 53:9.

Just because both religions use the term "God," it doesn't necessarily mean that they are talking about the same God. For example, if a husband is talking about his wife by name but gets many of her attributes wrong and describes her as tall when she is short, fat when she is thin, Hispanic when she is Caucasian, brunette when she is blonde, then he is actually talking about a different woman because his description simply does not match the description of his actual wife.

Similarly, the list of differences between the God of the Quran and the God of the Holy Bible is lengthy, but here are a few examples. In the Holy Bible, God loves all people including unbelievers—*"For God so loved the world, that he gave his only Son, that whoever believes in him should not perish but have eternal life"* (Jn. 3:16) ESV. In the Quran, Allah does not love unbelievers—"...He does not love the unbelievers (30:45)." In the Holy Bible, God forgives sin through His Son, Jesus Christ—*"For there is one God, and there is one mediator between God and men, the man Christ Jesus"* (1Ti. 2:5) ESV. In the Quran, Allah does not forgive the sin of those who associate Jesus with Him—"Surely Allah does not forgive that anything should be associated with Him..." (4:48). In the Holy Bible, Jesus is the Son of God—*"...This is my beloved Son; listen to him"* (Mk. 9:7) ESV. In the Quran, Jesus is not the Son of God—"...Allah, who has not taken a son..." (17:111). In the Holy Bible, God is our Father—*"Pray then like this: Our Father who art in heaven hallowed be your name."* (Mt. 6:9) ESV; and also in (Jn. 2:23) ESV we read, *"No one who denies the Son has the Father; whoever acknowledges the Son has the Father also."* The Quran very specifically denies that Allah is a Father (19:35; 112:1-4).

These contradictions clearly indicate that the God of Biblical Christianity and the God of Islam cannot be both the same God. Here are our only options—either they're both false or one is true and one is false. They both cannot be true at the same time when dealing with the same context, due to the well-established Law of Non-contradiction. Truth will never contradict itself and will always be that which conforms to reality, actuality, and fact.

Unfortunately, the problem is usually not in the term *truth* itself but in the application of it.

Is Islam a faith of peace?

The Quran says in Surah 5:51, "Believers, take neither the Jew nor the Christians for your friend." In Surah 5:17, "Infidels are those who declare: 'God is the Christ, the son of Mary.'" In Surah 9:123, "Make war on the infidels who dwell around you." In Surah 4:101, "The infidels are your sworn enemies." In Surah 2:191, "Kill the disbelievers wherever we find them."

Islamic oppression is one of the most widely-recognized sources of persecution for Christians and other non-Muslim groups in the world today, and it continues to spread.[136] According to a leading Christian persecution watch group, *Open Doors*,[137] in the year 2018 Christians found these top ten nations to be the most dangerous and difficult to practice their faith:

1. North Korea
2. Afghanistan
3. Somalia
4. Sudan
5. Pakistan
6. Eritrea
7. Libya
8. Iraq
9. Yemen
10. Iran

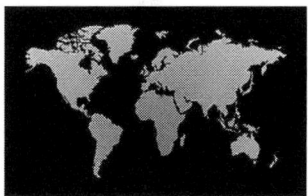

In these top 10 nations alone, we find in 2018 there were 3,066 Christians killed, 1,252 were abducted, 1,020 Christian women were raped or sexually harassed and 793 churches were attacked. According to the *Open Doors Persecution Watch Group*, Islamic sects fuel Christian persecution in eight of the top ten countries listed above.

Some religions teach that we can be reincarnated while others do not. Some religions teach there is a Hell and others do not.

As you can see there are major differences found in the teachings of world religions, but none come close to the structured content, consistency, and unity found in the Holy Bible.

James Orr, a professor of church history speaking of the Muslim, Zoroastrian, and Buddhist scriptures said: *"It is the simple fact that there is nothing that can be properly called history in these other sacred books of the world. They*

---

136 Islam is the world's second largest religious group, second to Christianity but, it is the fastest growing. Over 65 nations in the world today are Islamic. There are more Muslims in the United Kingdom than Methodists and Baptists combined. In 2015, Mosques and Islamic schools in the United States has exceeded 3,186–sources; Islamthreat.com, and pewresearch.org. Ron Rhodes, Islam: What You Need to Know (Eugene, OR; Harvest House Publishers, 2000).
137 www.opendoorsusa.org/christian-persecution/world-watch-list.

are, as every student of them knows, for the most part jumbles of heterogeneous material, loosely placed together, without order, continuity, or unity of any kind. There is no order, progress, or real connection of parts... The Bible, on the other hand, is a history with a beginning, a middle, and an end; a history of revelation; the history of a developing purpose of God, working up to a goal in the full-orbed discovery of the will of God for man's salvation in His Son, Jesus Christ. There is nothing like this, nothing even approaching it, in any other collection of sacred books in the world."[138]

Surprisingly, I've often heard people make the statement, "How can the Christian faith make claims of exclusivity?" The technical words for this view are called "religious exclusivism." What religious exclusivism teaches is that only one particular belief system can be true and all other competing contradictory belief systems are false—and constitutes religious intolerance. This view is in sharp contrast to religious pluralism which believes that all religions provide valid responses to the existence of God. I respond by saying, "How can the Christian faith be accused of intolerance simply because it does not place equal value on each spiritual or philosophical assertion?"

I admit to you that this accusation made against Biblical Christianity is true. It is also true that all belief systems in the world today make claims of exclusivity—even Hinduism.

This view of intolerance against Christianity has become widely accepted in western culture today, while Islam has become the most intolerant worldview in the world today, and Islam is spreading like a wildfire. Although Islam is currently the second largest religion in the world, it is the fastest growing, and at its current rate of growth, could possibly surpass Christianity by the end of 2060.[139]

In the United States of America, as of 2015, the number of Mosques and Islamic Schools has now exceeded 3,186. In 2006, Keith Ellison of Minnesota became the first Muslim elected to the U.S. Congress and was sworn in with a *Quran*. Niraj Warikoo, of the *Detroit Free Press* (12/25-26/06), quoted Ellison's speech:

---

138 *The Bible Under Trial* (New York: A. C. Armstrong, 1907), pp. 287-288.
139 Source: pewresearch.org.

"You can't back down. You can't chicken out. You can't be afraid. You got to have faith in Allah, and you've got to stand up and be a real Muslim."

Ellison, who said little of being a Muslim while campaigning, went on to tell his Islamic audience:

"We're going to continue to face them. They're not going to stop right away. But if you, and me too, stick together, if we believe in Allah, subhanahu wa ta'ala, if we turn to the Quran for guidance, we'll find an answer to the questions we have."

Since Ellison's election, two Muslim women have been sworn into Congress on a Quran as well, not on the Holy Bible.[140]

Do these successes of Muslim people prove the validity of Islam as a valid path to God, or are these accomplishments simply the result of a faith accomplishing its agenda without sufficient evidence to establish it as true?

Ultimately, we have to look at the real evidence for Islam and not just look at its successes alone. For example, if we take the Law of Non-contradiction seriously, we have to conclude that Islam and all the above-mentioned pseudo-Christian organizations and world religions cannot all be true at the same time, when dealing with the same context. Again, the Law of Non-contradiction, which states that something cannot be both true and not true at the same time when dealing with the same context, is one of the basic laws in classical logic that prohibits this.[141] For example, (A) cannot be both (A) and (non-A) at the same time.[142]

A lot of people conveniently misunderstand how much the Law of Non-contradiction is necessary and relied upon in their daily lives and how vital it is in understanding both God and reality. I think when people stop implementing the Laws of Logic correctly in their life, the concept of truth loses all meaning. This partially explains the reason why we see such a high level of legitimacy found in the illegitimate paths to God in the world today (i.e. blind or unreasonable faiths).

---

140 In 2006, the first Muslim member of Congress Keith Ellison was sworn in as a representative for Minnesota's Fifth Congressional District on a Quran, not a Bible; and, in 2017, Ilham Omar and Rashida Tlaib, were the first two female Muslim members of the U.S. Congress sworn in on a Quran, not a Bible.
141 Wikipedia.org; The Law of Non-contradiction.
142 Jevons, W. Stanley, ©1928. Elementary Lessons in Logic, London: Macmillan, p.117.

I find that a person will correctly use the Laws of Logic only when it is convenient. For example, it's our convenient use of logic that keeps us from going into an In-N-Out Burger® restaurant and ordering a pizza or a hot dog. It's not convenient for people to give submission and obedience to a Holy and Righteous God while they are living in rebellion against that God.

We have to also look at the evidence of Supernatural Intervention which confirms the Holy Bible's claim of Divine Origin and Inspiration. All other world religions claim to have Divine Authority, but unlike the Holy Bible, operate without proof of their authority (i.e. Supernatural Intervention and Confirmation).

After we've looked at some of the details found in the world's most popular belief systems, we can see some major differences in their teachings. These differences force us to come to the conclusion that they cannot all be true, based on the well-established Law of Non-contradiction. If they cannot all be true, it cannot be true that all religions lead to God.

Remember, truth will never contradict itself and the God of Biblical Christianity will not create contradictory belief systems in an attempt to get people to believe in Him. This is not only dishonest, but it would also cause major chaos and confusion. The God of Biblical Christianity is not the author of confusion (1Co. 14:33).

Five What-ifs

I want to look briefly at the logical outworking of denying Christ's truth claims, which would be necessary in order to accept that all other worldviews were legitimate paths to God.

Bear with me for a moment and let me throw five "what-ifs" at you.

If in fact Jesus Christ was not telling the truth, what would the logical outworking of such a position imply?

1. If Jesus Christ was not telling the truth, this would mean that He was either mentally imbalanced and/or deceptive.
2. If Jesus Christ was mentally imbalanced and/or deceptive, then He could not have been the Son of God.
3. If Jesus was not the Son of God, then the statements made by Him would be false.

4. If the statements made by Him were false, then the Holy Bible could not be true.
5. If the Holy Bible is not true, then all other worldviews could not be viewed as being false.

I'm reminded by the words of the late Dr. Walter Martin who said, *"Truth by definition is exclusive. If truth were all-inclusive, nothing would be false."*[143] I hope you can now understand why major world religions and cults believe it is so important to attack the person of Jesus Christ.

The proselytizing of disinformation by non-Biblical Christian worldviews, with regard to the person of Jesus Christ, is not only inconsistent internally with the well-established Biblical evidence, but is also inconsistent with the well-established historical evidence externally as well.

The one thing we must realize is that non-Christians attach the false information to the person of Jesus Christ through world religions, cults, and atheism in order to try to convince multitudes of people that they are legitimate explanations for our existence, purpose, and destination.

When Jesus Christ's truth claims are removed from reality, then spiritual truth seems to become subjective and all-inclusive. This creates a perfect platform for anti-Biblical belief systems to launch their false spiritual and philosophical assertions.

When doubt is placed upon the Holy Bible and its Authority, people can perceive the very foundation for Truth seems to be unreliable and, as a result, view the Holy Bible unauthoritative. The logical outworking of these non-factual, and untrue accusations, is that nothing would be able to be viewed as false.

There are some elements of good and truthfulness found in world religions and cults. This is because man was created in God's image and likeness and is capable of articulating these elements.

Non-Biblical Christian worldviews are unable to deny the reality of Christ's existence due to the well-documented Biblical, archaeological, and historical facts revealed about Him.[144] However, they still feel the need to

---

143 Walter Ralston Martin, author of *The Kingdom of the Cults*.
144 Cornelius Tacitus; Lucian of Samosata; Flavius Josephus; Suetonius; Plinius Secundus, Pliny the Younger; Tertullian; Thallus; Phlegon; Letter of Mara Bar-serapion. (See "A Ready Defense" by Josh McDowell and Bill

attack the person and Deity of Jesus Christ and cast doubt on the Authority of the Holy Bible.

The Holy Bible tells us, *"See to it that no one takes you captive through philosophy and empty deception, which are based on human tradition and the spiritual forces of the world rather than on Christ"* (Col. 2:8).

Because of the well-documented historical facts found both internally and externally in Biblical Christianity concerning the person of Jesus Christ, every major religious group must consider Jesus as an important religious figure. Incidentally, He is the One Religious Leader who is the most frequently mentioned by them, and they always have to make some kind of effort to account for Jesus' existence and teaching while completely disregarding the things Christ said about Himself.

He said, *"For God so loved the world, that he gave his only Son, that whoever believes in him should not perish but have eternal life. For God did not send his Son into the world to condemn the world, but in order that the world might be saved through him. Whoever believes in him is not condemned, but whoever does not believe is condemned already, because he has not believed in the name of the only Son of God"* (Jn. 3:16-18). He also said, *"I am the living bread that came down from heaven"* and *"I am the light of the world"* (Jn. 8:12) and *"I am the way, and the truth, and the life. No one comes to the Father except through me"* (Jn. 14:6) and *"I and the Father are one"* (Jn. 10:30).

I find it very interesting that even after Christ had made these statements about Himself, the majority of world religions still feel a need to include Jesus in their description of reality.

When Jesus asked His disciples a simple, but very important question (Mt. 16:15-17), *"But who do you say that I am?"* Simon Peter replied, *"You are the Christ, the Son of the living God."* Jesus answered him, *"Blessed are you, Simon Bar-Jonah! For flesh and blood has not revealed this to you, but my Father who is in heaven."* So according to Matthew 16:16, Christ agrees with Peter and attributes his answer as coming from His Father in Heaven.

These Biblical truths, however, are either ignored or explained away by all of the major world religions and Christian cults. Despite this, they still refer to Jesus Christ as a Wise and Enlightened Man, a Prophet, and a Good Teacher.

This is completely contradictory! Every world religion and Christian cult denies the truth claims Jesus Christ made about Himself, while at the same time they all agree that Jesus was a Good and Wise Man. How could He have been both a Good Man and a crazy man, or be both a Good Man and a liar?

Below are some examples of what world religions and Christian cults are saying about Jesus while completely disregarding the truth claims Jesus Christ made about Himself.

- **Judaists** believe Jesus was Mary's son, was a teacher (Rabbi), had many disciples, was respected, performed miracles, claimed to be the Messiah, and was crucified on a cross. They also acknowledge His followers reported Jesus was raised from the dead.[145]
- **Muslims** believe Jesus was born of a virgin,[146] is to be revered and respected,[147] was a Prophet,[148] a Wise Teacher[149] who worked miracles,[150] ascended to Heaven,[151] and will come again.[152]
- **Baha'ists** believe Jesus came from God,[153] was a Wise Teacher,[154] born of a virgin,[155] had a Divine and human nature, worked miracles,[156] and was crucified and resurrected as an atonement for humanity.[157]
- **Hindus** believe Jesus was a Holy Man[158] and a Wise Teacher.
- **Buddhists** believe Jesus was an Enlightened Man[159] and a Wise Teacher.[160]

---

[145] *The Talmud* is a central text of Rabbinic Judaism, Sanhedrin 34, Shabbat 11:15, 104; *Toledot Yeshu* (*The Life Story of Jesus*) a popular book in Hebrew literature.
[146] Quran 19:18-22.
[147] Quran 4:171.
[148] Quran 6:85.
[149] Quran 57:27.
[150] Quran 2:87; 3:46, 49.
[151] Quran 3:55.
[152] Quran 4:159.
[153] The Baha' faith describes Jesus as a "Manifestation" of God.
[154] *Gleanings from the Writings of Baha'a'llah*, p. 85.
[155] *The Promised Day Is Come,* by Shoghi Effendi, p. 109.
[156] *Gleanings from the Writings of Baha'u'llah*, p. 85
[157] *Gleanings from the Writings of Baha'u'llah*, p. 85.
[158] According to the teachings of Hinduism, Jesus qualified as a "Holy Man" or "Hindu Saint" on the basis of His life and teachings.
[159] 14th-Century Zen master, Gasan Joseki, referred to Jesus as an "Enlightened Man."
[160] The current Dalai Lama often describes Jesus as a "Holy Man." The Dalai Lama met frequently with the pope in the early part of the 21st-Century and showed great respect for the teachings of Jesus Christ.

John Stuart Mill, a British philosopher, skeptic, and antagonist of Christianity said this about Jesus: *"But about the life and sayings of Jesus, there is a stamp of personal originality combined with profundity of insight...in the very first rank of men of sublime genius of whom our species can boast. When this pre-eminent genius is combined with the qualities of probably the greatest moral reformer, and martyr to that mission, who ever existed upon earth, religion cannot be said to have made a bad choice in pitching on this man as the ideal representative and guide of humanity; nor, even now, would it be easy, even for an unbeliever, to find a better translation of the rule of virtue from the abstract into the concrete, than to endeavor so to live that Christ would approve our life."*[161]

What Mr. Mill is saying is that Jesus was a perfect example of everything He taught.

Also, let's look at a statement made by the noted Irish historian William Lecky who was a dedicated opponent of organized Christianity: *"It was reserved for Christianity to present to the world an ideal character, which through all the changes of eighteen centuries has inspired the hearts of men with an impassioned love; has shown itself capable of acting on all ages, nations, temperaments, and conditions; has been not only the highest pattern of virtue but the strongest incentive to its practice; and has exercised so deep an influence that it may be truly said that the simple record of [Jesus'] three short years of active life has done more to regenerate and to soften mankind than all the disquisitions of philosophers, and all other exhortations of moralists."*[162]

Given that Jesus is a Common Feature of most religions in the world and is spoken highly of from a famous antagonist of Christianity, non-Christian historians, philosophers, and skeptics, it might be important for us to learn more about Him. This ought to give seekers of truth a reason to pause and consider the life of Jesus more seriously.

After examining the major worldviews, while applying the well-established rules of logic—specifically, the Law of Non-contradiction—it can be determined that not all worldviews can be true regardless of whether or not

---

161 *The Creed & the Age, a Lecture* by Richard Hayes Robinson, p.28 (a quote of John Stuart Mill). London: Simpkin, Marshall & Co., Stationers' Hall Court. Bath: R. E. Peach, 8, Bridge Street, 1884.
162 Quote from his book, *History of European Morals from Augustus to Charlemagne*. Publisher: Kindle Direct Publishing, 2 vols., 1869 (Public Doman).

they claim to be true. There must be more than a mere claim—there must be *Proof of Authority*—which is to say, there must be Supernatural, Confirmational Evidence provided by a particular religion that would be sufficient to establish it as true, whereby produce belief in its message.

According to some estimates, there are roughly 4,200 religions in the world today[163] that people of faith regard as Divinely inspired, but surprisingly none of them have *Proof of Authority* as the Holy Bible.

Size and Projected Growth of Major Religious Groups

	2010 POPULATION	% OF WORLD POPULATION IN 2010	PROJECTED 2050 POPULATION	% OF WORLD POPULATION IN 2050	POPULATION GROWTH 2010-2050
Christians	2,168,330,000	31.4%	2,918,070,000	31.4%	749,740,000
Muslims	1,599,700,000	23.2	2,761,480,000	29.7	1,161,780,000
Unaffiliated	1,131,150,000	16.4	1,230,340,000	13.2	99,190,000
Hindus	1,032,210,000	15.0	1,384,360,000	14.9	352,140,000
Buddhists	487,760,000	7.1	486,270,000	5.2	-1,490,000
Folk Religions	404,690,000	5.9	449,140,000	4.8	44,450,000
Other Religions	58,150,000	0.8	61,450,000	0.7	3,300,000
Jews	13,860,000	0.2	16,090,000	0.2	2,230,000
World total	**6,895,850,000**	**100.0**	**9,307,190,000**	**100.0**	**2,411,340,000**

Source: The Future of World Religions: Population Growth Projections, 2010-2050
PEW RESEARCH CENTER

We must keep in mind that all religions were started by someone who claimed to have had either a vision or a message from God. Jesus never made that claim. He said that he is God,[164] that He came from Heaven[165] to teach us about His Father,[166] that no one can come to the Father except through Him (Jn. 14:6), that His Father sent Him to die for the sins of the world (Jn. 3:16-18; Ac. 4:12), and that He is the only Mediator between God and men (1Ti. 2:5). This means Jesus Christ is the Only Means and Provision provided by God for our restoration and reconciliation with Him (1Pe. 3:18). Muhammad, Buddha, and Joseph Smith never said they were God nor that they came from Heaven to die for anyone.

---

163 "World Religions, Religion Statistics, Geography Church Statistics. www.worldreligions.com; www.humanreligions.org.
164 Jn. 10:30; 14:9.
165 Jn. 6:38, 51; 8:12.
166 Mt. 11:27; Jn. 10:30; 14:6, 9.

The difference between them and Jesus is that Jesus was both God and man (Jn. 1:1; 8:58; Mk. 14:61-64) and revealed His Divine Authority in multiple ways.

In the New Testament, the book of John records Jesus Christ's direct claim of Deity (Jn. 8:58). He claims to be God, the Same One Who spoke to Moses at the burning bush (Ex. 3:14). The Jews certainly understood this as a claim of Deity because they immediately grabbed stones and tried to stone Him for blasphemy (Jn. 8:59).

Also, in the Gospel of John when Christ was talking to the Samaritan woman at the well, He claimed to be the Messiah (Jn. 4:25-26). Also, in the Gospel of Mark (Mk. 14:61-64) when Jesus was questioned by the High Priest, he asked Jesus if He was the Son of God. When Jesus said "I am," the High Priest tore his clothes and said, "Do we need any other witnesses? You have heard the blasphemy for yourself." They all condemned Him to be guilty of death.

There are many other examples that could be shown that include indirect claims of Deity. For example:
- He receives worship (Mt. 14:33; 21:9; 28:9), which is an action reserved for God alone.
- He forgives sin (Mk. 2:1-12; Lk. 5:20), which is also an action reserved for God alone.
- He claims to be equal with God (Jn. 5:17-18; 10:30).

Jesus accepted specific titles:
- King (Mk. 5:7, 13:26; Mt. 28:18; Jn. 18:36, 37)
- Messiah (Jn. 4:26; Mt. 16:14-17; Jn. 4:25, 26; 10:24, 25)
- Savior of the World (Jn. 4:42; 8:24)
- Son of Man (Mk. 14:62; Jn. 3:13, 14)
- Son of God (Lu. 1:35; Jn. 3:16; 5:18; 20:31)
- I Am (Jn. 8:58)

Jesus claimed to have control over the following:
- Life (Mk. 5:41; Lu. 11:17-27)
- Truth (Jn. 14:6)
- Death (Jn. 11:25-45)
- Eternal Destiny (Jn. 3:16-18)

Jesus claimed to have Authority regarding the following:
- To forgive sin (Mt. 9:2-6)
- Over the angels (Mt. 13:41-42; 24:30-31)
- Over demons (Mk. 5:1-20)
- All Authority in Heaven and on Earth (Mt. 11:27; 28:18-20)

Jesus was ultimately crucified for the charge of blasphemy. Jesus claimed to be none other than God in human flesh, and no other great world religious leader ever claimed to be God.

Jesus proved His Divine Authority in many other ways as well:
- Christ proved His Authority through physical healing and other miracles (Jn. 4:50; Mt. 8:5-7, 13; Mk. 5:8).
- Christ's Authority was established through His fulfillment of very specific Old Testament Messianic prophecies which were written hundreds of years before His birth.[167]
- Christ proved His Authority through the consistency and unity of His sinless (2Co. 5:21) Miraculous Life and Message.
- Christ proved His Authority through the Ultimate *Proof of Authority*, His death, and Resurrection (Ro. 1:4; Jn. 11:25, 26).

Remember, the Roman and Jewish authorities could not refute the Resurrection (Mt. 28:11-15). The Holy Bible tells us that the apostles had seen, heard, and touched the Risen Christ and He even ate with them over a 40-day period. Also, the Bible tells us that over 500 people saw the Resurrected Christ (1Co. 15:6-8).

The main purpose of Christ's life and death is told to us in the New Testament. The Apostle John records Christ's Words in His Gospel. We read in John 3:16-18:

> [16] "For God so loved the world that He gave His one and only Son, that everyone who believes in Him shall not perish but have eternal life. [17] For God did not send His Son into the world to condemn the world, but to save the world through Him. [18] Whoever believes in Him is not condemned, but whoever does not believe has already been condemned, because he has not believed in the name of God's one and only Son."

---

167 See *Proof of Authority*, chapter two, for additional information.

Only in Biblical Christianity do we see that God sent His Son as a sacrifice for the world so that all those who repent and believe in Him may have their sins forgiven and can have a personal relationship with God through Jesus Christ in both this life and the next.[168]

Only Biblical Christianity gives the promise of eternal life, which is not based on our good work but is based solely on His good grace, through faith in His Son, Jesus Christ (Ro. 3:24; 6:23).

Religion does not give one that opportunity because it relies heavily upon man's righteous efforts of diligent service and works. It relies upon expectations of earning an eternal reward through self-control, self-motivation, and self-determination, and achieving salvation through human effort.

In contrast, Biblical Christianity is a relationship with God through His One and Only Son, Jesus Christ and the opportunity for this relationship comes from God's amazing love and grace toward us.

Religion is essentially man's attempting to *reach up* to God through self-effort and good works. Biblical Christianity is God's *reaching down* to man through God's good grace, through Christ's voluntary sacrifice upon His cross.

We must understand that Christianity is not just a religion. It is a relationship with a loving God through His Son, the Only Mediator between God and men, Jesus Christ.

Again, we must understand that the individual writers of the Holy Bible, at the time it was written, would have had no idea that their writings would eventually be gathered together and put into One Book. *"Anyone who diligently studies the Bible will continually find a remarkable structured pattern throughout its pages, with intricacy and symmetry incapable of explanation by chance, common sense or collusion."*[169] What is amazing is that each individual, ancient, historical document fits perfectly together and each document has its own particular purpose in the Holy Bible as a whole. On the following pages, we will compare the major differences found in the most popular world religions in the form of charts.

---

168 Jn. 3:16-18; Ph. 2:9-11; Col. 1:20; Ac. 4:12; 1Ti. 2:5.
169 Dr. Norman L. Geisler (Th.B., William Tyndale College; A.B., Wheaton College; M.A., Wheaton College Graduate School; Ph.D., Loyola University) taught systematic theology at Dallas Theological Seminary.

BIBLICAL COMPARISON CHART OF OTHER RELIGIONS & CULTS

Christians Believe	Mormons Believe
GOD	
...that God is uniquely eternal and all-powerful, the only one God, and that He is a Spirit (Ps. 145:13; Jn. 4:24; 1Ti. 1:17)	...that God is a material creature who was once as we are now men. They say men can finally achieve godhood and that there are many gods.
THE BIBLE	
...that the Bible, given by God's Spirit, is complete in itself and needs no additions. In fact, additions to the Bible are forbidden (De. 4:2, 12:32; Pr. 30:5, 6; Ga. 1:8; He. 1:1, 2; Re. 22:18, 19).	...that they have "new Scripture" and that the writings of Joseph Smith are divinely inspired revelations—God's nineteenth century addition to the Bible.
SIN	
...that man is not godlike, but sinful and separated from God. We can only have a relationship with God through faith in Christ. Man, apart from Christ, is lost. (Jn. 1:29; Ro. 5:12-19, 6:23; Ga. 3:13; Ep. 2:1, 3).	...that man is progressively becoming a god. Mormons teach that Adam's sin in Eden was necessary in order to provide parentage for the spirit children of God who were ready and waiting for the experience of earth life.
SALVATION	
...that salvation is a free gift provided by the grace (unmerited love) of God for all who believe and accept His plan (Jn. 12:26; Ep. 2:8, 9; 14:1-3, 6; 1Jn. 3:1, 2).	...that salvation comes by works and that all will spend eternity on some level of multi-story heaven. The level will be determined by the scope of each man's good works.

BIBLICAL COMPARISON CHART OF OTHER RELIGIONS & CULTS

Christians Believe	Jehovah's Witnesses Believe
GOD	
...that God is an eternal, personal, spiritual Being in Three Persons—Trinity: Father, Son, and Holy Spirit (Mt. 3:13-17, 28:19; 2Co. 13:14).	...that there is One Solitary Being from all eternity, Jehovah God, the Creator and Preserver of the Universe and all things. They deny the doctrine of the Trinity.
IMMORTALITY	
...that Scripture teaches that man has an eternal, immortal soul (Ge. 1:26, 5:1; Jb. 32:8; Ac. 7:59; 1Co. 11:7).	...that man does not have an immortal soul. They teach that the soul is not separate from the body.
JESUS CHRIST	
...that Christ is Divine, a Part of the Trinity, God Himself (Jn. 1:1; Col. 1:15-19, 2:9; 1Jn. 5:7, 8).	...that Christ was not God but God's First Created Creature. They deny Christ's Deity.
ATONEMENT	
...that Christ's death was the complete payment for man's sins (Ro. 3:24, 25; 2Co. 5:20; Col. 1:20; 1Pe. 2:24).	...that Christ's death provides the opportunity for a man to work for salvation—Perfect Human Life for eternity on an Eden-like earth.
CHRIST'S RESURRECTION	
...that Christ was bodily resurrected from the grave (Lu. 24.43; Jn. 2:21; 20:24-29).	...that Christ was raised a "Divine Spirit." They deny the bodily resurrection of Christ.
CHRIST'S RETURN	
...that Christ will return to earth physically (Zec. 12:10; Mt. 24:30; 1Th. 4:16, 17; Re. 1:7).	...that Christ returned to Earth invisibly in 1915 and now rules Earth and Heaven.
HELL	
...there is eternal punishment for sin (Mt. 5:22, 8:11, 12; 13:42, 50; 22:13; Lu. 13:24-28; 2Pe. 2:17; Jude 13; Re. 14:9-11).	...that there is no Hell or eternal punishment. Those who do not measure up to Jehovah's standards will be annihilated.

BIBLICAL COMPARISON CHART OF OTHER RELIGIONS & CULTS

Christians Believe	Buddhist Believe
GOD	
...that God is Omniscient and Omnipotent (Jb. 42:2; Ps. 115:3; Mt. 19-26).	...that a personal God does not exist.
JESUS CHRIST	
...that He is the unique Son of God who died for man's sin (Mt. 14:33, 16:16; Jn. 1:34, 9:35-37; Ro. 5:6-8; 1Co. 15:3).	...that He was a good teacher who is less important than Buddha.
SIN	
...is any thought or deed contrary to the will of God. Man is spiritually dead in sin (Ro. 3:10, 23, 5:12; Ep. 2:1).	...is anything that hinders man's progress. Man is responsible for his own sin.
SALVATION	
...is through Christ's effort only (Ac. 4:12; Ep. 2:8-10; Tit. 3:5).	...is by self-effort only.

BIBLICAL COMPARISON CHART OF OTHER RELIGIONS & CULTS

Christians Believe	Hindus Believe
GOD	
...that God is a eternal, personal, spiritual Being in three persons—Trinity: Father, Son, and Holy Spirit (Mt. 3:13-17, 28:19; 2 Co. 13:14)..	...that Braham is a formless, abstract, eternal being without attributes. He takes form in a trinity as well as millions of lesser gods.
JESUS CHRIST	
...that Christ is the only begotten Son of God, the Father. He is God as well as man, sinless, and He died for our redemption (Mk. 10:45:1; Jn. 1:13, 14, 8:46, 10:30; He. 4;15; 1Pe. 2:24).	...that Christ is just one of many incarnations or sons of God. He was no more divine than any other man and He did not die for man's sins.
SIN	
...is proud, independent rebellion that separates men from God. It is falling short of the standards God has established in His Word to men. Sin must be punished, and its consequence is death and eternal separation from God (Ro. 3:23, 6:23).	Good and evil are relative terms. Whatever helps is good; whatever hinders is vice. Man cannot help "stumbling" over these obstacles as he strives to know himself. If he cannot succeed in this life, he may try again in a reincarnated form.
SALVATION	
Man is justified through the sacrificial death and resurrection of Jesus Christ who died in our stead (Ro. 3:24; 1 Co. 15:3).	Man is justified through devotion, meditation, good works, and self-control.

BIBLICAL COMPARISON CHART OF OTHER RELIGIONS & CULTS

Christians Believe	Muslims Believe
GOD	
...that one God is revealed in Scripture as Father, Son, and Holy Spirit. Within the one "essence" of the Godhead there are three persons who are co-equally and co-eternally God (Mt. 3:13-17, 28:19; 2Co. 13:14).	...that there is no God but Allah—*the* God.
JESUS CHRIST	
...that Jesus is the Christ, the Son of God, one with the Father, sinless redeemer of sinful man through His vicarious death on the cross and resurrection from the dead (Jn. 1:13, 14; 1Co. 15:3; He. 4:15; 1Pe. 3:18).	...that Jesus Christ was only a man, a prophet equal to Adam, Noah, Abraham, and Moses—all of whom are below Mohammad in importance. Christ did not die for man's sins; in fact, Judas—not Jesus—died on the cross.
SIN	
Sin is proud, independent rebellion against God in active or passive form (Ro. 1:18-23, 3:10, 23).	Sin is failure to do Allah's will; failure to do one's religious duties as outlined in the Five Pillars of Islam.
SALVATION	
Christ, God's Son, died for our sins (on the cross) according to the inspired Word of God (Jn. 3:16-18; 1Co. 15:3, 4).	Man earns his own salvation and pays for his own sins.

BIBLICAL COMPARISON CHART OF OTHER RELIGIONS & CULTS

Christians Believe	Roman Catholics Believe
INFALLIBILITY	
...that only God is infallible; men are corrupt (Je. 17:9; Ps. 51:5; Ro. 3:10-18, 23).	...that Roman Catholic popes are infallible.
SALVATION	
...that Jesus Christ is our only source for Salvation (Ep. 2:8, 9).	...that the Roman Catholic Church is the only source of salvation for sinners and the sacraments are essential for Salvation.
SAINTS	
...that all Christians are saints (Ro. 1:7; 1Co. 1:2; Ep. 1:1; Ph. 1:1).	...that a person can be recognized by the Catholic Church as having an exceptional degree of holiness or likeness to God.
IMMACULATE CONCEPTION	
...that Mary was blessed and called Jesus her Savior (Lu. 1:46-50).	...that the Virgin Mary was born without original sin.
MEDIATOR	
...that Christ is the only mediator between God and men (1Ti. 2:5; He. 12:24).	...that the Virgin Mary is a co-redeemer and savior.
INTERPRETATION	
...that every Christian can understand the Bible (Ep. 3:4).	...that the Catholic Church is the only correct interpreter of Scriptural doctrine.

Dogmas Declared by the Roman Catholic Church

Year	Statement
437	Proclamation that infant baptism regenerates the soul.
500	The Mass instituted as a re-sacrifice of Jesus for the remissions of sins.
593	Declaration that sin needs to be purged, established by Pope Gregory I.
600	Prayers directed to Mary, dead saints, and angels.
786	Worship of cross, images and relics authorized.
995	Canonization of dead people as saints initiated by Pope John XV.
1000	Attendance at Mass made mandatory under the penalty of mortal sin.
1079	Celibacy of priesthood, decreed by Pope Gregory XVI.
1090	Rosary, repetitious praying with beads, invented by Peter the Hermit.
1184	The Inquisitions, instituted by the council of Verona.
1190	The sale of indulgences established to reduce time in Purgatory.

Dogmas Declared by the Roman Catholic Church

Year	Statement
1215	Transubstantiation, proclaimed by Pope Innocent III.
1215	Confessions of sins to priests, instituted by Pope Innocent III.
1229	Bible placed on Forbidden Books in Toulouse.
1438	Purgatory elevated from doctrine to dogma by Council of Florence.
1545	Tradition claimed equal in authority with the Bible by the Council of Trent.
1546	Apocryphal Books declared cannon by The Council of Trent.
1854	Immaculate Conception of Mary proclaimed by Pope Pius IX.
1870	Infallibility of the Pope, proclaimed by Vatican Council.
1922	Virgin Mary proclaimed co-redeemer with Jesus by Pope Benedict XV.

Evidence to Evaluate

- All other religions believe that by just making a truth claim it becomes true. Anyone can make a truth claim, but only Biblical Christianity proves its Authority and is the only religious book in history that displays proof of Supernatural Intervention (i.e. Divine Origin and Inspiration). The Holy Bible backs up its truth claims through its Supernatural Intervention and Confirmation Evidence and is the greatest proof for God's Existence and Authority in confirming His Message, and Mission.
- All religions consist of some kind of work-based system for salvation and reject Jesus Christ's Deity and the Divine Inspiration of the Holy Bible. They also reject Jesus Christ Alone as the One and Only Provision provided by God for the forgiveness of sin and its consequences.

Notes

FINAL CONCLUSION

I have written *Proof of Authority* for people who have a desire to seek the truth, meaning, and purpose of this life, and to introduce those people to the amazing God Who has not only revealed Himself within the pages of His Holy Word (2Ti. 3:16), but He also has revealed Himself in other areas within our everyday human experience.

God has revealed Himself in our heart—also known as the place where human desires, feelings, thinking, and emotions begin—(He. 10:22; Ro. 2:15, 16), in creation (Ps. 8:3, 4; 19:1-6; Ro. 1:18-21), in other believers (1Pe. 2:12), and in Christ (Jn. 1:5; 12:45; 14:9; He. 1:1-14; Mt. 11:27). He made the universe and everything in it, and He gives us everything we need (Ge. 9:3; Lu. 12:22-24; 1Pe. 3:15; 2Pe. 1:1-11) such as oxygen, water and food—including meat, poultry, fruit, vegetables, fish, dairy, just to name a few. He has created us with the ability to see, smell, taste, touch, and hear so that we can enjoy flavor, fragrance, feelings, sounds, music, and beauty. He is infinite and eternal (De. 33:27). He has no beginning and no end (Re. 22:13). He is unchangeable in His being with regard to love, wisdom, power, holiness, justice, goodness, and truth. He is the same yesterday, today, and forever (He.13:8), and He is the Creator (Is. 40:28; Ge. 1:1), Preserver, and Sustainer (He. 1:3; Ps. 55:22) of all things (Ep. 3:9). The Holy Bible tells us that God's Word is living (He. 4:12), active, everlasting (1Pe. 1:23), God-breathed (2Ti. 3:16-17), and is as applicable today as it was yesterday (Ps. 119:89; 1Pe. 1:25).

These are very amazing statements made by the Holy Bible, but how can we know that these statements are true? The answer to this question can only be derived from the evidence that is provided by the Holy Bible's internal cohesiveness, unity, harmony, its external consistency with history, science, archaeology, mathematical probability, logic, reason and the evidence of fulfilled predictive prophecy. If the God of Biblical Christianity did not exist and the Holy Bible were not His Word, then we would need to ask ourselves and give an answer to these questions: How could the Holy Bible contain the level of consistency, accuracy, unity, and cohesiveness along with evidence of fulfilled predictive prophecy, (i.e. Supernatural Intervention and Confirmation)? How could it maintain the level of consistency in spite of the multiplicity of books, authors, years, locations, languages, circumstances, subjects, and literary genres found within its pages? How could any of the above listed phenomena occur without Supernatural Intervention, and why do these phenomena only occur in the Holy Bible? Why do not any other writings of any other religion exhibit evidence of Supernatural Intervention (i.e. *Proof of Authority*) as the Holy Bible? Could the reason for the phenomena found in the Christian Scriptures simply be because the Holy Bible is Divine in origin rather than human? Could this be proof that the Holy Bible is the Only True Inspired Word of God in existence today? Absolutely!

If the Holy Bible is the One and Only True Word of God, as the evidence suggests, then why doesn't the world wholeheartedly submit to its Message? In John 8:46, 47, Jesus Christ said, *"46 Which of you can prove Me guilty of sin? If I speak the truth, why do you not believe Me? 47 Whoever belongs to God hears the words of God. The reason you do not hear is that you do not belong to God."* Jesus gives us an answer to the question why the majority of people do not have a desire to submit to the One True God in their life. The answer is because they don't belong to God. The Apostle Paul tells us in Romans 1:18 that they suppress the truth in unrighteousness. Without a relationship with God, our heart, soul, and spirit will continue to operate from the position of a fallen and carnal state. Let's look at these three topics in a little more detail so that we can better understand them from a correct Biblical perspective.

The Human Heart

According to *Baker's Evangelical Dictionary of Biblical Theology,* the word *"heart"* is used over 1,000 times in the Holy Bible and is generally used as a reference to the spiritual make-up of human beings with regard to their physical, emotional, intellectual, and moral activities. This means that the term "heart" is synonymous with the place where human desires, feelings, thinking, and emotions start, which includes the mind (Ro. 8:6; 2Co. 5:17) and soul and is that which drives the will of men and women towards the things they say, do, and think.

The *"heart,"* according to the Holy Bible, is described primarily as the part of human beings that controls their will and behavior. In other words, the *"heart"* is synonymous with a moral conscience that steers our values and choices. In order for our *"heart"* to be transformed to have *"a good conscience and a sincere faith,"* we need to submit to God (Eze. 36:26-27; 1Ti. 1:5). That's because a Biblically-sound moral conscience is necessary for a Biblically-sincere and authentic Christian faith.

In order for God to get people to desire what He desires, He must purify, renew, and repair the human heart through the process of redemption, which includes justification and sanctification (Ps. 51:10; Col. 3:10; Tit. 3:7; Ga. 3:24; Ac. 26:18).

The redeemed, transformed, and renewed *heart* is the beginning point for our spiritual life with God that requires submission, repentance, and obedience. This reality is very difficult for many humans to accept. Most humans want to believe that the *heart* of people is basically good, and people have to be pushed, coerced, or forced into exhibiting bad behavior. However, Jesus Christ said the opposite: He said that the sins, such as evil thoughts, sexual immorality, theft, greed, murder, adultery, malice, deceit, lewdness, envy, slander, arrogance, and foolishness actually originate in the human *heart* (Mk. 7:21-23).

According to the Holy Bible, man's *heart, soul, and mind* were damaged because of the fall (Je. 31:33; Eze. 36:26) and need to be restored, transformed, and renewed—in other words, justified and sanctified (Tit. 3:4-7)—but it is only through submission and repentance that the **heart, soul, and mind** can be restored, transformed, and renewed (Ep. 4:22-24). When the Holy Bible speaks of belief, God tells us that it can start in one of three places. The Holy Scriptures reveal to us that belief can come from the **heart**

(Mk. 11:23; 16:14; Lu. 8:12; Ro. 10:9). 2.), the *mind* (Ro. 12.2; 2Co. 4:4), or the *soul* (Ps. 103:1-5; Ac. 14:22) and begins with God through your submission to the Work of the Holy Spirit.

The Holy Bible refers to God as also having a heart (Ac. 13:22) and emotions (Ge. 6:7) and desires that drive His behavior toward us. For example, He desires for people to draw close to Him (Ja. 4:7, 8) and to be saved by coming to the saving knowledge of His Son, Jesus Christ (1Ti. 2:4-6), which implies that the main desire of God's heart today is the same as it was in the beginning (Ge. 2), which is for human beings to know and to have a relationship with Him (Je. 31:33, 34; Ps. 46:10).

The Human Soul and Spirit

Throughout the pages of the Holy Bible, it consistently refers to people as "souls," (Ex. 31:14; Pr. 11:30). The Holy Bible tells us that the human soul and spirit are the entire inner person that is eternal and continues to live on after the fleshly carnal body dies and decays. The soul is regarded as a person's true self.[170] Both believers and non-believers will have resurrected bodies in the last day (Da. 12:1-2). The body of those who die in Christ will receive eternal life, and those who die without Christ will receive eternal death, including everlasting punishment and total separation from God (1Co. 15:52-55; Ro. 6:23; 2Th. 1:8-9).

What I mean by the statement *"total separation from God"* is as follows: The Holy Bible describes Everlasting Punishment in several different ways.

1. A lake of fire (Lu. 16:24).
2. Outer darkness (Mt. 8:12).
3. A prison (1Pe. 3:19).

And there will be:

4. No light (1Jn. 1:5).
5. No love (1Jn. 4:8).
6. No joy (Mt. 25:23).
7. No peace (Ep. 2:14).

---

170 Je. 17:9, 10; Ge. 6:5; Mk. 7:21-23; Ep. 4:18.

According to the Holy Bible, these four characteristics of God will be absent from Hell. This is what is meant by the statement *"total separation from God."*

We also must keep in mind that there is no Biblical support for the idea that humans get another chance after death. After death, the Judgment will come (He. 9:27). Jesus paid the price of our just punishment (Jn. 3:16-18). The spirit, soul, and body of those regenerated by the Holy Spirit will abide forever with God in a perfect state and place (1Jn. 3:2) which includes a New Heaven and New Earth (Is. 65:17-19; Re. 21; 2Pe. 3:10-13). The opposite is true for those who are in Hell (Is. 64:6). The souls of the righteous directly go into the presence of the Lord (Lu. 23:43; 2Co. 5:8; Ph. 1:23). The only way to be declared righteous before God is through faith in the death and Resurrection of Jesus Christ (Ro. 10:9).

Jesus said that we are not to fear men who can only kill the body but not the soul (Mt. 10:28). I want to give you some evidence that will suggest that, although in some passages they do overlap for obvious reasons, there are fundamental differences between the soul and the spirit, and they are actually two separate entities. The Holy Bible makes a distinction in 1Thessalonians 5:23 between the soul and the spirit. We read *"Now may the God of peace Himself sanctify you completely, and may your entire **spirit, soul,** and body be kept blameless at the coming of our Lord Jesus Christ."* In Hebrews 4:12 we read, *"For the word of God is living and active. Sharper than any double-edged sword, it pierces even to dividing **soul and spirit**, joints and marrow. It is able to judge the thoughts and intentions of the heart."*

The Holy Bible tells us that Jesus Christ was fully man and fully God. We also know that Christ has a soul because the Holy Bible tells us that Christ's soul experienced anguish at the Garden of Gethsemane while He prayed before going to the cross. He said, *"My soul is very sorrowful, even to death"* (Mt. 26:36-46). The Messianic psalm also speaks of the soul of the Messiah, saying that His soul will not be abandoned to Sheol, nor His body to corruption, or decay (Ps. 16:9-10; Ac. 13:35-37).

The Holy Bible also tells us that the human soul can be strong or weak (2Pe. 2:14), and that it can be saved or lost (Ja. 1:21; Eze. 18:4). The human soul was created by God (Je. 38:16). The human soul needs the protection, purification, and atonement of God (Le. 17:11; 1Pe. 1:22).

The human soul is eternal and will eternally exist in one of two places in the afterlife—Heaven or Hell—in a state of eternal life or eternal death.

All human beings will suffer physical death (i.e. the first death) when our time on Earth has ended. Jesus said that the believer will not experience the second death (1Jn. 5:4; Re. 2:11). The second death is a spiritual death and is synonymous with the Lake of Fire, mentioned several times in the Book of Revelation, which also includes total separation from God for eternity (Re. 21:8) and is exclusively for the Devil, his angels, and those who reject Jesus Christ (Mt. 25:41).

The Holy Bible teaches that those who are born twice (once physically and once spiritually) will experience just one death (once physically), but those who are born just once (physically) will suffer two deaths (once physically and once spiritually). The inevitable outcome for many human beings in this life is that they will reject the love and forgiveness of the One True God, which means they will have to pay and suffer for their own sins with the first and second death (Eze. 18; Ro. 3:21-24; 6:23) when their physical life comes to an end. Because the soul is eternal (Ge. 35:18), it will be an eternal death and punishment that includes total separation from God in a place of torment. However, those who accept the free gift of Christ's atonement will experience the opposite outcome (2Co. 5:21; 1Pe. 2:24; Ro. 5:8; 1Jn. 2:2) which includes eternal life and peace, both in the New Heaven and New Earth with God the Father, Son, and Holy Spirit. (Mt. 25:46; Jn. 3:36; 5:24; Ga. 6:7-8; 2Pe. 3:13; Ps. 23:2; Re. 21:1, 2; Is. 65:17; 66:22).

Finally, look specifically at how the *"spirit"* is described in Scripture. The Holy Bible says that the *"spirit"* is the very breath of Almighty God and was breathed into man at the beginning of God's creation: *"Then the LORD God formed a man from the dust of the ground and breathed into his nostrils the breath of life, and the man became a living being"* (Ge. 2:7). It is the human spirit that gives us a consciousness of self and other remarkable, although limited, "God-like" qualities. The human spirit includes our intellect, emotions, fears, passions, and creativity. It is this spirit that provides us with the unique ability to comprehend and understand (Jb. 32:8, 18). It is the intangible, unseen human spirit that influences man's mental and emotional reality.

Upon death "the spirit returns to God who gave it" (Ec. 12:7; see also Jb. 34:14-15; Ps. 104:29-30).

Every human being has a spirit, and it is distinct from the spirit of animals. God created humans differently from the animals in that He created humans *"In the image and likeness of God"* (Ge. 1:26-27). He created animals *"after their own kind"* (Ge. 1:24-25).

Therefore, because of the spirit, man is able to think, feel, love, design, create, and enjoy music, humor, and art; and it is because of the human spirit that humans have a "free-will" and, incidentally, there is no other creature on earth created with a "free will."

The Holy Bible tells us that the human spirit was damaged in the fall when Adam and Eve sinned, and their ability to directly have fellowship with God was severed, and they then had to approach God through a temporary sacrificial system implemented by God Himself.

The Holy Bible says in Genesis 3:21, *"The LORD God made garments of skin and clothed Adam and his wife."* Many scholars believe that this passage suggests God Himself taught and implemented the specifics to Adam and Eve about the new temporary sacrificial system. At the same time, God provided the first sacrifice after their sinful rebellion whereby re-establishing a temporary and limited relationship with God through the shedding of blood (He. 9:22). The killing of animals has no ability or worth by themselves to do away with our sin (He. 10:4). The sacrifices were sufficient at the time only because God chose them to be. It is because of the love of God that the blood of animals could temporarily cover our sin, and it is because of the love of God that the blood of Christ can permanently cover our sin now (Ga. 4:4-5). The Holy Bible tells us that sinners are slaves to sin (Jn. 8:34). The effects of our rebellion have been nullified through Christ (Ro. 5:12-21); and, of course, God looks for right disposition in His worshipers (1Ki. 8:47; Eze. 18:30-31), having repentance (Ac. 3:19; 1Jn. 1:8-9), submission (Ja. 4:7; Jb. 22:21), and obedience (Jn. 14:15; 1Jn. 5:3).

Although, the Holy Bible does not specifically tell us where God got the animal skins, He could have spoken them into existence if He had chosen to do so. However, if we observe the principles of atonement as they are revealed to us through Scripture, while implementing the well-established Laws of Logic, we would have to come to the conclusion that God obtained them through the sacrifice of two animals, most likely two perfect, unblemished lambs found among His creation. This theory is not only highly probable, but it also is consistent with the Old Testament teachings, specifically with regard to its principles of atonement (i.e. expiation and propitiation). The New Testament is consistent with the Old Testament teachings of atonement in that Christ died for our sins (1Co. 15:3; Jn. 3:16-18) and *"we were reconciled to God"* through the sacrifice of His Son (Ro. 5:10-11; 2Co. 5:18-20).

Adam and Eve died both physically and spiritually that day; and, as a consequence, so did all humanity, nature, and the universe. Scripture tells us that sin and death entered the world the moment of their rebellion. The Holy Bible tells us in Romans 5:12, *"Therefore, just as sin entered the world through one man, and death through sin, so also death was passed on to all men, because all sinned."* Jesus restores our fellowship with the Father through His permanent sacrificial system. Romans 5:19 tells us, *"For just as through the disobedience of the one man the many were made sinners, so also through the obedience of the one Man the many will be made righteous."* Ever since the day of the rebellion, the human body, soul, and spirit have suffered the effects and consequences of that fall. In God's Word prior to Christ's sacrifice, a person is characterized as spiritually "dead" (Ep. 2:1-5; Col. 2:13). However, after Christ's death and Resurrection, a person that comes to God through Christ is now characterized as spiritually made "alive" (1Co. 15:22; Ep. 2:5; Col. 2:13; 1Pe. 3:18).

A relationship with Christ revitalizes our carnal and fallen spirit and renews us day by day (2Co. 4:16). Adam was originally made alive by the breath of God, and we are made alive by God's Holy Spirit through Christ. (2Co. 5:17; Jn. 3:3; Ro. 6:4).

Upon our acceptance of Jesus Christ as Lord and Savior, the Holy Spirit of God joins with our own spirit in ways that we could never imagine. The apostle John said, *"This is how we know that we live in Him and He in us: He has given us of His Spirit"* (1Jn. 4:13).

When we allow the Spirit of God to lead our lives, *"the Spirit Himself testifies with our spirit that we are God's children"* (Ro. 8:16). As children of God, we are no longer led by the spirit of our carnal flesh, but by the Holy and Righteous Spirit of God Who leads us to eternal life; but without the joining of God's Spirit with our spirit, pleasing God becomes impossible, and the desire to seek, submit, and obey God becomes unattainable. Anyone who wants to come to God must first believe that God exists (He.11:6; Mt. 19:26; 1Co. 2:14).

In order for God to get people to desire what He desires, there must be a submission to God's truth which itself is, in fact, a work of the Holy Spirit that requires our submission.

In John 16:8 we read, *"And when He comes, He will convict the world in regard to sin and righteousness and judgment."* If people have a desire to submit to the truth found in God's Word, then the God of Biblical Christianity is operating at His proper position of authority in their lives.

The biggest problem on the earth today is that the majority of its inhabitants are proclaiming *"my will be done,"* not *"God's will be done."* As a result, the humans on this planet have their greatest desires focused on something or someone else and not toward the One True God and Creator of the universe.

We must understand that everyone has a "god" that they serve, whether they realize it or not. For some people, their god might be an object, a person, or an image; for others it could even be themselves. It is these desires that determine who the God of our life really is. As a result of these misplaced desires, God is no longer operating in His proper position of authority in their lives.

In the New Testament, when Jesus was teaching His disciples how to pray, He told them that they were to pray directly to God the Father and to make Him the priority in their life (Mt. 6:9-15).

I am completely convinced that when people begin to recognize that the Holy Bible is not just some foolish or irrational group of thoughts, but is actually the most compatible, helpful, and reliable tool ever produced for the human race's condition, and that through the study of the Holy Bible and submission to the work of the Holy Spirit and Christ, all their spiritual needs will be met and satisfied.

Again, the rejection of God and His Word is not because there is a lack of evidence to support the Holy Bible's claim of Divine Origin and Inspiration (i.e. Supernatural Intervention and Confirmation), but rather, it is due to the condition of man's heart (Ge. 6:5; Ep. 4:18). In Jeremiah 17:9 we read: *"The heart is deceitful above all things and beyond cure—who can understand it?"* Also, we read in the Gospel of Mark 7:21-23, *"21For from within the hearts of men come evil thoughts, sexual immorality, theft, murder, adultery, 22 greed, wickedness, deceit, debauchery, envy, slander, arrogance, and foolishness. 23 All these evils come from within, and these are what defile a man."*

According to the Word of God, the natural condition of man's heart is far from having a desire to obtain any sort of moral accountability towards a holy and righteous God.

Unfortunately, the undeniable facts about God are denied in an attempt to remove moral accountability from their life. British journalist Malcolm Muggeridge said,

> *"The depravity of man is at once the most empirically verifiable reality but at the same time the most intellectually resisted fact."*

Muggeridge also said,

> *"One of the peculiar sins of the twentieth century which we've developed to a very high level is the sin of credulity. It has been said that when humans stop believing in God they believe in nothing. The truth is much worse: they believe in anything."*

This is one of many reasons why the Holy Bible has received so much opposition and why people have laughed, scorned, ridiculed, and burned it and even made laws against it.[171]

The Holy Bible also tells us in the Book of Proverbs that *"there is a way that seems right to a man, but its end is the way to death"* (Pr. 14:12). Another truth found in Scripture, with regard to the fallen condition of man, is that

---
171 Ro.3:10,11; www.opendoorsusa.org/christian-persecution/world-watch-list/

the heart of man has become spiritually dead (Ep. 4:18) and, as a result, has become spiritually blind (2Co. 4:3, 4) and needs to experience a rebirth.[172] Without that rebirth, it is impossible to please God, but the Holy Bible also tells us that if we diligently seek Him, He will reward those who do (He. 11:6).

When the desire to draw close to the One True God, through prayer and the reading of Scripture is removed from the human consciousness, then truth becomes suppressed (Ro. 1:18), and people are essentially saying by their actions that the One True God does not exist. As a result, they fashion beliefs according to their own feelings, aspirations, and desires without any absolute moral standards of right or wrong. Without these absolute moral standards, people begin to assume that they are free to act any way they want. If you try to suggest to them a better way in Jesus Christ, they accuse you of being narrow-minded or guilty of bigotry because you are unwilling to agree with another philosophy or teaching that is contrary to the clear teachings of the Holy Bible (Col. 2:8).

As the majority of these people try to understand themselves independently apart from God, they will give their devotion to the other gods in this life. Because of this decision, there will always remain emptiness in their heart because the god they are serving is unable to fill the Christ-shaped void that exists in their heart, soul, and spirit. If they try to put anything else inside their Christ-shaped void, it won't fit. It won't fill the need they have inside their heart, soul, and spirit; and they will try to cover their feelings of guilt, shame, unworthiness, and insecurities by increasing the quantity of achievements and activities in their lives.

However, the more time they spend in their good and loving activities that help others, the more they will drift toward the false understanding that God's love is something that can be earned through work, commitment, and dedication, like a paycheck or an award. The reasons for these feelings are basically because the majority of these people misunderstand the love, purpose, character, and true nature of God.

Let's look at the seven attributes of God so we can better understand this topic from a correct Biblical perspective:

---

172 Jn. 3:3; 1Pe. 1:23; Jn. 2:14-16; 2Co. 5:17-19.

1. **God is Love** It's true that the Holy Bible tells us that God is love and that He loves us, but God's love is more than just an attribute; it is a part of His essence (1Jn. 3:1; 4:7-21; Ro. 5:8; 1Ti. 4:10; Ps. 86:15). God's love is the highest expression of love in existence. It is a pure, perfect, holy, just, selfless, unconditional love that involves faithfulness and commitment. The word for God's love in the Greek language is "Agape."
Agape love is used 106 times throughout the New Testament and is beautifully described in 1 Corinthians 13: 4-8:

⁴Love is patient, love is kind. It does not envy, it does not boast, it is not proud. ⁵It is not rude, it is not self-seeking, it is not easily angered, it keeps no account of wrongs. ⁶Love takes no pleasure in evil, but rejoices in the truth. ⁷It bears all things, believes all things, hopes all things, endures all things. ⁸Love never fails.

2. **God is Sovereign** He is the Supreme Authority and all things are under His control. He is the Creator of the universe. As the Creator, He is the Incontestable Owner and Possessor of the universe and everything in it. God is subject to no one and no one can tell God what to do or judge His actions (Ro. 9:1-25; Ps. 115:3; 135:6). He has the absolute right and full authority to do or allow whatever He desires.

3. **God is Holy** He is "set apart." God is set apart from all other things and is 100% pure in everything. He is set apart because of Who He is. His very nature and attributes set Him apart as unique from all else, and holiness is His central attribute (Ps. 99:9; 33:21; 77:13; 89:18).

4. **God is Omnipotent** He is all-powerful. There is no limit to His might (Is. 43:13; Jb. 42:2).

5. **God is Omniscient** He knows everything. He knows our thoughts, our sins, our innermost desires (He. 4:13), and He knows our destiny. Nothing can be hidden from Him (Jb. 34:21-23). God also has foreknowledge, which is a concept with two aspects—prescience and preacquaintance. Prescience refers to God's knowledge of events, situations, and persons in general, before they happen or come into being (Is. 42:9). Preacquaintance[173] refers to God's personal foreknowledge of

---

[173] Definition of preacquaintance: www.collinsdictionary.com

His people. He knows them in an intimate, personal sense—meaning He does not just know about them, He knows them (Je. 1:5; Ro. 8:29; 11:2-5; 1Pe. 1:1-2).
6. **God is Immutable** God does not change (He. 6:17; 13:8; Mal. 3:6; Ja. 1:17).
7. **God is Wrathful** It's a scary thing when you start to think about an all-powerful God Who gets angry. But God turns aside His wrath (applies propitiation) for believers through the blood of Christ (Ro. 3:25-26; 5:8-9).

Because God's wrath toward sin is so great, He sent His Son to die for those who would be redeemed. When humans deny the Gospel Message, they are essentially denying the wrath of God. When we understand God's attributes and characteristics from a correct Biblical perspective, we can better understand our horrific condition, both spiritually and physically; and our desperate need for reconciliation becomes apparent.

Only Jesus Christ satisfies God's requirements—which are eternal, perfect, human, and sinless. Jesus is the Only Person Who could have been the Sacrifice for the sins of the world; and, because Christ Himself is infinite and eternal, the value of His sacrifice becomes infinite and eternal as well. Therefore, Jesus is the Only One Who could have performed this task. This is exactly the reason why Jesus is described as the Only Way to the Father and the Only Mediator between God and men in Scripture.

According to the Holy Bible, humans were created as trichotomous creatures, meaning that a human possesses a body, soul, and spirit. I want to break down these three parts of a human being so we can better understand each part's function.

The Body

The five senses of the human body are as follows:
1. Hearing
2. Vision
3. Taste
4. Smell
5. Touch

God created these five senses so that human beings can experience all the things capable of being perceived. In other words, humans can exist and experience all the things in our physical reality that God created for them. It is through our body that we experience things in the physical realm, but the Holy Bible tells us that we are more than just a physical body of flesh and bones—we also possess a soul.

The Soul

Although the soul is invisible, the Holy Bible tells us that it is as real as our physical body. It is through our soul that we experience things in the psychological realm. In fact, the Greek word for *soul* used in the Holy Bible is *psuche* which is the root word for our English word "psychology."

The soul is composed of the **mind** and is responsible for our ability to think, reason, consider, remember, and wonder. Also, it is where we get our **emotions**, which enable us to have feelings like happiness, relief, anger, and compassion. The soul is also responsible for the **will** of humans and is what enables humans to choose and make decisions.

Our ***mind, emotion, and will*** together make up our soul; and, according to the Holy Bible, we are not just a body and a soul, but we also have a spirit.

The Spirit

Although the spirit is invisible like the soul, it is through our spirit that we experience things in the spiritual realm. It's through our spirit that we can enter into a relationship with God. No other creature was created on planet Earth with this third part. Because humans have a conscience, they have the capability to determine right from wrong. Animals were not given the ability to choose right from wrong or to accept or reject salvation (Ps. 32:9). God has created only humans with the ability to make choices and to reason. The Holy Bible tells us that man, not animals, is the only creature made in the image and likeness of God. Animals were made according to their own kind (Ge.1:24-25). Therefore, man is the only creature in creation that—without Christ—will be held accountable for the rebellion against God. Although all of creation has suffered the consequences of man's rebellion, animals will not directly suffer eternally for man's rebellion—only humans—without Christ—will.

It is through our spirit that we can communicate with God, receive Him, and experience fellowship with Him, and worship Him.

The reason why God created us with a spirit is that He wants to know us intimately (Jn. 17:22-23; Ja. 4:8), He wants to have fellowship with us (Is. 43:7; 1Co. 1:9), and He wants to live within us (Jn. 15:5; Ro. 8:10; 2Co. 13:5; Ga. 2:20; 4:19). In John 4:24 we read, *"God is Spirit, and His worshipers must worship Him in spirit and in truth."*

What God desires from all human beings is that they would put Him back in His proper position of authority in their lives. He desires that they would use their three God-given parts—body, soul and spirit—as voluntary vessels in conveying and expressing His thoughts and feelings to both themselves and to others who so desperately need to hear them—planet Earth's spiritually lost and dying inhabitants.

When human beings fail to submit to Jesus Christ, they will be operating without the redemptive, transforming, and regenerating effects of the Holy Spirit within their body, soul, and spirit. As a result, all human thought, ideas, and desires will be operating from the position of a spiritually-fallen and carnal state. When this happens, making God-pleasing decisions will be completely impossible to achieve. Making God-pleasing decisions will be contingent upon our submission to the Father, Son, and Holy Spirit which includes repentance and obedience. However, once we submit to the work of God and begin our new life in Christ, then God's Spirit will live in us, we will begin to express God's desire instead of our own, and He will lead and transform every part of our body, soul, and spirit, which includes regeneration, restoration, and transformation. When we live by God's Spirit, our body, soul, and spirit will experience a new resurrected and glorified body, soul, and spirit at the End of the Age (1Co. 15:26, 53-54). The person who rejects Jesus Christ as Lord and Savior will also experience a resurrected body, soul, and spirit, but this resurrection will lead to damnation; and this resurrection is referred to in Scripture as "the second death" (Re. 2:11).

The purpose of God for our life can only be obtained through our submission to His will. We must come to God on His terms, not our own. God's purpose for us is clear and includes that we turn from our sinful rebellion against Him, submit to His will, and come to Him through the only means of atonement provided by Him through His Son, Jesus Christ. When people come to the saving knowledge of Jesus Christ through the submission to the work of the Holy Spirit, God will give them the desire and ability to please Him in the things they say, do, and think.

When this occurs, the new believer will experience new desires that glorify God in their life and exclude their own natural and carnal desires. They will have a desire to study the Scriptures, pray daily, and share their faith with others. When God's gift of the Gospel of Jesus Christ is received, then that person will begin to understand their level of moral depravity and corruption from a correct Biblical perspective as the Holy Spirit begins to transform their life through their submission and obedience to the Father. When this happens, then the realization of God's amazing, redemptive gift becomes by far the most incredible gift ever bestowed upon a human being and cannot be achieved through self-effort, but can be achieved only through the work of the Holy Spirit and Christ's atoning sacrifice on His cross.

Again, for humans to experience the loving act of God's redemption in this life, it will require two conscious submissions prompted and maintained by the work of the Holy Spirit. These two submissions are 1) Repentance (2Pe. 3:9) and 2) Obedience (Jn. 3:36). These are two actions that say, "I want to come to God on His terms." They are not only critically important elements in achieving salvation, but, according to Scripture, salvation cannot be achieved without these submissions through the atoning sacrifice of God's Son, Jesus Christ (2Co, 5:21; Jn. 5:21), which are themselves a work of the Holy Spirit (Jn. 16:8-11).

Sin has hindered our ability to clearly reflect God's image in our life correctly and completely. God uses the Holy Bible and the Holy Spirit to work together to achieve a common goal, which is transforming us to better reflect the image and likeness of Jesus Christ in every aspect of our lives. This happens as we read the Holy Bible as individuals and in groups. God uses His Holy Spirit and His Word to grow us in Godliness. God has given us other Christians to learn from and to learn with as we walk through both this physical and spiritual journey called life.

We must remember that the Holy Bible is *God-breathed* (2Ti. 3:16) which means that God spoke through various human authors using their unique personalities and writing styles to communicate exactly what He wanted to say (2Pe. 1:20-21).

> [20] *Above all, you must understand that no prophecy of Scripture comes from the prophet's own interpretation.* [21] *For no prophecy was ever brought about through human initiative, but men spoke from God as they were carried along by the Holy Spirit.*

There is no part of our lives to which the Holy Bible does not speak. At the foundation of the Christian experience, there is a pattern of both repentance and faith, which are really two sides of the same coin. Repentance is turning away from our sinful rebellion, and faith is turning to God in trust for our salvation. Repentance and salvation are the two greatest words in the Christian vocabulary and are the starting and ending points in our ongoing relationship with God through His Son, Jesus Christ. The reason for this is that you can't have one without the other. You can't experience salvation without repentance. Again, the goal of our faith is salvation (1Pe. 1:9).

Jesus said in John 14:15, *"If you love me keep my commandments."* The Holy Bible makes it very clear that since the fall of Adam, sin and its consequences have spread through every part of the human race (Ge. 3; Ro. 5:12). It may seem wrong to some people to say that we are born bad and sinful. However, it's worse than that. The Holy Bible not only tells us that we are born with sin and separated from God, but that sin is not just something we do—sin is something that we *are*. Our whole being has been affected by the rebellion. The theological term for this condition is called *Total Depravity*. The Holy Bible depicts the sinful nature as a consistent theme that runs throughout its pages. The Holy Bible tells us that sin is rebellion against God and it deserves death—*"The wages of sin is death"* (Ro. 6:23). Sinful people need a mediator who can approach God on their behalf. That person is Jesus Christ Who is both God and man, Who is innocent of sin, and the Only One Who could perform this task (1Ti. 2:5, 6).

Only in an ongoing relationship with the One True God can anyone find the ultimate peace, intimacy, forgiveness, and joy for which their heart is searching. I have revealed to you the nine amazing categories of Supernatural Intervention and Confirmation for the Divine Inspiration and Authority that sets the Holy Bible apart from the sacred writings of all other worldviews.

I have shown you that all worldviews today claim to be the Inspired Word of God, but according to the well-established Law of Non-contradiction, they can't all be right. The Quran,[174] the Bhagavad Gita,[175] the Book of Mormon,[176] and many other worldviews claim to be Divinely Inspired but are unable to substantiate their claims with Supernatural Intervention and Confirmation (i.e. *Proof of Authority*) like that found in the Holy Bible.

The reason the topic of Divine Origin and Inspiration is so important is that all worldviews attempt to give answers to four of the most important and controversial questions known to man but only Biblical Christianity gives the answers to these questions with absolute consistency, accuracy, coherency, and unity.

The four most important and controversial questions known to man are these:

1. What is our purpose?
2. Where did we come from?
3. Where are we going?
4. How should we live our lives?

I want to take the four most important and controversial questions known to man and use the acronym M.O.D.E. to help you remember them. They are as follows:

- M = Meaning—What is the purpose of life?
- O = Origin—Where did we come from?
- D = Destiny—Where is mankind headed?
- E = Ethics—How should we live?

Let's take a concise look at the Biblical answers to the four most important and controversial questions known to man as they are revealed to us through Scripture.

1. Meaning: What is the purpose of life?

The Holy Bible is very clear on the answer to what our purposes are in this life. One of the most important purposes for man is to glorify God

---
174 A sacred and central religious text of Islam.
175 A sacred religious text and chief devotional for the Hindu worldview.
176 A sacred text of the Church of Jesus Christ of Latter-day Saints.

by doing His will,[177] and the most important will of God is for people to receive Jesus Christ as Lord and Savior.

We must also understand that something cannot be God's will if it's contrary or not in accordance with what is taught in His Word. The will of God for our life will always have reason and purpose, and it's only through Scripture that we find the meaning and the principles for understanding God's will. These Scriptures include the command to love one another (Jn.13:34, 35), to follow Jesus Christ at the cost of denying our own desires (Mt. 16:24), to care for the poor and needy (Ja.1:27), not to habitually sin as those who don't know God (1Th. 5:6-8), and to share the Gospel of Jesus Christ with a lost and dying world.

Another part of our purpose in this life is to know the Father through abiding in Christ. In Jesus' prayer for His disciples prior to His crucifixion, He prayed, *"I do not ask for these only, but also for those who will believe in me through their word, that they may all be one, just as you, Father, are in me, and I in you, that they also may be in us, so that the world may believe that you have sent me. The glory that you have given me I have given to them, that they may be one even as we are one, I in them and you in me, that they may become perfectly one, so that the world may know that you sent me and loved them even as you loved me. Father, I desire that they also, whom you have given me, may be with me where I am, to see my glory that you have given me because you loved me before the foundation of the world. O righteous Father, even though the world does not know you, I know you, and these know that you have sent me. I made known to them your name, and I will continue to make it known, that the love with which you have loved me may be in them, and I in them"* (Jn. 17:20-26). Jesus has given us another glimpse with regard to the unique relationship between the Father and Himself (Jn. 6:40). He told His disciples that they may all be one with Him and His Father just as He and the Father are one (Jn. 17:21, 22). Jesus is making it very clear in this passage that His desires are one and the same with His Father's desires and that Their desire is to have a relationship with people and that this relationship can only be achieved through Jesus Christ Who is the Only Mediator between God and men (1Ti. 2:5). When Jesus Christ was asked the question, *"What is the greatest commandment in the Law?"* we can see the will and purpose of God for man in His answer. He

---

177 1Jn. 2:16-17; Jn. 6:40; Ac. 22:14; Mt. 7:21; Ga. 1:4.

said, *"You shall love the Lord your God with all your heart and with all your soul, and with your entire mind. This is the first and greatest commandment. And the second greatest commandment is to love your neighbor as yourself"* (Mt. 22:36-40). When Paul and Silas were asked the question by the jailer, *"What must I do to be saved?"* we see their answer reveals the will and purpose of God as well. Incidentally, this is the most important will and purpose of God that man could ever discover in this life. They answered, *"believe in the Lord Jesus, and you will be saved"* (Acts 16:31).

The book of Psalms gives us some insight on the purpose for man as having a correct perspective in this life. King David was focusing not only on his satisfaction with God in this life, but also on the satisfaction with God in the life to come. He said, *"And I in righteousness, I will see your face when I wake, I will be satisfied with seeing your likeness"* (Ps. 17:15).

Solomon also gives us some insight with these concluding remarks in his book of Ecclesiastics (12:13, 14). This is his conclusion on the matter of purpose: *"Fear God and His commandments. For this is the whole duty of man, for God will bring every deed into judgment, including every hidden thing, whether it is good or evil."* Our purpose, according to the wisest and richest man on earth at the time, is to glorify God by fearing and obeying Him, which could also be translated "respect and submit" to God and His Will.

The Apostle Paul was a highly educated Pharisee and could speak in multiple tongues or languages (1Co. 14:18), such as Greek (Ac. 21:37), Hebrew (Ac. 21:40; 22:2), and probably Aramaic. He studied Law under the great Pharisee and teacher Gamaliel (Ac. 22:3). Most scholars believe that Paul's educational level would have been the equivalent of a PhD today. He talked about how everything that he had achieved religiously prior to his encounter with Jesus on the road to Damascus is like manure or rubbish when compared to the excellence of knowing Christ (Ph. 3:7-10). Paul says that he wants nothing more than to know Christ and "be found in Him" (Ph. 3:9), to have His righteousness, and to live by faith in Him—even if it meant suffering or dying. Paul said that his purpose in life was to know God and to know Him intimately and to live in fellowship with Him, and that this can only be obtained through our faith. This is synonymous with belief which includes obedience and commitment to Jesus Christ (2Ti. 3:12).

We receive fulfillment from God by following His purposes for our life, which enables us to experience true and lasting joy and the abundant life that He desires for us. Those who wish to give their life to the God of Biblical Christianity must first submit to the work of the Holy Spirit (Tit. 2:11, 12) by repenting of their sinful rebellion (Mk. 1:15) and come to God through the saving knowledge of Jesus Christ (Ro. 10:9, 10; Mk. 16:16). They must trust in Jesus Christ and what He did on His cross (1Co. 15:1-4) and stop trusting in what they can achieve for themselves apart from Christ (Ep. 2:8, 9).

We must seek God through His Word and through prayer. The reason for this is that God's Word is the primary way God communicates His truth to human beings and prayer is the primary way that human beings communicate their needs to God (Mt. 6:9-13).

The Holy Bible also tells us that without submission to the work of the Holy Spirit in our life, which includes repentance and obedience, that we cannot understand God's Word correctly (1Co. 2:13, 14). The Holy Bible also tells us that without repentance and obedience, the Holy Spirit will not be given because the Holy Spirit is only given to those who submit to God and obey His Word (Ac. 5:32).

This relationship with God that the Holy Bible talks about can only be achieved by submitting to the Holy Spirit. This submission is essential for the proper application of God's will in our life. Without it, the will and purpose of God can never be properly understood and implemented correctly.

Living for God means putting Him in His proper position of authority. We have to give up our desires and desire God's will above all else. Unfortunately, because of man's fall into sin, our fellowship with God has been broken. Only by restoring our fellowship with God, through faith in Jesus Christ, can our purpose in this life be rediscovered and the will of God be satisfied (Ga. 1:4; Jn. 6:40).

2. Origin: From where did we come?

In the Holy Bible, God has revealed to us our origin. We read that *God created man in His own image and likeness, in the image of God He created him; male and female He created them.*[178]

---

[178] Ge. 1:27; Mt. 19:4; Jn. 1:2-3; Col. 1:16.

When the Holy Bible uses the terminology, "created in the image and likeness of God," it is saying that people are comprised of mind, emotion, and will. We are able to perceive and feel things and have conscious knowledge of our own abilities and character or self-awareness. We are moral beings with a "moral compass" born within us, which was given to us from God as a natural orientation of "right" and "wrong." We have instinctive capacity to develop and appreciate beauty, drama, art, and story in all forms. We will naturally seek out and develop relationships and friendships with others. We are *all of this* because God is *all of this* and we are made in God's image and likeness. These above mentioned human characteristics are both consistent with what we observe about ourselves in reality and the teachings about God's nature and character found in the Holy Bible.

3. Destiny: Where is mankind headed?

Physical death is one fact about man's destiny that is unquestioned and undisputed, but what do we really know about life after death? In answering this question, we are left really with only two possible sources to consult. Either we turn to the non-Biblical religious systems with their unsupported theories for answers that are without Supernatural Intervention and Confirmation, or we can turn to the Holy Bible for answers on this topic. It is the only religious writing in history with Supernatural Intervention and Confirmation (i.e. *Proof of Authority*). For example, the Holy Bible tells us in the book of Hebrews that it is appointed for man to die once and after that comes judgment (He. 9:27), and the book of John tells us that whoever believes in God's Son may have eternal life and that without Christ man is already condemned (Jn. 3:16-18).

In the book of Matthew, we read that we should not fear those who can kill the body but fear God who can destroy both the body and the soul in hell (Mt. 10:28), and that the believer's citizenship is in heaven which will include both a new heaven and a new earth (2Pe. 3:13), and when we die, we will be in the presence of the Lord (2Co. 5:6-8) and we will have glorified bodies (Ph. 3:20-21). Jesus said, in his Father's house there are many rooms and that He is going to prepare a place for His disciples (Jn. 14:2-3).

Paul said in the book of Philippians that we should live our life for Christ and that death was far better (Ph. 1:21). In the book of 1st Corinthians, we read that nobody has seen or heard, nor the heart of man can imagine, what God has prepared for those who love him (1Co. 2:9).

The Holy Bible also talks about the destiny for those who die without Christ. In the book of Matthew, we are told that the nonbeliever will go away into eternal punishment and there would be gnashing of teeth and utter darkness (Mt. 8:12), but the righteous will go into eternal life (Mt. 25:46).

In the book of Revelation, we read that those without Christ will spend eternity in the lake that burns with fire and sulfur (Re. 21:8), and in the book of 2 Thessalonians we read that those without Christ will suffer the punishment of eternal destruction forever separated from God (2Th. 1:9).

The Holy Bible tells us everyone will exist eternally—either in Heaven or hell—when they die and everyone has only one life in which to determine their eternal destiny. Heaven or hell is determined by whether or not a person puts their trust in Jesus Christ alone to save himself or herself. I hope and pray that you choose Christ.

4. Ethics: How should we live?

The Holy Bible is all we need for determining how we should live our life. This is precisely where Biblical ethics come into play. The *Oxford Dictionary* defines ethics as, "the moral principles that govern a person's or groups' behavior; the moral correctness of specified conduct." Therefore, Biblical ethics consists of the principles derived from the Word of God. God's Word may not cover exactly every detail of a given situation, but its principles do and give us the standards by which we can conduct ourselves.

The rule is, where there are no explicit instructions, we use the principles found in Scripture. For example, the Holy Bible does not say anything explicitly about the use of illegal drugs; yet, based on the principles that we learn through Scripture, we can know it is wrong, and this is why.

The Bible tells us in 1Corinthians 6:19-20 that our body is a temple of the Holy Spirit and that we should honor God with it. Because we know that illegal drugs can cause harm to our body, then we also know that the use of them can potentially harm or destroy the temple of the Holy Spirit.

The Holy Bible also tells us that we are to submit to the authorities established by God himself (Ro. 13:1). Because of the illegal nature of drugs and by using them, we are not submitting to the authority established by

God, but actually, are rebelling against them, and this behavior is certainly not God-honoring. Does this mean that if illegal drugs were legalized that it would be okay to use them? No, because by using them we would be violating the principles found in God's Word. By using the principles found in Scripture, people will be able to determine the ethical course for any given situation.

The book of Colossians (Col. 3:1-6) summarizes Biblical ethics well, especially when it talks about setting our hearts and minds on things above and not on earthly things. It tells us to put to death whatever belongs to our earthly nature, such as sexual immorality, impurity, lust, evil desires, and greed, which is idolatry. Because of these things, the wrath of God will come.

The Holy Bible can guide us in any situation. In some cases, it will be simple, like in the book of Ephesians (Ep. 5:18) where it directly tells us not to get drunk with wine, or the rules found in Colossians 3. In other cases, it will be a bit harder and will require diligent study (2Ti. 2:15). When it comes down to it, for the answer to the question of how we should live our life, we need to look for Biblical principles that can be applied to our situation. By living through these principles, we can know how to glorify God with our lives in the things we say, do, and think. This is the reason why understanding the teachings and principles found in Scripture is so important because by doing so, we can correctly determine all the necessary Biblical elements for a healthy and well-balanced Christian worldview.

A person's worldview is formed in many ways. It is formed through our metaphysical, philosophical, and ideological reality. It can be developed through the exposure to our particular culture, which includes our education, religious beliefs, emotions, and environment. The exposure to these various realities will, in fact, dictate (either consciously or subconsciously) how we think, how we discern between right and wrong, and what we do with what is right and what is wrong. Because of this, our worldview is directly shaped by our opinions, and our worldview and opinion become synonymous. Because worldviews are like opinions and everyone has one, each person will judge every experience, every fact, and every feeling through certain internal presuppositions. This is what people mean by a worldview.

Let me put it another way: A worldview is a set of predetermined rules of reality and beliefs that someone uses to interpret and form opinions about his humanity—rules to determine purpose in life, duties in the world, responsibilities to family, interpretation of truth, social issues, etc. As a result, not everyone's worldview or interpretation of reality will be exactly the same.

Developing a correct worldview is critically important because, according to the teachings of every religion in the world, your worldview will determine where and how you will or will not spend eternity. This is why it is so important that the foundation of our belief be anchored in truth and that truth must be validated by the evidence as it relates to reality.

I've often heard people say, "How can I know which religion is the right one? I would have to study them all to find out." This is true, but really a person could save a lot of time by first looking at each religion's claim of *Proof of Authority*, which is to say what Supernatural Intervention and Confirmation evidence could be provided by a particular religion that would be sufficient to establish it as true and produce belief in its message.

I do understand that all religions have some similarities in that:
1. They all have their own versions of the truth.
2. They all give their own answer about the meaning and purpose of this life.
3. They all give their own answer to the question, "What happens after death?"
4. They all have a book or books that form the foundation of their beliefs.
5. They all were started by a spiritual leader who had developed a following.

Before we can acquire a truthful understanding to these five topics, we will need to first ask ourselves this one question: "What distinguishes truth from non-truth?"

The only way we can check the validity of a truth claim is on the basis of its evidence. The answer to the question, "What is Truth?" is always going to be contingent upon the validity of the evidence as it relates to reality.

For example, if I told you that I was wearing brown shoes and I did, in fact, have brown shoes on at the time while making that statement, you would immediately validate my claim as truthful based solely on my claim's agreement with reality; but if I had white shoes on at the time while making that statement, you would automatically think one of two things: 1) I was not being truthful, or 2) I was delusional. Why would you automatically come to such a conclusion? The reason is that my truth claim was not consistent with reality. The description of reality and reality itself must always agree with each other, and truth is always going to be the following:

1. Logically consistent.
2. Factual.
3. Viable.
4. Feasible.

Truth is always going to be characterized by clear, sound, rational reasoning and will always be factual to what is actual reality rather than our interpretations of it or reaction to it. Truth is always going to be viable in the sense that it is capable of working successfully with reality and will always be feasible. Doing what is true will always be possible to achieve easily or conveniently. However, the absence of the laws of logic from the human thought process actually becomes a necessary component in denying that truth even exists. You can run from it, pervert it, twist it, spin it, and deny it; but, at the end of the day, truth will always be truth, and it will never cease to exist. Proving something to be true always requires us to ask the right questions.

Let me ask you a question. If you automatically use this kind of logic and reasoning in everyday life on matters and issues that are eternally insignificant, like the color of my shoes, then why would you not automatically apply the same kind of logic and reasoning to important matters that have eternal significance—such as where you will spend eternity?

Is it possible that one's unbelief in the One True God is actually an unwillingness to submit to Him and His authority? Is the conscious or subconscious removal of truth and logic from the reasoning process really a necessary convenience for rejecting the truth about the One True God and His moral accountability? Again, it is very important that we understand that people do not reject God and His Truth due to a lack of evidence—they reject God and His Truth due to the condition of their heart (Je. 17:9; Mk. 7:21-23).

There is no doubt, nor may there ever be, that the Holy Bible claims Divine Origin and Inspiration as its cause. We find in the Holy Bible the repeated claim that the words and deeds it records come from a living God. In hundreds of passages, both in the Old and New Testaments, the Bible plainly declares to be the very Word of the Living God. Some 3,800 times the Bible declares, "God said," or "Thus says the Lord."

Jesus said that the words He spoke were given to Him by the Father (Jn. 17:8) and that they are truth (Jn. 17:17). Divine Origin and Inspiration is also clearly seen in Paul's letter to Timothy. We read in 2Timothy 3:16,17:

16All Scripture is God-breathed and is useful for instruction, for conviction, for correction, and for training in righteousness, 17so that the man of God may be complete, fully equipped for every good work.

The Bible tells us that the writers were speaking on behalf of the One Who claims to have authored it. The Bible explains this in 2Peter 1:21:

21For no prophecy was ever brought about through human initiative, but men spoke from God as they were carried along by the Holy Spirit.

By making such claims of itself, the Holy Bible implies that it is either inspired by God or a fraud. These are the only two choices. If these claims are true, we would expect to see evidence that is consistent with reality and beyond human capability, and this is exactly what we see in the Holy Bible.

Because God does not expect His creation to follow Him blindly, He has given us overwhelming proofs that give authority to His Message. Because of this fact, we can see Supernatural Intervention (i.e. *Proof of Authority*) established in Biblical Christianity— unlike any other worldview in history.

The internal and external evidence seen in its accuracy, unity, and coherency with reality will show the Holy Bible to be the One and Only True Word of God. I believe that I've presented a strong case for Biblical Christianity's uniqueness with regard to the human mind, laws of science, laws of logic, ethical and moral values, justice, love, the meaning to life, the problem of evil, suffering, truth, and its consistency with everyday issues in life. Biblical Christianity corresponds with the reality of our present condition unlike any other worldview on earth. It would be reasonable for us to ask ourselves at least five questions concerning the Holy Bible and Biblical Christianity:

1. How could the internal and external coherency, unity and accuracy throughout the 66 individual historical documents be achieved apart from Supernatural Intervention?
2. How could the predictive prophecy found in the Old Testament be fulfilled in the New Testament through the person of Jesus Christ with 100-percent accuracy and be achieved apart from Supernatural Intervention?
3. Who claims responsibility for the Supernatural Intervention found in the Holy Bible?
4. What is the Message and Purpose of the One Who claims responsibility for the Supernatural Intervention found in the Holy Bible?
5. Why does the proof of Supernatural Intervention only occur in the Christian and Jewish Scriptures, and not in any other religious writings in the world?

Another extraordinary thing we've seen in the Holy Bible is that it has one consistent theme through Genesis to Revelation about God's great work in the redemption of His creation through His One and Only Son Jesus Christ, Who is the Center of God's Revelation, Redemption, and the Christian Hope; and this Truth is consistent in both the Old and New Testaments.

We also have seen amazing compatibility and accuracy in scientific statements made in the Holy Bible that are consistent with reality like no other writings found in any other religion.

Another big difference that I have shown you with Biblical Christianity is in its Message and Purpose. Biblical Christianity is about

- Reconciliation[179]
- Redemption[180]
- Relationship[181]

---
179 Ro. 5:10; 2Co. 5:18-20.
180 Jn. 3:16-18; He. 9:12; Col. 1:13, 14.
181 1Ti. 2:5; He. 8:6; 9:15.

Jesus came to forgive, redeem, and reconcile mankind to God (Mk. 2:10; Ro. 3:24; Col. 1:20).

Although some Christian doctrines may transcend our comprehension, unlike the claims of other religions, they are never irrational or contradictory. In most cases, other religions contradict themselves and lack coherency, consistency, and unity in their writings.

The well-established laws of logic, particularly the Law of Non-contradiction, tell us if one proposition is known to be true, its opposite must be false. For example, if it is true that I presently exist, it cannot also be true that I presently do not exist. Even if you claim that the Law of Non-contradiction is false, you are asserting that this statement is true and its opposite is false. You end up appealing to the very law you are trying to deny, and your argument becomes self-defeating.

Uniting the *Proof of Authority* found in the Holy Bible with the laws of logic will lead to the conclusion that all other opposing worldviews cannot be true. This does not mean, however, that other religions do not contain some elements of truth in their writings. As I have already pointed out, the Holy Bible declares that all people are created in the image and likeness of God[182] and can articulate principles that are true. However, only the Holy Bible can prove its claims of Divine Origin and Inspiration through its *Proof of Authority* (i.e. Supernatural Intervention and Confirmation). All other claims of Divine Origin and Inspiration made by other belief systems, without evidence of *Proof of Authority* as the Holy Bible, are false.

I have shown you that, among all the major religious books ever written, the Holy Bible is absolutely unique. I have shown you that the Holy Bible is not just one book, but actually 66 individual books with One Amazing Unifying Message. No other religious book has ever been compiled by so many writers over such an expanse of time, with such cohesive unity and accuracy.

The Holy Bible is essentially a book about God's relationship with man throughout history and His redemptive rescue operation for mankind. It has a lot to say about the nature of man, the world, purpose, truth, and morality; but so does the world and its religions.

---

182 Ge. 1:26, 27; 9:6.

More often than not, other religions' teachings are in conflict with the views of Biblical Christianity.

For example, religion tells us that there are many paths to God, but the Holy Bible says there is only *One Way* to God.[183] The world proclaims to us that man evolved, but the Holy Bible says he was *created* by the God of Biblical Christianity and ultimately is responsible and will be held accountable to Him.

The world tells us that truth is relative, but the Holy Bible tells us that truth is absolute. The world tells us that there is no need for salvation and redemption, but the Holy Bible clearly states that we are in need of deliverance from our sinful rebellion. The differences are obvious. The list of conflicting teachings between the Holy Bible, the world's religions, and their philosophies are many. We must not forget that two opposing views cannot both be true at the same time when dealing with the same context, due to the well-established Law of Non-contradiction.

From the very beginning (Ge. 3:1-24), God made a perfect world (Ge. 1:31) for us. However, the majority of His creation has continually rejected His authority and has sought to determine truth for itself. Despite this rebellion, God promised to bestow His love (1Jn. 4:8), grace (Ro. 3:23-24), and mercy (Ps. 145:9) to an unworthy people. People only deserve His eternal judgment as the consequence of our rebellion. Instead God offers redemption to mankind as a free gift (Ep. 2:8) through the sacrifice of His One and Only Son, Jesus Christ (He. 10:10). The grace of God means that He loves, forgives, and saves us not because of what we do, or who we are, but because of Who *He* is. Biblical Christianity teaches that salvation is reliant upon God's good grace, not on our good deeds. Incidentally, the Gospel story is the only story where the superhero comes to die for the villain.

God's plan of redemption has now been permanently secured (Ac. 10:43). All man is required to do for the forgiveness of our sins is to submit to the work of the Holy Spirit by repenting, believing, and abiding in Jesus Christ (Ac. 4:12) Who is the Only Mediator between God (He, 9:15) and men (Ro. 3:23-25). Jesus removed the judgment against man and made it possible

---

183 Jn. 14:6; 17:3; Ac. 4:12; 13:38-39; 1Jn. 2:12; Ro. 3:22.

for God's enemies to reconcile to Him (Ro. 5:10), and to restore their fellowship (Col. 1:13-14), as they commit and dedicate their lives to Him out of love and adoration (Jn. 15:4-10).

In the book of Romans (Ro. 1:19-25), the Apostle Paul gives the Biblical explanation for why there are so many religions. We read that the truth of God is seen and known by every human being because God has made it so. Instead of accepting the truth about God and submitting to Him, most human beings reject it and seek their own way to understanding God.

This doesn't lead to a better understanding of God—but renders humans completely incapable of producing any truthful results in their thinking about this topic from a correct Biblical perspective. The Holy Bible frequently speaks about the concept of wisdom, knowledge, and learning. In fact, the Scriptures call for its readers to practice good thinking, and this is associated with the correct understanding and proper perspective about God (Ph. 4:8).

I think that everyone reading this book would agree that the only reason to believe something is that it is true—no other reason. Because belief is a matter of the will, no matter how much logical evidence is presented, some will still choose to deny God and miss the One and Only True Path to reconciliation with Him. The decision to embrace the truth about God is important for the simple reason that eternity is an awfully long time to be wrong.

This book was written in an attempt to reach a lost and dying world with the truth of the One True God as it has been revealed through the Person of Jesus Christ, His Word, and creation. The evidence shown to you in this book is not hidden but is in plain sight for all to find.

Again, people do not reject God and His Truth due to a lack of evidence; they reject God and His Truth due to the condition of their heart (Je. 17:9-10).

Do all Religions Lead To God?

According to www.census.gov, the U.S. population is just over 330 million, the world population is just under 7.8 billion as of February 2021, and the death rate on planet earth is still 100-percent. Statistics show that worldwide approximately 250,000 people die every day—that translates to about 11,000 people per hour or 180 people per minute or three people per second, which means that no matter what religion we embrace, everyone will meet God after death (He. 9:27). The answer to the question "Do all religions lead to God?" is actually, "Yes." All religions will lead to God, but only one religion will result in God's forgiveness and acceptance. Only through faith in His Son, Jesus Christ can anyone approach Him with the confidence of forgiveness, salvation, and eternal life. This is why right thinking about God is so critically important because— again I emphasize to you—eternity is an awfully long time to be wrong.

The Worldview Puzzle

When it's all said and done, the truth about God can be found and the worldview puzzle can be successfully pieced together by simply testing each puzzle piece and truth claim and systematically pushing aside false pieces of the puzzle so that only true pieces of the puzzle remain.

Using correct logic and reasoning together with the right questions will lead to truthful and reasonable conclusions about religion, the world, and God. Again, within the pages of the Holy Bible, God has revealed to us His plan of salvation,[184] His will for mankind,[185] the futility of our works,[186] and the proof of His authority in validating His truth claims.

According to the Holy Bible, our correct understanding about the relationship between God and human beings is really the whole reason and purpose for human existence. If people want to know about the specifics of God's will for their life, they must have knowledge about Biblical Truth which is essential for the correct understanding about this topic. The essential truths necessary for understanding God's will and purpose in the life of humans can only be found within the pages of the Holy Bible. Human beings must come to God on *His* terms, not their own, and the reason for this is that He is God and we are not.

God's truth is here for all to see, and I hope you will agree that there is no other faith on the planet that can match the mountain of evidence that exists for the reality of the Biblical Judaic/Christian God. Because the majority of people have rebelled against God, they have become His enemy. Jesus

---

[184] Jn. 1:12; 3:16-18; 1Jn. 5:11, 12; Ro. 3:23; 5:8.
[185] Jn. 3:16; 2Pe. 3:9; Mt. 5:8; 22:37-39; 1Th. 4:3; 5:16-18; 2Chr. 16:9; Ps. 40:8; Pr. 3:5; Ro. 8:29.
[186] Ro. 3:10; Ep. 2:8-9; Tit. 3:5-7; Ro. 1:4; 4:1-5, 25; 2Co. 5:21; 1Pe. 3:18.

made it possible for God's enemies to reconcile with Him and has revealed this important truth to a lost and dying world. He did this with one incredible, unifying theme about grace and forgiveness for sinners by God through the redeeming work of His Son, Jesus Christ. Without the submission to the Holy Spirit and to the saving knowledge of Jesus Christ abiding within us, a person cannot discern the things of God and obtain salvation (1Co. 2:14; Jn. 3:16-18; 1Ti. 3:5; 1Jn. 1:9, 10).

The Holy Bible tells us that the Creator of the universe loved His creation so much that He became flesh like us, dwelt among us (Jn. 1:14), and died for us to save us (Jn. 3:16-18) from the eternal consequences of our sinful rebellion (Ro. 6:23). Paul Washer has so eloquently put it in this way: *"God has saved us **for** Himself, God has saved us **by** Himself, and God has saved us **from** Himself."* What amazes me is that He has performed this incredible act of love while man was in rebellion against Him (Ro. 5:8).

The Bottom Line

The God of Biblical Christianity is unimaginably perfect, merciful, righteous, and just (De. 32). All that we have and all that we own is a testimony of His goodness, love, and grace (Ja. 1:17). Every breath that we take and every beat of our heart is a gift from God (Ac. 17:28). The God of Biblical Christianity is a wonderful God, and He is worthy of our utmost admiration and honor.

Fellowship with God is a privilege and a great blessing, and there is nothing greater in this life that a person can achieve. When we know God, we are granted the ability to experience His amazing characteristics and attributes and to be blessed through our relationship with Him.

When we have a desire to seek and know God, the Holy Bible is clear that we begin to understand and experience His love and forgiveness (Ro. 5:5; 1 Jn. 1:9), hear His voice (Jn. 10:27), and feel His peace (2Th. 3:16). We can become partners in His plan and purpose (1Pe. 2:9), experience His freedom (Ro. 6:4), and rest in His Presence (Ps. 16:11). When we focus our lives on knowing and abiding in God through His Holy Word, we can experience Him like we do in any other relationship. For example, I don't desire to just hear my wife's voice; rather, I desire to know her through conversation and to participate in real interaction with her as a consequence of that communication. I don't desire just the emotion of love from my wife; rather, in getting to know her and walking in relationship with her, I experience her affections and feelings toward me. The same is true in our relationship with God. When we seek to know Him, we experience His love, peace, freedom, and rest through our relationship with Him.

That's why our fellowship with God through Jesus Christ should be the number one priority in our life. Jesus Christ said in John 8:31, 32 that, *"If you continue in My word, you are truly My disciples. 32 Then you will know the truth, and the truth will set you free,"* and in John 14:15 Christ said, *"If you love Me, you will keep My commandments."* These verses are telling us that Jesus is not just satisfied with a mere intellectual understanding about Himself or even our profession of faith alone, but He requires repentance, obedience, and commitment.

The first most important thing a person can achieve in this life, according to the Holy Bible, is to receive Jesus Christ as Lord and Savior. The second most important thing a person can achieve in this life, according to the Holy Bible, is to share Jesus Christ as Lord and Savior. Once people become believers and place their trust in Christ, then the Holy Spirit will come and take residency within them (Ep. 5:17-21), and then they will be able to understand the Words of Christ as they let His Word dwell in them richly in all wisdom (Col. 3:16).

The majority of the Christian churches today have minimized the importance of discipleship and evangelism. Jesus Christ told His disciples in Matthew 28:19, 20, *"19 Go therefore and make disciples of all nations, baptizing them in the name of the Father and of the Son and of the Holy Spirit, 20 teaching them to observe all that I have commanded you."* I think because of the minimizing of Christ's command to evangelize and make disciples, that many self-professing Christians are setting themselves up for hearing these words from Christ: *"Away from me, I never knew you"* (Mt. 7:23). Our greatest opportunity is set before us in the Person of Jesus Christ. If we choose to follow Him according to His commands, with everything we have, we can expect to hear these words from Christ: *"Well done, good and faithful servant"* (Mt. 25:21). The choice is ours.

Biblical Christianity teaches that salvation comes by grace through faith in Jesus Christ, that it is a gift from God, and it can't be earned apart from our submission to the work of the Holy Spirit and obedience to Jesus Christ (Ep. 2:8). The logical outworking of true conversion will always include the desire to evangelize and to make disciples. If evangelism and discipleship is absent from the Christian experience, then our reconciliation through Christ must be re-evaluated (Mt. 28:18-20).

The Biblical Judaic/Christian worldview is the only belief system in the world that has *Proof of Authority* attached to its Message which cannot be separated from it.

A Matter of Life and Death

The Holy Bible is clear that human beings have a huge problem—that problem is called sin (Ro. 3:23)—and because of our sin there is a high price that needs to be paid (Ro. 6:23). Once you realize the severity of your problem Biblically, then and only then, can you begin to understand the value of God's only Solution for this problem. Knowing that the One and Only Solution for the human condition is available to us as a free gift from God in the Person of Jesus Christ is the most important piece of information that you can ever receive or obtain in this life (Jn. 3:16-18).

Our relationship to Jesus Christ will determine the answers to the two most important questions in this life (1Jn. 5:13):

1. What happens after I die?
2. Where will I spend eternity?

The events of 2020/2021 have been very difficult, to say the least, with the U.S. government's mishandling of the COVID-19 pandemic to the recent Presidential election controversy, the disinformation of the mainstream media, Hollywood's acceptance of the LGBTQ agenda, and the acceptance of abortion. From 1973–2018, more than 61.8 million babies have been aborted in the U.S. In 2018 only, the U.S. aborted 862,320 babies. That is more than 2,362 abortions per day in America, more than 98 abortions per hour, or one abortion every 32 seconds. Major cities in America are being wrecked and ruined through open lawlessness and rebellion. These are all signs of a culture that has reached rock-bottom in their corrupt and evil condition (Mt. 15:19; Mk. 7:21-23). The Apostle Paul talked about this in Romans 1:21-32. These people not only commit and approve of wickedness and evil, but they demand that everyone participate in their public glorification of it. Our culture's dilemma is a deep, spiritual one that goes far below the surface of our physical reality and can't be fixed through politics. No political party can fix this problem and that's because humans are a fallen creation. And remember, if righteousness could come through the law, then Christ died without reason (Ga. 2:21). Moreover, Christ is not trying to restore a culture. He is calling out a people unto Himself (Ac. 15:14).

I hope and pray that when you study the Holy Bible, you'll find what millions of people have discovered throughout the centuries, and that is that you're reading the authentic Word of the One and Only True Living God!

You have seen and read the evidence found in God's Word for *Proof of Authority*. Now you must decide for yourself—the choice is yours.

I hope and pray that the information presented in this book has helped you to better understand the uniqueness found only in the Holy Bible and Biblical Christianity, and as a result, you will submit to the Work and Message of the One True God and come to Him through the saving knowledge of His Son, Jesus Christ. Amen.

In Christ's service,
David Wayne Meeker

RATIONALIZATIONS OF UNBELIEF

I'M NOT GOOD ENOUGH.

Hebrews 7:25 Therefore He is able to save completely those who draw near to God through Him, since He always lives to intercede for them.

Isaiah 1:18 "Come now, let us reason together," says the LORD. Though your sins are like scarlet, they will be as white as snow; though they are as red as crimson, they will become like wool.

THERE'S TOO MUCH TO SURRENDER.

Mark 8:36 What does it profit a man to gain the whole world, yet forfeit his soul?

1John 2:15 Do not love the world or anything in the world. If anyone loves the world, the love of the Father is not in him.

1John 2:16 For all that is in the world—the desires of the flesh, the desires of the eyes, and the pride of life—is not from the Father but from the world.

1John 2:17 The world is passing away along with its desires, but whoever does the will of God remains forever.

I'M AFRAID I COULDN'T CONTINUE INDEFINITELY.

1Peter 1:5 who through faith are protected by God's power for the salvation that is ready to be revealed in the last time.

Philippians 1: 6 For I am confident of this, that He who began a good work in you will continue to perfect it until the day of Christ Jesus.

I'M AFRAID OF WHAT OTHER PEOPLE MIGHT PRESUME.

Matthew 10:32 Therefore everyone who confesses Me before men, I will also confess him before My Father in heaven.

Matthew 10:33 But whoever denies Me before men, I will also deny him before My Father in heaven.

NOT NOW, MAYBE LATER.

Proverbs 27:1 Do not boast about tomorrow, for you do not know what a day may bring.

2Corinthians 6:2 For He says: "In the time of favor I heard you, and in the day of salvation I helped you." Behold, now is the time of favor; now is the day of salvation!

I'M DOING THE BEST I POSSIBLY CAN.

Ephesians 2:8 For it is by grace you have been saved through faith, and this not from yourselves; it is the gift of God,

Ephesians 2:9 not by works, so that no one can boast.

Ephesians 2:10 For we are God's workmanship, created in Christ Jesus to do good works, which God prepared in advance as our way of life.

Isaiah 64:6 All of us have become like one who is unclean, and all our righteous acts are like a polluted garment; we all wither like a leaf, and our iniquities carry us away like the wind.

I'M NOT THAT BAD.

James 2:10 Whoever keeps the whole Law but stumbles at just one point is guilty of breaking all of it.

Isaiah 53:6 We all like sheep have gone astray, each one has turned to his own way; and the LORD has laid on Him the iniquity of us all.

GOD WILL NOT JUDGE ANYONE.

John 3:18 Whoever believes in Him is not condemned, but whoever does not believe has already been condemned, because he has not believed in the name of God's one and only Son.

John 3:36 Whoever believes in the Son has eternal life. Whoever rejects the Son will not see life. Instead, the wrath of God remains on him."

Hebrews 9:27 Just as man is appointed to die once, and after that to face judgment,

HOW DO I KNOW GOD WILL NOT EXCLUDE ME?

John 6:37 Everyone the Father gives Me will come to Me, and the one who comes to Me I will never drive away.

2Peter 3:9 The Lord is not slow to fulfill His promise as some understand slowness, but is patient with you, not wanting anyone to perish, but everyone to come to repentance.

I CAN'T COMPREHEND THE BIBLE.

1Corinthians 2:14 The natural man does not accept the things that come from the Spirit of God. For they are foolishness to him, and he cannot understand them, because they are spiritually discerned.

2Corinthians 5:7 For we walk by faith, not by sight.

HOW DO I KNOW JESUS IS THE ONLY WAY TO GOD?

John 14:6 Jesus answered, "I am the way, the truth, and the life. No one comes to the Father except through Me.

Acts 4:12 Salvation exists in no one else, for there is no other name under heaven given to men by which we must be saved."

I'D RATHER ENJOY MY LIFE TODAY.

Ecclesiastes 11:9 Rejoice, O young man, while you are young, and let your heart be glad in the days of your youth. Walk in the ways of your heart and in the sight of your eyes, but know that for all these things God will bring you to judgment.

THE COST OF FOLLOWING CHRIST IS TOO MUCH FOR ME.

Mark 8:36 What does it profit a man to gain the whole world, yet forfeit his soul?

Luke 18:29 "Truly I tell you," Jesus replied, "no one who has left home or wife or brothers or parents or children for the sake of the kingdom of God

Luke 18:30 will fail to receive many times more at the proper time—and in the age to come, eternal life."

WAS JESUS REALLY GOD?

Hebrews 1:3 The Son is the radiance of God's glory and the exact representation of His nature, upholding all things by His powerful word. After He had provided purification for sins, He sat down at the right hand of the Majesty on high.

John 10:30 "I and the Father are one."

IT DOESN'T SOUND LOGICAL.

Isaiah 55:8 "For My thoughts are not your thoughts, neither are your ways My ways," declares the LORD.

Isaiah 55:9 "For as the heavens are higher than the earth, so My ways are higher than your ways and My thoughts than your thoughts."

1 Corinthians 1:18 For the message of the cross is foolishness to those who are perishing, but to us who are being saved it is the power of God.

1Corinthians 1:23 but we preach Christ crucified, a stumbling block to Jews and foolishness to Gentiles,

I'LL TAKE THE RISK.

Hebrews 10:31 It is a fearful thing to fall into the hands of the living God.

Luke 12:16 Then He told them a parable: "The ground of a certain rich man produced an abundance.

Luke 12:17 17 So he thought to himself, 'What shall I do, since I have nowhere to store my crops?'

Luke 12:18 Then he said, 'This is what I will do: I will tear down my barns and will build bigger ones, and there I will store up all my grain and my goods.'

Luke 12:19 19 Then I will say to myself, 'You have plenty of good things laid up for many years. Take it easy. Eat, drink, and be merry!'

Luke 12:20 20 But God said to him, 'You fool! This very night your life will be required of you. Then who will own what you have accumulated?'

Luke 12:21 This is how it will be for anyone who stores up treasure for himself but is not rich toward God."

I DON'T BELIEVE IN JESUS CHRIST.

Romans 3:3 What if some did not have faith? Will their lack of faith nullify God's faithfulness?

Acts 4:12 Salvation exists in no one else, for there is no other name under heaven given to men by which we must be saved.

1Timothy 2:5-6 For there is one God and one mediator between God and men, the man Christ Jesus, 6 who gave Himself as a ransom for all—the testimony that was given at just the right time.

A BIBLICAL WORLDVIEW CREED

We believe there is a God (Is. 43:10, 11; 44:6-8; 45:5). We believe the Christian Trinity is the only God (Ge.1:26; Zec. 12:10; 2 Co. 13:14; Jn. 1:1). We believe God has revealed Himself in four ways: through creation, the Bible, the Holy Spirit, and in the person of Jesus Christ (Ro. 1:18-20; 1Co. 15:3; Jn. 5:39; 14:9; Ac. 10:43; He. 1:1-3). We believe God is the creator of the world and the universe (Ge. 1:1) and He created everything that is in it with order and design, which means that the universe is not an accident (Ge. 1; Is. 44:24; 45:18; Je. 27:5; Ne. 9:6). We believe all life on earth was created by God with a design and a purpose and life did not evolve (Ge. 1:11, 12, 21, 24, 25; 1Co. 15:38, 39). We believe the unseen supernatural world is just as real as the physical world (Ep. 6:12; Jb. 1:6; Mk. 5:2; Mt. 12:22). We believe God made man in His own image, distinct from the animals, and man did not evolve (Ge. 1:26, 27; 2:7; 1Co. 11:7). We believe Man from conception is human and possesses dignity due to being made in God's image (Jb. 31:15; Ps. 22:10; 139:13; Hos. 12:3; Lu. 1:41-44). We believe the first humans were Adam and Eve (Ge.2; Ro.5:14; 1Co. 15:22, 45; 1Ti. 2:13). We believe Adam and Eve were the first family (male and female) according to the purpose of God for procreation and glorifying Him, and homosexuality, therefore, is unnatural (Ge. 1:28; 2:21-25). We believe man is morally responsible and answerable to God (Ex. 15:26; 1Ki. 11:38; Ro. 2:16; Ps.50:6; 82:8; Ja. 1:21). We believe God gave dominion of the earth to Adam and Eve and to their descendants (Ge. 1:28; Tit. 1:7). We believe man is a steward of God's creation and is to subdue the world in a manner consistent with Biblical revelation (Ge. 1-2; 2Ti. 3:16, 17). We believe sin entered the world through

Adam and Eve (Ge. 3:1-6; Ro. 5:12-14). We believe all people have sinned and are in need of salvation (Ro. 3:23). We believe only God can save. Man cannot save himself (Mt. 19:25, 26). We believe that Jesus Christ is the only begotten Son and He lived a sinless life (2Co. 5:21; He. 4:15) and God sent Him to die for the sins of the world (Jn. 3:16-18; Jn. 4:9-10). We believe that salvation can only be obtained through individual faith in Christ's finished work on the cross (Jn. 19:30) and cannot be earned (Ep. 2:8-9). Jesus is the only way to escape the judgment of God (Ac. 4:12; Jn. 14:6). We believe the Christian Gospel is the key to the conversion of all people (1Co. 15:1-4; Mk. 8:35; 13:10; Ro. 1:16). We believe the Bible is the inspired revelation of God and correct and authoritative in all it addresses (2Ti. 3:16, 17; Ac. 17:11; Am. 3:7). We believe the Holy Bible is God's Word for mankind and is completely accurate and reflects the true and moral character of God; therefore, truth and morals are knowable and absolute, not relative (Ex. 20:1-17). We believe because of the *Proof of Authority* found only in the Holy Bible that absolute truth exists (Ps. 102:25-27; Mal. 3:6). We believe the government is ordained by God and is God's provision for order and safety in society (Ro. 13:1-7; Jn. 19:11). We believe Christians are to follow the laws of the land except where they contradict the Bible (Ac. 5:29; 4:19). We believe Christians are to evangelize the world (Mt. 28:18, 19; Ps. 22:17). We believe all areas of life are subject to God and should have Christian principles guiding them: personal, public, and political matters, as well as medicine, science, art, literature, etc. (Ge. 1:28; Mt. 28:19, 20). We believe all areas of life are a Christian mission field: family, political, medicine, science, art, literature, education, technology, economics, etc. (Ge. 1:28; Mt. 28:19, 29). We believe Satan is a real being (not symbolic) and seeks to defeat God's plan for man (1Pe. 5:8).

EXAMINE YOURSELF TEST

Examine yourselves to see whether you are in the faith; test yourselves. Can't you see for yourselves that Jesus Christ is in you—unless you actually fail the test? 2Corinthians 13:5.

1. Do you believe in Jesus Christ?
   Yes☐   No☐   Seldom☐

1John 5:13 I have written these things to you who believe in the name of the Son of God, so that you may know that you have eternal life.

1John 5:1 Everyone who believes that Jesus is the Christ is born of God, and everyone who loves the Father also loves the one born of Him.

2. Do you practice sin regularly?
   Yes☐   No☐   Seldom☐

1John 3:9 Anyone born of God refuses to practice sin, because God's seed abides in him; he cannot go on sinning, because he has been born of God.

Romans 6:1 What then shall we say? Shall we continue in sin so that grace may increase?

Romans 6:2 By no means! How can we who died to sin live in it any longer?

3. Do you study God's Word daily?
Yes☐   No☐   Seldom☐

2Timothy 2:5 Make every effort to present yourself approved to God, an unashamed workman who accurately handles the word of truth.

2Timothy 3:16 All Scripture is God-breathed and is useful for instruction, for conviction, for correction, and for training in righteousness,

2Timothy 3:17 so that the man of God may be complete, fully equipped for every good work.

4. Do you abide in Christ?
Yes☐   No☐   Seldom☐

John 15:4 Remain in Me, and I will remain in you. Just as no branch can bear fruit by itself unless it remains in the vine, neither can you bear fruit unless you remain in Me.

John 15:5 I am the vine and you are the branches. The one who remains in Me, and I in him, will bear much fruit. For apart from Me you can do nothing

5. Are you indifferent to sin?
Yes☐   No☐   Seldom☐

1John 1:6 If we say we have fellowship with Him yet walk in the darkness, we lie and do not practice the truth.

1John 1:7 But if we walk in the light as He is in the light, we have fellowship with one another, and the blood of Jesus His Son cleanses us from all sin.

1John 1:8 If we say we have no sin, we deceive ourselves, and the truth is not in us.

6. Do you obey Christ?
   Yes☐   No☐   Seldom☐

1 John 2:3 By this we can be sure that we have come to know Him: if we keep His commandments.

1 John 2:4 If anyone says, "I know Him," but does not keep His commandments, he is a liar, and the truth is not in him.

1 John 2:5 But if anyone keeps His word, the love of God has been truly perfected in him. By this we know that we are in Him:

1 John 2:6 Whoever claims to abide in Him must walk as Jesus walked.

7. Do you practice righteousness?
   Yes☐   No☐   Seldom☐

1 John 3:7 Little children, let no one deceive you: The one who practices righteousness is righteous, just as Christ is righteous.

8. Do you pray for the lost?
   Yes☐   No☐   Seldom☐

Matthew 9:37 Then He said to his disciples, "The harvest is plentiful, but the workers are few.

Matthew 9:38 Ask the Lord of the harvest, therefore, to send out workers into His harvest."

9. Do you go to church regularly?
   Yes☐   No☐   Seldom☐

Hebrews 10:25 Let us not neglect meeting together, as some have made a habit, but let us encourage one another, and all the more as you see the Day approaching.

10. Do you pray to God daily?
Yes☐   No☐   Seldom☐

1Thessalonians 5:17 Pray without ceasing.

1Thessalonians 5:18 Give thanks in every circumstance, for this is God's will for you in Christ Jesus.

1Timothy 2:8 Therefore I want the men everywhere to pray, lifting up holy hands, without anger or dissension.

11. Do you share the Gospel regularly?
Yes☐   No☐   Seldom☐

2Timothy 1:8 So do not be ashamed of the testimony of our Lord, or of me, His prisoner. Instead, join me in suffering for the gospel by the power of God.

2Timothy 1:9 He has saved us and called us with a holy calling, not because of our own works, but by His own purpose and by the grace He granted us in Christ Jesus before time eternal.

12. Do you keep yourself pure?
Yes☐   No☐   Seldom☐

1John 5:18 We know that anyone born of God does not keep on sinning; the One who was born of God protects him, and the evil one cannot touch him.

13. Do you love your neighbor?
Yes☐   No☐   Seldom☐

Matthew 22:37 Jesus declared, "Love the Lord your God with all your heart and with all your soul and with all your mind. Matthew 22:38 This is the first and greatest commandment. Matthew 22:39 And the second is like it: 'Love your neighbor as yourself.'"

14. Do you believe that Jesus is God?
   Yes☐   No☐   Seldom☐

John 1:1 In the beginning was the Word, and the Word was with God, and the Word was God.

Colossians 2:9 For in Christ all the fullness of the Deity dwells in bodily form.

15. Do you know and love Christ?
   Yes☐   No☐   Seldom☐

John 14:15 If you love Me, you will keep My commandments.

1John 2:3 By this we can be sure that we have come to know Him: if we keep His commandments.

1John 2:4 If anyone says, "I know Him," but does not keep His commandments, he is a liar, and the truth is not in him.

1John 2:5 But if anyone keeps His word, the love of God has been truly perfected in him. By this we know that we are in Him.

16. Do you worship God daily?
   Yes☐   No☐   Seldom☐

Psalm 63:3 Because Your loving devotion is better than life, my lips will glorify You.

Psalm 63:4 So I will bless You as long as I live; in Your name I will lift my hands.

Psalm 59:16 But I will sing of Your strength and proclaim Your loving devotion in the morning. For You are my fortress, my refuge in times of trouble.

17. Do you desire to serve others?
   Yes☐   No☐   Seldom☐

Galatians 5:13 For you, brothers, were called to freedom; but do not use your freedom as an opportunity for the flesh. Rather, serve one another in love.

Ephesians 6:7 Serve with good will, as to the Lord and not to men.

18. Do you love the things of this world?
   Yes☐   No☐   Seldom☐

Titus 2:12 It instructs us to renounce ungodliness and worldly passions, and to live sensible, upright, and godly lives in the present age.

1John 5:4 because everyone born of God overcomes the world. And this is the victory that has overcome the world: our faith.

1John 5:5 Who then overcomes the world? Only he who believes that Jesus is the Son of God.

19. Do you love other Christians?
   Yes☐   No☐   Seldom☐

1John 3:14 We know that we have passed from death to life, because we love our brothers. The one who does not love remains in death.

John 13:34 A new commandment I give you: Love one another. As I have loved you, so also you must love one another.

John 13:35 By this all men will know that you are My disciples, if you love one another."

20. Do you forgive others?
   Yes☐   No☐   Seldom☐

Mark 11:26 But if you do not forgive, neither will your Father in Heaven forgive your trespasses.

21. Do you enjoy reading your Bible?
   Yes☐   No☐   Seldom☐

2Timothy 3:16 All Scripture is God-breathed and is useful for instruction, for conviction, for correction, and for training in righteousness.

2Timothy 3:17 so that the man of God may be complete, fully equipped for every good work.

22. Do you love God with all your heart, mind, soul, and strength?
   Yes☐   No☐   Seldom☐

Mark 12:30 and you shall love the Lord your God with all your heart and with all your soul and with all your mind and with all your strength.

23. Do you desire to serve the Lord?
   Yes☐   No☐   Seldom☐

Romans 12: Do not let your zeal subside; keep your spiritual fervor, serving the Lord.

24. Do you confess your sin?
   Yes☐   No☐   Seldom☐

1John 1:9 If we confess our sins, He is faithful and just to forgive us our sins and to cleanse us from all unrighteousness.

Romans 6:1 What then shall we say? Shall we continue in sin so that grace may increase?

Romans 6:2 By no means! How can we who died to sin live in it any longer?

25. Is your life dedicated to Jesus?
   Yes☐   No☐   Seldom☐

Matthew 10:33 But whoever denies Me before men, I will also deny him before My Father in heaven.

Matthew 16:4 Then Jesus told His disciples, "If anyone would come after Me, he must deny himself and take up his cross and follow Me.

26. Do you believe that Christ is the only way to Heaven?
    Yes☐   No☐   Seldom☐

John 14:6 Jesus answered, "I am the way, the truth, and the life. No one comes to the Father except through Me.

1 Timothy 2:5 For there is one God and one mediator between God and men, the man Christ Jesus.

THE THREE STEPS OF BECOMING A CHRISTIAN

1. *Repent*
Admit to God that you are a sinner. Repent, and turn away from your sin.
- Romans 3:23 *for all have sinned and fall short of the glory of God,*
- Romans 3:24 *and are justified by his grace as a gift, through the redemption that is in Christ Jesus.*
- Romans 6:23 *For the wages of sin is death, but the free gift of God is eternal life in Christ Jesus our Lord.*
- Acts 3:19 *Repent therefore, and turn again, that your sins may be blotted out.*
- 1John 1:9 *If we confess our sins, he is faithful and just to forgive us our sins and to cleanse us from all unrighteousness.*

2. *Believe*
Believe that Jesus Christ is God's Son and accept God's gift of forgiveness from sin.
- John 3:16 *For God so loved the world, that he gave his only Son, that whoever believes in him should not perish but have eternal life.*
- John 3:17 *For God did not send his Son into the world to condemn the world, but in order that the world might be saved through him.*
- John 3:18 *Whoever believes in him is not condemned, but whoever does not believe is condemned already, because he has not believed in the name of the only Son of God.*
- John 14:6 *Jesus said to him, "I am the way, and the truth, and the life. No one comes to the Father except through me."*

- Act 4:12 *And there is salvation in no one else, for there is no other name under heaven given among men by which we must be saved.*
- Romans 5:8 *but God shows his love for us in that while we were still sinners, Christ died for us.*
- Ephesians 2:8 *For by grace you have been saved through faith. And this is not your own doing; it is the gift of God,*
- Ephesians 2:9 *not a result of works, so that no one may boast.*
- John 1:11 *He came to his own, and his own people did not receive him.*
- John 1:12 *But to all who did receive him, who believed in his name, he gave the right to become children of God,*
- John 1:13 *who were born, not of blood nor of the will of the flesh nor of the will of man, but of God.*

3. *Confess*
Confess your faith in Jesus Christ as Savior and Lord.
- Romans 10:9 *because, if you confess with your mouth that Jesus is Lord and believe in your heart that God raised him from the dead, you will be saved.*
- Romans 10:10 *For with the heart one believes and is justified, and with the mouth one confesses and is saved.*
- Romans 10:13 *For "everyone who calls on the name of the Lord will be saved."*

TERMS AND DEFINITIONS

Adoption   The giving to anyone the same name and privileges of a child who is not a child by birth. This term is found in the New Testament in Paul's letters. It is the process by which a man or woman might be brought into God's family with all the same benefits and privileges through Jesus Christ. (Jn. 1:12; Ep. 1:5; Ga. 3:26; 4:5; Ro. 8:15, 23.)

Apologetics   The English word comes from a Greek root meaning "to defend, to make reply, to give an answer, to legally defend oneself." In the New Testament times *apologia* was a formal courtroom defense of something (2Ti. 4:16).

Apostle   A title referencing any of Jesus' 12 disciples after the resurrection of Christ, but sometimes references other Christ-followers with whom Jesus revealed Himself physically after the resurrection, such as Paul (Ac. 9:1-19; 22:6-21; 26:12-18).

Atonement   The repair of the broken relationship between God and man restored by the death and resurrection of Jesus Christ (Ex. 12:5; Le. 17:11; Is. 53:3-12; Lu. 4:18, 19; Jn. 3:16; 10:17; Ac. 20:28; Ro. 3:23-25; 1Co. 7:23; 15:3; Ep. 2:13; Col. 1:12, 13; Tit. 2:14; He. 9:22; 1Pe. 2:21-24; 3:18).

Belief   The thing believed. Our belief is only as true, reliable, and good as the object in which it is placed. Christ is the object in which Christian belief is placed. Our Christian belief is in the person of Jesus Christ. (Mk. 1:15; Ac. 20:21; Ro. 10:9; 2Th. 2:13.)

Body of Christ   Christians make up the Body of Christ (1Co. 12:27). Jesus is the head of the Body (Col. 1:18) and should be the center of everything we say, do, and think (Mt. 18:20). The Body of Christ meets together to pray

(Ep. 6:18), worship (Ex. 34:14), share in suffering (2Ti. 2:3), encourage (Ep. 4:12), and teach (2Ti. 2:2) about Christ in love (Jn. 13:34) and unity (Ep. 4:3). The Body of Christ is responsible for the preaching of the Gospel to others (Mt. 28:18, 19) with gentleness and respect (1Pe. 3:15).

Conversion The moment an individual repents and places their faith upon Jesus for their salvation. When they are declared righteous and forgiven by God, thus converted from being far from God to now being accepted and justified in Christ (2Chr. 7:14; Jn. 3:5; Ac. 2:38; Ro. 12:2; Ep. 4:22; 2Co. 5:17; Re. 3:20).

Covenant A treaty, or promise, between two people or groups. Biblically, it is a promise made by God to His people for salvation (Je. 31:31-34; Mt. 26:28; Lu. 22:20; He. 8:6, 8; 9:15; 12:24; 13:20; 1Co. 11:25).

Cult A cult is a religious group that denies one or more of the fundamentals of Biblical truth. Specifically, it is a group that claims to be Christian, but whose teachings, if believed, would prevent someone from having a saving relationship with Jesus Christ (1Ti. 6:20; Col. 2:8).

Disciple A person who follows a teacher. This person does what their teacher says to do (Jn. 14:15; Lu. 11:28; 1Jn. 5:3; 1Ti. 6:14; Ja. 1:22).

Doctrine A statement(s) describing a set of beliefs that is grounded in the Word of God and are theologically sound.

Doubt A lack of faith or a trust in something or someone. To not be sure (Pr. 3:5-8; Mt. 21:21; Ja. 1:5-8; Mk. 11:22-25; He. 11:6).

Doxology The study or act of worship by which believers ascribe worth, glory, and praise to God.

Election In the New Testament it occurs six times (Ro. 9:11; 11:5; 11:7, 28; 1Th. 1:4; 2Pe. 1:10). In all these passages it appears to denote an act of Divine selection upon human beings to bring them into a special and saving relationship with God.

Evil Bad. Wicked. Doing things that do not please God (Is. 5:20; Pr. 8:13; Ro. 3:23; 12:9; Ep. 6:12; 1Th. 5:22).

Expiation The prefix *ex* means "out of" or "from," so *expiation* has to do with removing something or taking something away. In Biblical terms, it has to do with taking away guilt through the payment of a penalty or offering of atonement.

Fact An isolated piece of information that is indisputable. Information used as evidence or as part of a news report, news article or evidence in a legal court case.

Faith The on-going and personal commitment to trust and believe. What we believe. We can only be a Christian if we have faith in Christ (Ep. 3:7; Ga. 3:26). Our faith is the relationship we have with God through Jesus Christ (Jn. 14:6). Faith justifies not on its own worthiness and value, but by the worthiness and value of Him in Whom is our faith (Ac. 20:21; Col. 2:9). Faith makes the connection by which our sin is imputed to Christ, and Christ's righteousness is imputed to us (2Co. 5:19, 21; 1Co. 1:30). Without faith, we cannot please God (He. 11:6). We are saved by grace through faith in Christ (Ep. 2:8, 9).

Father, The God. The first person of the Trinity. The Father shares the same attributes and characteristics as Jesus and the Holy Spirit. He is holy (Is. 6:3; Le. 19:2), eternal (De. 33:27; Ps. 90:2), omnipresent (Ps. 139:7-12), omnipotent (Re. 19:6), omniscient (Ps. 139:2-6; Pr. 15:3), immutable (Mal. 3:6), righteous (Ps. 119:137), truth (Je. 10:10), good (Ps. 107:8), merciful (Ps. 103:8-17), gracious (Ps. 111:4), faithful (De. 7:9), and loves us (Jn. 3:16; 1Jn. 4:8).

Forgiveness An act of pardon by God through the completed work of His Son, Jesus Christ. It is a gift from God (Jn. 3:16; Ro. 6:23) through faith (Ep. 2:8, 9; Ro. 10:9, 10, 13) in Jesus Christ (Jn. 10:17). Forgiveness is promised by God when we repent of our sin and believe and trust in Jesus for our salvation (Jn. 3:16-18; 1Jn. 1:8-10), but we have to forgive others if we want God to forgive us (Ep. 4:32).

God The Creator (Ge. 1:1) of the universe and everything that exists (Ac. 17:24). The Bible teaches that there is one God (1Ti. 2:5) revealed in three persons, the Father, the Son, and the Holy Spirit (Mt. 3:16, 17;

> 1Pe. 1:2), Who all share the same attributes and characteristics. He is omnipresent (Ps. 139:7-12), omniscient (Ps. 139:2-6; Pr. 15:3), omnipotent (Re. 19:6), eternal (Ps. 45:6), holy (Is. 6:3), righteous (Ps. 119:137), merciful (Ps. 103:8-17), gracious (Ps. 111:4), faithful (De. 7:9), immutable (Mal. 3:6), truthful (Je .10:10) , spirit (Jn. 4:24), good (Ps. 107:8), and love (1Jn. 4:8).

Gospel, The Paul tells us what the Gospel is, that Christ died for our sin and was buried and rose again on the third day (1Co. 15:3,4) to save us from the eternal consequences of our sin (Jn.3:16). Salvation is a gift from God through faith in Jesus Christ (Ro. 6:23) because He loves us. The Gospel is the grace of God (Ac. 20:24). (Jn. 3:16-18; Ro. 1:16; Ac. 13:47; 16:17; 1Co. 15:2-6; Ep. 1:7; 1Co. 1:30.)

Grace The loving act of God in a person's life, making possible their salvation, sanctification, and justification. It is by grace that God makes salvation possible through His Son, Jesus Christ's death and resurrection (Ro. 6:23) and it's through grace that He sustains the Body of Christ (Ex. 34:6; Ep. 1:7, 8; 2:8, 9; 1Pe. 1:13). Grace is a gift from God (Ro. 3:24). God's grace is revealed in His Gospel (Ac. 20:24).

Heaven The dwelling place of God and the hope and destiny of believers of Jesus Christ either by way of the grave or His coming (Is. 25:8; Mt. 5:17-20; 7:13,14; Jn. 14:2,3; 2Co. 5:2; He. 8:1; Col. 1:5; Ph. 1:23; 3:7; 2Pe. 3:13; Re. 7:17; 21:4; 22:5).

Hell A permanent place of torment for those who are condemned by sin because of their rejection of God's only provision for our sin, His Son, Jesus Christ, where they are eternally separated from God in a place of torment (Mt. 8:12; 25:41; Ro. 1:18-20; 2Pe. 2:4-9; Jude 1:7; Re. 21:8).

Hermeneutics The word *hermeneutics* comes from a Greek root meaning *"Interpreter"* or *"Interpret"*. Thus, hermeneutics is an interpretation. **Merriam-Webster Dictionary** defines hermeneutics as *"the study of methodological principles of interpretation" (as of the Holy Bible" and a method or principles of interpretation."* and is also referred to as the *Art and Science of Biblical Interpretation*. The Holy Bible commands the followers of Christ, in 2Timothy 2:15, to be involved in hermeneutics. The five basic foundational rules of hermeneutics are as follows: A) Scripture must be used to interpret itself. B) Scripture itself is its best commentary. C) Scripture must be taken literally allowing for normal use of figurative language, allegory, narrative, poetry and parables. D) Scripture must be interpreted in the context by which the passage was originally intended. Correct context will help determine the correct

meaning. E) Be sensitive to the type of literature you are reading. Biblical hermeneutics must also follow these 15 fundamental rules:
1. Understand the author (Who wrote the book?).
2. Understand the audience (Why was the book written?).
3. Understand the meaning of words (*Strong's Dictionary* is recommended).
4. Understand the historical setting.
5. Understand the grammar.
6. Understand the textual issues.
7. Understand the syntax (the set of rules for the analysis or arrangement of words and phrases to create well-formed sentences in a language).
8. Understand the form and genre of the literature (Is it legal, historical narrative, figures of speech, analogies, parables, Hebrew poetry and song, wisdom sayings and proverbs, the Gospels, prophecy, genealogy, letters or Epistles, Apocalyptic, etc.?).
9. Understand the immediate context (and remember a text out of context becomes a pretext).
10. Understand the document's context.
11. Understand the author's context.
12. Understand the Biblical context (Biblical passages must be consistent with the whole of scripture. Scripture is never contradictory of itself).
13. Understanding the difference between prescriptive and descriptive statements in the Holy Bible. (Is the verse telling us to do something, or does it describe an action someone does).
14. Build all doctrine on necessary rather than possible inferences (A necessary inference is something that is clearly taught in scripture. Its conclusion is conclusive. A possible inference is something that could or might be true, but not something actually stated by the text).
15. Interpret the unclear passages in scripture in light of the clear.

God has given us His Holy Spirit to illuminate His Word and has created us with the ability to logically reason which include, investigate, analyze and review. This is obviously one of the main reasons why God has equipped humans with the capacity for clear and sound reasoning in conducting or assessing factually based information according to strict principles of validity. Biblical interpretation implements the same rules found in the logical reasoning process. He has also given us many people throughout history to help us interpret His Word, which includes, gifted and anointed Bible teachers (Ep. 4:8-12).

Hypothesis A proposition not yet tested to the point of general acceptance. An unscientifically supported theory.

Holy Spirit, The God. The third person of the Trinity active in creation (Ge. 1:2; Jb. 33:4; Ps. 104:30) and throughout history, indwelling believers (Ro. 8:11) and directs and guides the Church (Jn. 16:12, 13) and is the Source of Scripture. The Holy Spirit shares the same attributes and characteristics in Scripture as the Father and Jesus Christ. He is omnipresent (Ps. 139:7-10), omniscient (Jn. 14:26; 16:12,13), omnipotent (Lu. 1:35), eternal (He. 9:14), holy (Ro. 1:4), merciful (Ga. 5:22), immutable (Ga. 4:6), truthful (Jn. 16:13), and He teaches (Jn. 14:26), leads us (Ro. 8:14), gives us joy (1Th. 1:6), seals us (Ep. 4:30), intercedes for us (Ro. 8:26), regenerates us (He. 9:14), reminds us (Jn. 14:26), reveals to us (1Co. 2:10), communes with us (2Co. 13:14; 1Jn. 3:24), convicts us (Jn. 16:8-11) loves us (Ro. 5:5; 15:30; Ga. 5:22), is involved in salvation (Tit. 3:5), and sanctifies us (Ro. 15:16). The Holy Spirit's ministry is both personal and permanent (Jn. 14:16-17).

Imago Del The Latin translation of "image of God," this term is used to describe God creating mankind in His image and likeness (Ge. 1:26-28), resulting in every single person having immense worth, value, and the unique ability to reflect and connect with God the Creator.

Image of God When the Bible uses the terminology "created in the image of God" (Ge. 1:26-28), it is talking about how people are made in God's image, comprised of mind, emotion, and will. We are able to perceive and feel things and have conscious knowledge of our own abilities and character or self-awareness. We are moral beings with a "moral compass" inborn within us, which was given to us from God, as a natural orientation of "right" and "wrong." We have an instinctive capacity to develop and appreciate beauty, drama, art, and story in all forms. And we will naturally seek out and develop relationships and friendships with others. We are all this because God is all this and we are made in God's image and likeness. All these conclusions are consistent with what we observe about ourselves in reality and the overall teachings of the Holy Bible.

Jesus Christ God. The second person of the Trinity. The Creator of the universe and everything that exists (Jn. 1:1-3; Col. 1:16, 17). He is sinless (2Co. 5:21; 1Jn. 3:5). Jesus shares the same attributes and characteristics in Scripture as the Father and Holy Spirit. He is omnipresent (Mt. 18:20; 28:18-20), omniscient (Jn. 16:30; 21:17), omnipotent (He. 1:3), eternal (Jn. 1:1,2; 17:5,24), holy (Lu. 1:35), righteous (1Jn. 2:1), merciful (Jude 1:21), faithful (Re. 1:5), immutable (He. 13:8), truthful (Jn. 14:6), good (Lu. 18:18,19), gracious (1Pe. 2:3), and loves us (Jn. 15:13; Ga.2:20). Jesus is called God in the New Testament (Jn. 1:1; 10:20-33; 20:28; Ro. 9:5; Col. 2:9; Tit. 2:13; He. 1:8).

Judgment God will bring every work and secret thing into judgment, whether good, or evil, believer or non-believer (Da. 7:10; Jb. 34:23; Ps. 9:7; Ec. 3:17; 11:9; 12:14; Mal. 3:5; Mt. 12:36; 25:32; Jn. 5:24; 7:24; Ro. 14:10; 1Co. 3:12-15; 2Co. 5:10; 2Ti. 4:8; He. 9:27; 12:23; Re. 11:18; 20:11-15).

Justification The gift of God by which He restores us to a right relationship with Himself through the death and resurrection of His Son, Jesus Christ (1Jn. 2:23, 24; 5:1; 2Jn. 1:9; Ro. 3:23, 24).

Law, Scientific A statement describing how some phenomena of nature behaves. Laws are generalizations from data. They express regularities and patterns in the data. A law is usually limited in scope, to describe a particular process in nature.

Mediator Jesus Christ stands between God and man in establishing our relationship with God. Jesus is the guarantee of our relationship with God. Jesus Christ is the only mediator between God and men. (Jn. 14:6; Ac. 4:12; 1Ti. 2:5.)

Messiah A Hebrew word that means "The anointed One." It means the same thing as the Greek word "Christ." See also "Jesus."

Mercy God's mercy and compassion to help those in need or in distress. God's mercy cannot be separated from His love, grace, and faithfulness.

God's ultimate mercy was shown through His willingness to send His Son, Jesus Christ as a sacrifice for the world. (Mi. 6:8; Lu. 6:36; Ro. 11:30; Ep. 2:4; 1Ti. 1:2; 2Ti. 1:2; Tit. 3:5; 1Pe. 1:3; 2:10; Jude 1:21; 1Jn. 1:3.)

Obey To do what you are told to do. To carry out God's commands. According to Scripture, God demands that His revelation be taken as a rule for man's whole life in both heart and conduct (Je. 7:22; 1Sa. 15:22; 1Co. 14:21; Tit. 3:1). The disobedience of Adam and Eve plunged mankind into guilt, condemnation, and death (Ro. 5:19; 1Co. 15:22). Christ's unfailing obedience "unto death" (Ph. 2:8; He. 5:8; 10:5-10) won righteousness (acceptance with God) and life (fellowship with God) for all who believe on Him (Ro. 5:15-19). Faith in the Gospel and in Jesus Christ is obedience (Ac. 6:7; Ro. 6:17; He. 5:9; 1Pe. 1:22), for God commands it (Jn. 6:29; 1Jn. 3:23). A life of obedience to God is the fruit of faith (Ge. 22:18; He. 11:8; 17; Ja. 2:2). Unbelief is disobedience) Ro. 10:16; 2Th. 1:8; 1Pe. 2:8; 3:1; 4:17).

Paradise A perfect place. Another name used for Abraham's bosom or heaven (Lu. 16:19-31; 23:43; 2Co. 12:3; Re. 2:7).

Pardon The forgiveness of sins granted freely by God as a gift (Ro. 3:23) through faith in Jesus Christ (Is. 43:25; Ps. 65:3; Ps. 86:5; Is. 1:18; Eze. 36:25; Mt. 6:14, 15; 18:21-35; Col. 3:13; 1Jn. 1:8, 9).

Prayer Prayer is talking with and being with God. Through adoration, confession, thanksgiving, and supplication, believers are able to worshipfully communicate with God in order to build intimacy with Him (Je. 29:12; Ph. 4:6; Ps. 102:17; Ja. 5:16; Mt. 6:6; 26:41; Lu. 6:27-28; 1Th. 5:16-18; 1Jn. 1:9).

Propitiation The removal of God's judgment on mankind through the death and resurrection of Jesus Christ (Jn. 3:16; 1Jn. 5:3, 11).

Reconciliation Man is restored to God, through Christ, to friendship or harmony. When Christ died on the cross, He satisfied God's judgment and made it possible for God's enemies to reconcile with Him. (Ro. 5:10; 2Co. 5:18-20; Col. 1:20, 21.)

Redemption The restoring of our fellowship with God through Jesus Christ's death and resurrection (Jn. 3:16-18; He. 9:12; Col. 1:13, 14).

Regeneration Believers are new creations through their belief in the Gospel of Jesus Christ as they commit and dedicate their lives (Jn. 15:4-9) to Jesus Christ (2Co. 5:17).

Religion   Is a fundamental set of beliefs and practices generally agreed upon by a like minded group of people. These set of beliefs concern the cause, nature, and purpose of the universe and involve devotional and ritual observances. They also often contain a moral code governing the conduct of human affairs also known as a worldview (1Co. 2:1-5; Col. 2:8).

Repentance   Confession of and turning away from your sin through the conviction from the Holy Spirit (Jn.16:8) and turning to God for mercy through Jesus Christ with a desire to obey and serve Him (Eze. 18:30; Lu. 3:7, 8; 13:3-5; Ac. 2:38; 3:19; 8:22; 17:30; 2Co. 7:9,10; 2Pe. 3:9; Mt. 3:2; 4:17).

Salvation   Salvation refers to the process of sinners becoming justified, sanctified, and glorified through the death and resurrection of Jesus Christ. Deliverance from the physical and spiritual bondage of sin by God's grace through faith in Jesus Christ and His completed work on the cross. Salvation is a gift from God by grace through faith and cannot be achieved through self-effort apart from Christ. (Jn. 1:12, 13; 3:1-18; 14:6; 17:1-5; Ac. 2:37, 38; Ro. 6:23; 10:8-10; Ep. 2:1-9; Col. 1:13,14; 1Pe. 1:18,19; He. 5:9; Tit. 2:11; 2Co. 7:10; 1Th. 5:9).

Sanctification   The completing to perfection the work begun in regeneration and it extends to the whole person (Ro. 6:9, 13, 22; 1Co. 1:30; 6:19, 20; 2Co. 4:6; 1Th. 4:3; 2Th. 2:13; Col. 3:10; 1Jn. 4:7; 1Pe. 1:2).

Sin   To disobey or displease God. Lawlessness (1Jn. 3:4), the result of disobedience (Ro. 5:19) and rebellion (Is. 1:2) against God. Sin is unbelief (1Jn. 1:10). The result of sin is death (Ro. 5:12). Jesus Christ is God's remedy for sin (2Co. 5:21). Christ has saved us from the power, control, and consequences of sin, and from eternal separation from God (Ge. 3:1-19; Ps. 51; Ro. 3:23; 6:23; 1Jn. 1:8, 9).

Soul   A person's true inner self.

Theory   A supposition or system of ideas intended to explain something, especially one based on general principles independent of the thing to be explained. A model (usually mathematical) that links and unifies a broader range of phenomena, and that links and synthesizes the laws that describe those phenomena. In science they do not grant an idea the status of theory until its consequences have been very well tested.

The Trinity   The word "Trinity" is not used in the Holy Bible, but the concept is throughout. For example: **1).** Who raised Jesus from the dead? Well, it was God the Father (Ga. 1:1; 1Th. 1:10), it was also Jesus Himself (Jn. 2:19; 10:17, 18, and it was the Holy Spirit (Ro. 8:11). **2).** Who gave the new covenant? The Father (Je. 31:33, 34), Jesus (He. 8:1-13; 10:29; 12:24; 13:20), and the Holy Spirit (He. 10:15-17). **3).** Who sanctifies believers? The Father (1Th. 5:23), Jesus (He. 13:12), and the Holy Spirit (1Pe. 1:2). **4).** Who is the Creator? The Father (Ge. 1:1; Is. 44:24; Ac. 17:24; Ep. 3:9), Jesus (Jn. 1:3; Col. 1:16; He. 1, 10), and the Holy Spirit (Jb. 33:4). **5).** Who indwells believers? The Father (1Co. 3:16a; 2Co. 6:16; 1Jn. 3:24), Jesus (Jn. 6:56; Ro. 8:10; Ep. 3:17), and the Holy Spirit (Jn. 14:16, 17; Ro. 8:9, 11; 1Co. 3:16b). The Holy Bible even describes this in terms of different combinations: Father and Son (Jn. 14:23), Father and Holy Spirit (Ep. 2:21, 22; 1Jn. 3:24), and Son and Holy Spirit (Ga. 4:6).

Witnessing   In the New Testament believers are instructed to be a good witness with both their speech and their lifestyle (1Ti. 4:12; Ga. 5:22,23), which includes sharing their faith with others (Is. 52:7; Eze. 3:18,19; Mt. 5:14-16; 28:18-20; Lu. 12:8,9; Ac. 1:8; 1Co. 3:5-9; 2Co. 5:18-21; 1Pe. 3:15).

Worldview   A perspective of reality itself; a view of life; a comprehensive conception or apprehension of the world from a specific point of view. A worldview is a formal philosophy that is consistent and non-contradictory and explains all the facts of our life's experiences. Every individual has a worldview, a perspective that both interprets and guides life. In this sense, a worldview consciously or subconsciously answers four questions: Who am I? (What is the nature of human beings?) Where am I? (What is the nature of the world?) What is wrong? (What is the nature of evil?) What is the solution? (What is the nature of good and salvation?).

HELPFUL RESOURCES AND ORGANIZATIONS

Books On:
- **Worldviews:**

Johnson, Philip. *Reason in the Balance.* Downers Grove, IL: InterVarsity Press, 1995.

McCallum, Dennis, ed. *The Death of Truth.* Minneapolis, MN: Bethany House, 1996.

Noebel, David. *The Battle for Truth.* Eugene, OR: Harvest House, 1991.

Ridenour, Fritz. *So What's the Difference?* Regal Books by Gospel Light Publications, Glendale, 1976.

Schaeffer, Francis. *The Complete Works of Francis A. Schaeffer.* Vol.1-5. Wheaton, IL: Crossway, 1982.

Sire, James. *The Universe Next Door.* Downers Grove, IL: InterVarsity, 1997.

White, James Emery. *What is Truth?* Nashville, TN: Broadman & Holman Publishers, 1994.

- **Theology:**

Bilezekian, Gilbert. *Christianity 101.* Grand Rapids, MI: Zondervan, 1993.

Bloech, Gilbert. *Essentials of Evangelical Theology.* Vols. 1-2. Peabody, MA: Prince Press, 1998.

Erickson, Millard. *Introducing Christian Doctrine.* Grand Rapids, MI: Baker Books, 2001.

Evan, William. *The Great Doctrines of the Bible.* Chicago, IL: Moody, 1974.

Oden, Thomas. *The Word of Life.* Peabody, MA: Prince Press, 1998.

- **Apologetics:**

Geisler, Norman. *Christian Apologetics.* Grand Rapids, MI: Baker Books, 1976.

Grenz, Stanley. *What Christians Really Believe and Why.* Louisville, KY: Westminster John Knox, 1998.

Johnson, Alan, and Robert Webber. *What Christians Believe.* Grand Rapids, MI: Zondervan, 1993.

Wallace, J. Warner. *Person of Interest.* Grand Rapids, MI: Zondervan, 2021.

McDowell, Josh. *The New Evidence That Demands a Verdict.* Nashville, TN: Thomas Nelson, 1999.

Sproul, R.C. *Essential Truths of the Christian Faith.* Wheaton, IL: Tyndale, 1998.

Meyers, Steven C. *Darwin's Doubt.* San Francisco, CA: HarperOne/Harper Collins, 2010.

Meyers, Steven C. *Signature in the Cell.* San Francisco, CA: HarperOne/Harper Collins, 2012.

- **Other Published Resources:**

Archer, Gleason. *Encyclopedia of Bible Difficulties.* Grand Rapids, MI: Zondervan, 1982.

Comfort, Philip.ed. *The Origin of the Bible.* Wheaton, IL: Tyndale, 1992.

Geisler, Norman and William E. Nix. A General *Introduction to the Bible.* Chicago, IL: Moody Press, 1986.

Geisler, Norman and Ron Rhodes. *When Cultists Ask.* Grand Rapids, MI: Baker Books, 1997.

Stott, John. *Understanding the Bible.* Grand Rapids, MI: Zondervan, 1976.

Kaiser, Davids, Bruce, Brauch. *Hard Sayings of the Bible.* Downers Grove, IL: InterVarsity Press, 1996.

HELPFUL WEBSITES

Apologetics:
- Dr. William Lane Craig, www.reasonablefaith.org
- Ray Comfort, www.fullyfreefilms.com
- The Christian Research Institute, www.equip.org
- Josh McDowell Ministry, www.josh.org
- Ron Rhodes Ministry, www.ronrhodes.org
- John Macarthur Ministry, www.gty.org
- R.C. Sproul Ministry, www.ligonier.org
- Paul Washer Ministry, www.heartcrymissionary.com
- Got a Bible Question?, www.gotquestions.org
- www.evidenceforchristianity.org
- www.truelife.org

Bible Study Tools:
- www.biblestudy.org
- www.biblehub.com
- www.blueletterbible.org
- www.biblestudytools.com
- www.biblequestions.org
- www.e-sword.org

Bible Translations:
- www.youversion.com

Archaeology:
- www.Biblicalarchaeology.org
- www.baslibrary.org
- www.biblearchaeology.org

Creation:
- The Institute for Creation Research, www.icr.org
- www.answersingenesis.org

Manuscript Evidence:
- Daniel Wallace, The Center for the Study of New Testament Manuscripts @ www.csntm.org
- www.icr.org/bible-manuscripts
- www.carm.org/manuscript-evidence
- www.josh.org/manuscript-validate-old-testament

Watch word-for-word Gospel movies at the Jesus Film Project® at www.jesusfilm.org>watch
- Gospel of Luke—(Good News Translation). www.jesusfilm.org/watch/jesus.html/english/html
- Gospel of John—(Good News Translation). www.jesusfilm.org/watch/life-of-jesus-gospel-of-john.html/english/html
- The Book of Acts—(New International Version). www.jesusfilm.org/watch/book-of-acts.html/english/html

LAST CHANCE MUSIC MINISTRY PRODUCTS BY DAVID AND LAURA MEEKER

These Christian products by Last Chance Music Ministry can be found at: Amazon.com/Kunaki.com/Cdbaby.com/iTunes/Bookbaby.com/Youtube.com

Last Chance Music Ministry Gospel Tract CD is available now at **Kunaki.com**.

Just go to https://kunaki.com/mSales.asp?PublisherId=113289 or contact lastchancemusic1@aol.com to order.

This Last Chance Music Ministry Gospel Tract is actually the ***Unable to Deny*** CD with the Biblical description and references to the Gospel of Jesus Christ printed right on the disc itself. Included are 10 original songs that glorify God, edify the Body of Christ and reach a lost and dying world. These songs are currently playing on FM Christian radio in Austin, Texas The Gospel tract CD is a great way to share the Biblical truth of Jesus Christ to a lost and dying world, and we have discovered that non-believers are less likely to throw away a compact disk tract into the trash as opposed to a paper tract.

MORE LAST CHANCE MUSIC MINISTRY PRODUCTS BY DAVID AND LAURA MEEKER FROM KUNAKI.COM

Just go to https://kunaki.com/mSales.asp?PublisherId=113289 or contact lastchancemusic1@aol.com to order.

THE GOSPEL OF JOHN

John 1

The Beginning (Genesis 1:1-2)
¹In the beginning was the Word, and the Word was with God, and the Word was God. ²He was with God in the beginning. ³Through Him all things were made, and without Him nothing was made that has been made. ⁴In Him was life, and that life was the light of men. ⁵The Light shines in the darkness, and the darkness has not overcome it.

The Witness of John (Malachi 3:1-5)
⁶There came a man who was sent from God. His name was John. ⁷He came as a witness to testify about the Light, so that through him everyone might believe. ⁸He himself was not the Light, but he came to testify about the Light. ⁹The true Light who gives light to every man was coming into the world. ¹⁰He was in the world, and though the world was made through Him, the world did not recognize Him. ¹¹He came to His own, and His own did not receive Him. ¹²But to all who did receive Him, to those who believed in His name, He gave the right to become children of God— ¹³children born not of blood, nor of the desire or will of man, but born of God.

The Word Became Flesh (Psalm 84:1-12)
¹⁴The Word became flesh and made His dwelling among us. We have seen His glory, the glory of the one and only Son from the Father, full of grace and truth. ¹⁵John testified concerning Him. He cried out, saying, "This is He of whom I said, 'He who comes after me has surpassed me because He

was before me.' ¹⁶From His fullness we have all received grace upon grace. ¹⁷For the Law was given through Moses; grace and truth came through Jesus Christ. ¹⁸No one has ever seen God, but the one and only Son, who is Himself God and is at the Father's side, has made Him known.

The Mission of John the Baptist (Isaiah 40:1-5; Matthew 3:1-12; Mark 1:1-8; Luke 3:1-20)

¹⁹And this was John's testimony when the Jews of Jerusalem sent priests and Levites to ask him, "Who are you?" ²⁰He did not refuse to confess, but openly declared, "I am not the Christ." ²¹"Then who are you?" they inquired. "Are you Elijah?" He said, "I am not." "Are you the Prophet?" He answered, "No." ²²So they said to him, "Who are you? We need an answer for those who sent us. What do you say about yourself?" ²³John replied in the words of Isaiah the prophet: "I am the voice of one calling in the wilderness, 'Make straight the way for the Lord.'" ²⁴Then the Pharisees who had been sent ²⁵asked him, "Why then do you baptize, if you are not the Christ, nor Elijah, nor the Prophet?" ²⁶"I baptize with water," John replied, "but among you stands One you do not know. ²⁷He is the One who comes after me, the straps of whose sandals I am not worthy to untie." ²⁸All this happened at Bethany beyond the Jordan, where John was baptizing.

Jesus the Lamb of God (Matthew 3:13-17; Mark 1:9-11; Luke 3:21-22)

²⁹The next day John saw Jesus coming toward him and said, "Look, the Lamb of God, who takes away the sin of the world! ³⁰This is He of whom I said, 'A man who comes after me has surpassed me because He was before me.' ³¹I myself did not know Him, but the reason I came baptizing with water was that He might be revealed to Israel." ³²Then John testified, "I saw the Spirit descending from heaven like a dove and resting on Him. ³³I myself did not know Him, but the One who sent me to baptize with water told me, 'The man on whom you see the Spirit descend and rest is He who will baptize with the Holy Spirit.' ³⁴ I have seen and testified that this is the Son of God."

The First Disciples (Matthew 4:18-22; Matthew 13:47-52; Mark 1:16-20; Luke 5:1-11)

³⁵The next day John was there again with two of his disciples. ³⁶When he saw Jesus walking by, he said, "Look, the Lamb of God!" ³⁷And when the

two disciples heard him say this, they followed Jesus. ³⁸Jesus turned and saw them following. "What do you want?" He asked. They said to Him, "Rabbi" (which means Teacher), "where are You staying?" ³⁹"Come and see," He replied. So they went and saw where He was staying, and spent that day with Him. It was about the tenth hour. ⁴⁰Andrew, Simon Peter's brother, was one of the two who heard John's testimony and followed Jesus. ⁴¹He first found his brother Simon and told him, "We have found the Messiah" (which is translated as Christ). ⁴²Andrew brought him to Jesus, who looked at him and said, "You are Simon son of John. You will be called Cephas" (which is translated as Peter).

Jesus Calls Philip and Nathanael
⁴³The next day Jesus decided to set out for Galilee. Finding Philip, He told him, "Follow Me." ⁴⁴Now Philip was from Bethsaida, the same town as Andrew and Peter. ⁴⁵Philip found Nathanael and told him, "We have found the One Moses wrote about in the Law, the One the prophets foretold— Jesus of Nazareth, the son of Joseph." ⁴⁶"Can anything good come from Nazareth?" Nathanael asked. "Come and see," said Philip. ⁴⁷When Jesus saw Nathanael approaching, He said of him, "Here is a true Israelite, in whom there is no deceit." ⁴⁸"How do You know me?" Nathanael asked. Jesus replied, "Before Philip called you, I saw you under the fig tree." ⁴⁹"Rabbi," Nathanael answered, "You are the Son of God! You are the King of Israel!" ⁵⁰Jesus said to him, "Do you believe just because I told you I saw you under the fig tree? You will see greater things than these." ⁵¹Then He declared, "Truly, truly, I tell you, you will see heaven open and the angels of God ascending and descending on the Son of Man."

John 2

The Wedding at Cana
¹On the third day a wedding took place at Cana in Galilee. Jesus' mother was there, ²and Jesus and His disciples had also been invited to the wedding. ³When the wine ran out, Jesus' mother said to Him, "They have no more wine." ⁴"Woman, why does this concern us?" Jesus replied. "My hour has not yet come." ⁵His mother said to the servants, "Do whatever He tells you."

⁶Now six stone water jars had been set there for the Jewish rites of purification. Each could hold from twenty to thirty gallons. ⁷Jesus told the servants, "Fill the jars with water." So they filled them to the brim.
⁸"Now draw some out," He said, "and take it to the master of the banquet." They did so, ⁹and the master of the banquet tasted the water that had been turned into wine. He did not know where it was from, but the servants who had drawn the water knew. Then he called the bridegroom aside ¹⁰and said, "Everyone serves the fine wine first, and then the cheap wine after the guests are drunk. But you have saved the fine wine until now!"
¹¹Jesus performed this, the first of His signs, at Cana in Galilee. He thus revealed His glory, and His disciples believed in Him.

Jesus Cleanses the Temple (Matthew 21:12-17; Mark 11:15-19; Luke 19:45-48)

¹²After this, He went down to Capernaum with His mother and brothers and His disciples, and they stayed there a few days. ¹³When the Jewish Passover was near, Jesus went up to Jerusalem. ¹⁴In the temple courts He found men selling cattle, sheep, and doves, and money changers seated at their tables. ¹⁵So He made a whip out of cords and drove all from the temple courts, both sheep and cattle. He poured out the coins of the money changers and overturned their tables. ¹⁶To those selling doves He said, "Get these out of here! How dare you turn My Father's house into a marketplace!" ¹⁷His disciples remembered that it is written: "Zeal for Your house will consume Me." ¹⁸On account of this, the Jews demanded, "What sign can You show us to prove Your authority to do these things?" ¹⁹Jesus answered, "Destroy this temple, and in three days I will raise it up again." ²⁰"This temple took forty-six years to build," the Jews replied, "and You are going to raise it up in three days?" ²¹ But Jesus was speaking about the temple of His body. ²²After He was raised from the dead, His disciples remembered that He had said this. Then they believed the Scripture and the word that Jesus had spoken. ²³While He was in Jerusalem at the Passover Feast, many people saw the signs He was doing and believed in His name. ²⁴But Jesus did not entrust Himself to them, for He knew all men. ²⁵He did not need any testimony about man, for He knew what was in a man.

John 3

Jesus and Nicodemus

¹Now there was a man of the Pharisees named Nicodemus, a leader of the Jews. ²He came to Jesus at night and said, "Rabbi, we know that You are a teacher who has come from God. For no one could perform the signs You are doing if God were not with him." ³Jesus replied, "Truly, truly, I tell you, no one can see the kingdom of God unless he is born again." ⁴"How can a man be born when he is old?" Nicodemus asked. "Can he enter his mother's womb a second time to be born?" ⁵Jesus answered, "Truly, truly, I tell you, no one can enter the kingdom of God unless he is born of water and the Spirit. ⁶Flesh is born of flesh, but spirit is born of the Spirit. ⁷Do not be amazed that I said, 'You must be born again.' ⁸The wind blows where it wishes. You hear its sound, but you do not know where it comes from or where it is going. So it is with everyone born of the Spirit." ⁹"How can this be?" Nicodemus asked. ¹⁰"You are Israel's teacher," said Jesus, "and you do not understand these things? ¹¹Truly, truly, I tell you, we speak of what we know, and we testify to what we have seen, and yet you people do not accept our testimony. ¹²If I have told you about earthly things and you do not believe, how will you believe if I tell you about heavenly things? ¹³No one has ascended into heaven except the One who descended from heaven—the Son of Man. ¹⁴Just as Moses lifted up the snake in the wilderness, so the Son of Man must be lifted up, ¹⁵ that everyone who believes in Him may have eternal life.

For God So Loved (Genesis 22:1-10; Romans 5:6-11)

¹⁶For God so loved the world that He gave His one and only Son, that everyone who believes in Him shall not perish but have eternal life. ¹⁷For God did not send His Son into the world to condemn the world, but to save the world through Him. ¹⁸Whoever believes in Him is not condemned, but whoever does not believe has already been condemned, because he has not believed in the name of God's one and only Son. ¹⁹And this is the verdict: The Light has come into the world, but men loved the darkness rather than the Light, because their deeds were evil. ²⁰Everyone who does evil hates the Light, and does not come into the Light for fear that his deeds will be

exposed. ²¹But whoever practices the truth comes into the Light, so that it may be seen clearly that what he has done has been accomplished in God."

John's Testimony about Jesus

²²After this, Jesus and His disciples went into the Judean countryside, where He spent some time with them and baptized. ²³Now John was also baptizing at Aenon near Salim, because the water was plentiful there, and people kept coming to be baptized. ²⁴(For John had not yet been thrown into prison.) ²⁵A dispute arose between John's disciples and a certain Jew over the issue of ceremonial washing. ²⁶So John's disciples came to him and said, "Look, Rabbi, the One who was with you beyond the Jordan, the One you testified about—He is baptizing, and everyone is going to Him." ²⁷John replied, "A man can receive only what is given him from heaven. ²⁸You yourselves can testify that I said, 'I am not the Christ, but am sent ahead of Him.' ²⁹The bride belongs to the bridegroom. The friend of the bridegroom stands and listens for him, and is overjoyed to hear the bridegroom's voice. That joy is mine, and it is now complete. ³⁰He must increase; I must decrease. ³¹The One who comes from above is above all. The one who is from the earth belongs to the earth and speaks as one from the earth. The One who comes from heaven is above all. ³²He testifies to what He has seen and heard, yet no one accepts His testimony. ³³Whoever accepts His testimony has certified that God is truthful. ³⁴For the One whom God has sent speaks the words of God, for God gives the Spirit without limit. ³⁵The Father loves the Son and has placed all things in His hands. ³⁶Whoever believes in the Son has eternal life. Whoever rejects the Son will not see life. Instead, the wrath of God remains on him."

John 4

Jesus and the Samaritan Woman

¹When Jesus realized that the Pharisees were aware that He was gaining and baptizing more disciples than John ²(although it was not Jesus who baptized, but His disciples), ³He left Judea and returned to Galilee.

⁴Now He had to pass through Samaria. ⁵So He came to a town of Samaria called Sychar, near the plot of ground Jacob had given to his son Joseph. ⁶ Since Jacob's well was there, Jesus, weary from His journey, sat down by the well. It was about the sixth hour. ⁷When a Samaritan woman came to draw water, Jesus said to her, "Give Me a drink." ⁸(His disciples had gone into the town to buy food.) ⁹"You are a Jew," said the woman. "How can You ask for a drink from me, a Samaritan woman?" (For Jews do not associate with Samaritans.) ¹⁰Jesus answered, "If you knew the gift of God and who is asking you for a drink, you would have asked Him, and He would have given you living water." ¹¹"Sir," the woman replied, "You have nothing to draw with and the well is deep. Where then will You get this living water? ¹²Are You greater than our father Jacob, who gave us this well and drank from it himself, as did his sons and his livestock?" ¹³Jesus said to her, "Everyone who drinks this water will be thirsty again. ¹⁴But whoever drinks the water I give him will never thirst. Indeed, the water I give him will become in him a fount of water springing up to eternal life."
¹⁵The woman said to Him, "Sir, give me this water so that I will not get thirsty and have to keep coming here to draw water." ¹⁶Jesus told her, "Go, call your husband and come back." ¹⁷"I have no husband," the woman replied. Jesus said to her, "You are correct to say that you have no husband. ¹⁸In fact, you have had five husbands, and the man you now have is not your husband. You have spoken truthfully." ¹⁹"Sir," the woman said, "I see that You are a prophet. ²⁰Our forefathers worshiped on this mountain, but you Jews say that the place where one must worship is in Jerusalem." ²¹"Believe Me, woman," Jesus replied, "a time is coming when you will worship the Father neither on this mountain nor in Jerusalem. ²²You worship what you do not know; we worship what we do know, for salvation is from the Jews. ²³But a time is coming and has now come when the true worshipers will worship the Father in spirit and in truth, for the Father is seeking such as these to worship Him. ²⁴God is Spirit, and His worshipers must worship Him in spirit and in truth." ²⁵The woman said, "I know that Messiah" (called Christ) "is coming. When He comes, He will explain everything to us." ²⁶Jesus answered, "I who speak to you am He."

The Disciples Return and Marvel

²⁷Just then, His disciples returned and were astonished that He was speaking with a woman. But no one asked Him, "What do You want from her?" or, "Why are You talking with her?"

²⁸Then the woman left her water jar, went back into the town, and said to the people, ²⁹"Come, see a man who told me everything I ever did. Could this be the Christ?" ³⁰So they left the town and made their way toward Jesus. ³¹Meanwhile, the disciples urged Him, "Rabbi, eat something." ³²But He told them, "I have food to eat that you know nothing about." ³³So the disciples asked one another, "Could someone have brought Him food?" ³⁴Jesus explained, "My food is to do the will of Him who sent Me and to finish His work. ³⁵Do you not say, 'There are still four months until the harvest'? I tell you, lift up your eyes and look at the fields, for they are ripe for harvest. ³⁶Already the reaper draws his wages and gathers a crop for eternal life, so that the sower and the reaper may rejoice together. ³⁷For in this case the saying 'One sows and another reaps' is true. ³⁸I sent you to reap what you have not worked for; others have done the hard work, and now you have taken up their labor."

Many Samaritans Believe

³⁹Many of the Samaritans from that town believed in Jesus because of the woman's testimony, "He told me everything I ever did." ⁴⁰So when the Samaritans came to Him, they asked Him to stay with them, and He stayed two days. ⁴¹And many more believed because of His message. ⁴²They said to the woman, "We now believe not only because of your words; we have heard for ourselves, and we know that this man truly is the Savior of the world."

Jesus Heals the Official's Son (Matthew 8:5-13; Luke 7:1-10)

⁴³After two days, Jesus left for Galilee. ⁴⁴Now He Himself had testified that a prophet has no honor in his own country. ⁴⁵Yet when He arrived, the Galileans welcomed Him. They had seen all the great things He had done in Jerusalem at the feast, for they had gone there as well. ⁴⁶So once again He came to Cana in Galilee, where He had turned the water into wine. And there was a royal official whose son lay sick at Capernaum. ⁴⁷When he heard that Jesus had come from Judea to Galilee, he went and begged Him to come

down and heal his son, who was about to die. ⁴⁸Jesus said to him, "Unless you people see signs and wonders, you will never believe." ⁴⁹"Sir," the official said, "come down before my child dies." ⁵⁰"Go," said Jesus. "Your son will live." The man took Jesus at His word and departed. ⁵¹And while he was still on the way, his servants met him with the news that his boy was alive. ⁵²So he inquired as to the hour when his son had recovered, and they told him, "The fever left him yesterday at the seventh hour." ⁵³Then the father realized that this was the very hour in which Jesus had told him, "Your son will live." And he and all his household believed. ⁵⁴This was now the second sign that Jesus performed after coming from Judea into Galilee.

John 5

The Pool of Bethesda

¹Some time later there was a feast of the Jews, and Jesus went up to Jerusalem. ²Now there is in Jerusalem near the Sheep Gate a pool with five covered colonnades, which in Aramaic is called Bethesda. ³On these walkways lay a great number of the sick, the blind, the lame, and the paralyzed. ⁵One man there had been an invalid for thirty-eight years. ⁶When Jesus saw him lying there and realized that he had spent a long time in this condition, He asked him, "Do you want to get well?" ⁷"Sir," the invalid replied, "I have no one to help me into the pool when the water is stirred. While I am on my way, someone else goes in before me." ⁸ Then Jesus told him, "Get up, pick up your mat, and walk." ⁹Immediately the man was made well, and he picked up his mat and began to walk. Now this happened on the Sabbath day, ¹⁰so the Jews said to the man who had been healed, "This is the Sabbath! It is unlawful for you to carry your mat." ¹¹But he answered, "The man who made me well told me, 'Pick up your mat and walk.'" ¹²"Who is this man who told you to pick it up and walk?" they asked. ¹³But the man who was healed did not know who it was, for Jesus had slipped away while the crowd was there. ¹⁴Afterward, Jesus found the man at the temple and said to him, "See, you have been made well. Stop sinning, or something worse may happen to you." ¹⁵And the man went away and told the Jews that it was Jesus who had made him well.

The Father and the Son

[16]Now because Jesus was doing these things on the Sabbath, the Jews began to persecute Him. [17]But Jesus answered them, "To this very day My Father is at His work, and I too am working." [18]Because of this, the Jews tried all the harder to kill Him. Not only was He breaking the Sabbath, but He was even calling God His own Father, making Himself equal with God. [19]So Jesus replied, "Truly, truly, I tell you, the Son can do nothing by Himself, unless He sees the Father doing it. For whatever the Father does, the Son also does. [20]The Father loves the Son and shows Him all He does. And to your amazement, He will show Him even greater works than these. [21]For just as the Father raises the dead and gives them life, so also the Son gives life to whom He wishes. [22]Furthermore, the Father judges no one, but has assigned all judgment to the Son, [23]so that all may honor the Son just as they honor the Father. Whoever does not honor the Son does not honor the Father who sent Him. [24]Truly, truly, I tell you, whoever hears My word and believes Him who sent Me has eternal life and will not come under judgment. Indeed, he has crossed over from death to life.

[25]Truly, truly, I tell you, the hour is coming and has now come when the dead will hear the voice of the Son of God, and those who hear will live. [26]For as the Father has life in Himself, so also He has granted the Son to have life in Himself. [27]And He has given Him authority to execute judgment, because He is the Son of Man. [28]Do not be amazed at this, for the hour is coming when all who are in their graves will hear His voice [29]and come out—those who have done good to the resurrection of life, and those who have done evil to the resurrection of judgment. [30]I can do nothing by Myself; I judge only as I hear. And My judgment is just, because I do not seek My own will, but the will of Him who sent Me.

Testimonies about Jesus

[31]If I testify about Myself, My testimony is not valid. [32]There is another who testifies about Me, and I know that His testimony about Me is valid. [33]You have sent to John and he has testified to the truth. [34]Even though I do not accept human testimony, I say these things so that you may be saved. [35]John was a lamp that burned and gave light, and you were willing for a season to

bask in his light. ³⁶But I have testimony more substantial than that of John. For the works that the Father has given Me to accomplish—the very works I am doing—testify about Me that the Father has sent Me. ³⁷And the Father who sent Me has Himself testified about Me. You have never heard His voice nor seen His form, ³⁸nor does His word abide in you, because you do not believe the One He sent.

The Witness of Scripture (Luke 16:19-31)
³⁹You pore over the Scriptures because you presume that by them you possess eternal life. These are the very words that testify about Me, ⁴⁰yet you refuse to come to Me to have life. ⁴¹I do not accept glory from men, ⁴²but I know you, that you do not have the love of God within you. ⁴³I have come in My Father's name, and you have not received Me; but if someone else comes in his own name, you will receive him. ⁴⁴How can you believe if you accept glory from one another, yet do not seek the glory that comes from the only God? ⁴⁵Do not think that I will accuse you before the Father. Your accuser is Moses, in whom you have put your hope. ⁴⁶If you had believed Moses, you would believe Me, because he wrote about Me. ⁴⁷But since you do not believe what he wrote, how will you believe what I say?"

John 6

The Feeding of the Five Thousand (Matthew 14:13-21; Mark 6:30-44; Luke 9:10-17)
¹After this, Jesus crossed to the other side of the Sea of Galilee (that is, the Sea of Tiberias). ²A large crowd followed Him because they saw the signs He had performed on the sick. ³Then Jesus went up on the mountain and sat down with His disciples. ⁴Now the Jewish Feast of the Passover was near. ⁵When Jesus looked up and saw a large crowd coming toward Him, He said to Philip, "Where can we buy bread for these people to eat?" ⁶But He was asking this to test him, for He knew what He was about to do. ⁷Philip answered, "Two hundred denarii would not buy enough bread for each of them to have a small piece." ⁸One of His disciples, Andrew, Simon Peter's brother, said to Him, ⁹"Here is a boy with five barley loaves and two small fish.

But what difference will these make among so many?" ¹⁰"Have the people sit down," Jesus said. Now there was plenty of grass in that place, so the men sat down, about five thousand of them. ¹¹Then Jesus took the loaves and the fish, gave thanks, and distributed to those who were seated as much as they wanted. ¹²And when everyone was full, He said to His disciples, "Gather the pieces that are left over, so that nothing will be wasted." ¹³So they collected them and filled twelve baskets with the pieces of the five barley loaves left over by those who had eaten. ¹⁴When the people saw the sign that Jesus had performed, they began to say, "Truly this is the Prophet who is to come into the world." ¹⁵Then Jesus, realizing that they were about to come and make Him king by force, withdrew again to a mountain by Himself.

Jesus Walks on Water (Matthew 14:22-33; Mark 6:45-52)
¹⁶When evening came, His disciples went down to the sea, ¹⁷got into a boat, and started across the sea to Capernaum. It was already dark, and Jesus had not yet gone out to them. ¹⁸A strong wind was blowing and the sea grew agitated. ¹⁹When they had rowed about three or four miles, they saw Jesus approaching the boat, walking on the sea—and they were terrified. ²⁰But Jesus spoke up: "It is I; do not be afraid." ²¹Then they were willing to take Him into the boat, and at once the boat reached the shore where they were heading.

Jesus the Bread of Life
²²The next day, the crowd that had remained on the other side of the sea realized that only one boat had been there, and that Jesus had not boarded it with His disciples, but they had gone away alone. ²³However, some boats from Tiberias arrived near the place they had eaten the bread after the Lord had given thanks. ²⁴So when the crowd saw that neither Jesus nor His disciples were there, they got into the boats and went to Capernaum to look for Him. ²⁵When they found Him on the other side of the sea, they asked Him, "Rabbi, when did You get here?" ²⁶Jesus replied, "Truly, truly, I tell you, it is not because you saw these signs that you are looking for Me, but because you ate the loaves and had your fill. ²⁷Do not work for food that perishes, but for food that endures to eternal life, which the Son of Man will give you. For on

Him God the Father has placed His seal of approval." ²⁸Then they inquired, "What must we do to perform the works of God?" ²⁹Jesus replied, "The work of God is this: to believe in the One He has sent." ³⁰So they asked Him, "What sign then will You perform, so that we may see it and believe You? What will You do? ³¹Our forefathers ate the manna in the wilderness, as it is written: 'He gave them bread from heaven to eat.' ³²Jesus said to them, "Truly, truly, I tell you, it was not Moses who gave you the bread from heaven, but it is My Father who gives you the true bread from heaven. ³³For the bread of God is He who comes down from heaven and gives life to the world." ³⁴"Sir," they said, "give us this bread at all times." ³⁵Jesus answered, "I am the bread of life. Whoever comes to Me will never hunger, and whoever believes in Me will never thirst. ³⁶But as I told you, you have seen Me and still you do not believe. ³⁷Everyone the Father gives Me will come to Me, and the one who comes to Me I will never drive away. ³⁸For I have come down from heaven, not to do My own will, but to do the will of Him who sent Me. ³⁹And this is the will of Him who sent Me, that I shall lose none of those He has given Me, but raise them up at the last day. ⁴⁰For it is My Father's will that everyone who looks to the Son and believes in Him shall have eternal life, and I will raise him up at the last day."

⁴¹At this, the Jews began to grumble about Jesus because He had said, "I am the bread that came down from heaven." ⁴²They were asking, "Is this not Jesus, the son of Joseph, whose father and mother we know? How then can He say, 'I have come down from heaven?' ⁴³"Stop grumbling among yourselves," Jesus replied. ⁴⁴"No one can come to Me unless the Father who sent Me draws him, and I will raise him up at the last day. ⁴⁵It is written in the Prophets: 'And they will all be taught by God.' Everyone who has heard the Father and learned from Him comes to Me—⁴⁶not that anyone has seen the Father except the One who is from God; only He has seen the Father. ⁴⁷Truly, truly, I tell you, he who believes has eternal life. ⁴⁸I am the bread of life. ⁴⁹Your forefathers ate the manna in the wilderness, yet they died. ⁵⁰This is the bread that comes down from heaven, so that anyone may eat of it and not die. ⁵¹I am the living bread that came down from heaven. If anyone eats of this bread, he will live forever. And this bread, which I will give for the life of the world,

is My flesh." ⁵²At this, the Jews began to argue among themselves, "How can this man give us His flesh to eat?" ⁵³So Jesus said to them, "Truly, truly, I tell you, unless you eat the flesh and drink the blood of the Son of Man, you have no life in you. ⁵⁴Whoever eats My flesh and drinks My blood has eternal life, and I will raise him up at the last day. ⁵⁵For My flesh is real food, and My blood is real drink.

⁵⁶Whoever eats My flesh and drinks My blood remains in Me, and I in him. ⁵⁷Just as the living Father sent Me and I live because of the Father, so also the one who feeds on Me will live because of Me. ⁵⁸This is the bread that came down from heaven. Unlike your forefathers, who ate the manna and died, the one who eats this bread will live forever."

Many Disciples Turn Back (Matthew 8:18-22; Luke 9:57-62; Luke 14:25-33)

⁵⁹Jesus said this while teaching in the synagogue in Capernaum. ⁶⁰On hearing it, many of His disciples said, "This is a difficult teaching. Who can accept it?" ⁶¹Aware that His disciples were grumbling about this teaching, Jesus asked them, "Does this offend you? ⁶²Then what will happen if you see the Son of Man ascend to where He was before? ⁶³The Spirit gives life; the flesh profits nothing. The words I have spoken to you are spirit and they are life. ⁶⁴However, there are some of you who do not believe." (For Jesus had known from the beginning which of them did not believe and who would betray Him.) ⁶⁵Then Jesus said, "This is why I told you that no one can come to Me unless the Father has granted it to him."

Peter's Confession of Faith (Matthew 16:13-20; Mark 8:27-30; Luke 9:18-20)

⁶⁶From that time on, many of His disciples turned back and no longer walked with Him. ⁶⁷So Jesus asked the Twelve, "Do you want to leave too?" ⁶⁸Simon Peter replied, "Lord, to whom would we go? You have the words of eternal life. ⁶⁹We believe and know that You are the Holy One of God." ⁷⁰Jesus answered them, "Have I not chosen you, the Twelve? Yet one of you is a devil!" ⁷¹He was speaking about Judas, the son of Simon Iscariot. For although Judas was one of the Twelve, he was later to betray Jesus.

John 7

Jesus Teaches at the Feast

¹After this, Jesus traveled throughout Galilee. He did not want to travel in Judea, because the Jews there were trying to kill Him. ²However, the Jewish Feast of Tabernacles was near. ³So Jesus' brothers said to Him, "Leave here and go to Judea, so that Your disciples there may see the works You are doing. ⁴For no one who wants to be known publicly acts in secret. Since You are doing these things, show Yourself to the world." ⁵For even His own brothers did not believe in Him. ⁶Therefore Jesus told them, "Although your time is always at hand, My time has not yet come. ⁷The world cannot hate you, but it hates Me, because I testify that its works are evil. ⁸Go up to the feast on your own. I am not going up to this feast, because My time has not yet come." ⁹Having said this, Jesus remained in Galilee. ¹⁰But after His brothers had gone up to the feast, He also went—not publicly, but in secret. ¹¹So the Jews were looking for Him at the feast and asking, "Where is He?" ¹²Many in the crowds were whispering about Him. Some said, "He is a good man." But others replied, "No, He deceives the people." ¹³Yet no one would speak publicly about Him for fear of the Jews. ¹⁴About halfway through the feast, Jesus went up to the temple courts and began to teach. ¹⁵The Jews were amazed and asked, "How did this man attain such learning without having studied?" ¹⁶"My teaching is not My own," Jesus replied. "It comes from Him who sent Me. ¹⁷If anyone desires to do His will, he will know whether My teaching is from God or whether I speak on My own. ¹⁸He who speaks on his own authority seeks his own glory, but He who seeks the glory of the One who sent Him is a man of truth; in Him there is no falsehood. ¹⁹Has not Moses given you the Law? Yet not one of you keeps it. Why are you trying to kill Me?" ²⁰"You have a demon," the crowd replied. "Who is trying to kill You?" ²¹Jesus answered them, "I did one miracle, and you are all astonished. ²²But because Moses gave you circumcision, you circumcise a boy on the Sabbath (not that it is from Moses, but from the patriarchs.) ²³If a boy can be circumcised on the Sabbath so that the Law of Moses will not be broken, why are you angry with Me for making the whole man well on the Sabbath? ²⁴Stop judging by outward appearances, and start judging justly."

Is Jesus the Christ?

²⁵Then some of the people of Jerusalem began to say, "Isn't this the man they are trying to kill? ²⁶Yet here He is, speaking publicly, and they are not saying anything to Him. Have the rulers truly recognized that this is the Christ? ²⁷But we know where this man is from. When the Christ comes, no one will know where He is from." ²⁸Then Jesus, still teaching in the temple courts, cried out, "You know Me, and you know where I am from. I have not come on My own accord, but He who sent Me is true. You do not know Him, ²⁹but I know Him, because I am from Him and He sent Me." ³⁰So they tried to seize Him, but no one laid a hand on Him, because His hour had not yet come. ³¹Many in the crowd, however, believed in Him and said, "When the Christ comes, will He perform more signs than this man?" ³²When the Pharisees heard the crowd whispering these things about Jesus, they and the chief priests sent officers to arrest Him. ³³So Jesus said, "I am with you only a little while longer, and then I am going to the One who sent Me. ³⁴You will look for Me, but you will not find Me; and where I am, you cannot come." ³⁵At this, the Jews said to one another, "Where does He intend to go that we will not find Him? Will He go where the Jews are dispersed among the Greeks, and teach the Greeks? ³⁶What does He mean by saying, 'You will look for Me, but you will not find Me,' and, 'Where I am, you cannot come'?"

Living Water

³⁷On the last and greatest day of the feast, Jesus stood up and called out in a loud voice, "If anyone is thirsty, let him come to Me and drink. ³⁸Whoever believes in Me, as the Scripture has said: 'Streams of living water will flow from within him.'" ³⁹He was speaking about the Spirit, whom those who believed in Him were later to receive. For the Spirit had not yet been given, because Jesus had not yet been glorified.

Division Regarding Jesus

⁴⁰On hearing these words, some of the people said, "This is truly the Prophet." ⁴¹Others declared, "This is the Christ." But still others asked, "How can the Christ come from Galilee? ⁴²Doesn't the Scripture say that the Christ will come from the line of David and from Bethlehem, the village where David

lived?" ⁴³So there was division in the crowd because of Jesus. ⁴⁴Some of them wanted to seize Him, but no one laid a hand on Him.

Unbelief of the Jewish Leaders

⁴⁵Then the officers returned to the chief priests and Pharisees, who asked them, "Why didn't you bring Him in?" ⁴⁶"Never has anyone spoken like this man!" the officers answered. ⁴⁷"Have you also been deceived?" replied the Pharisees. ⁴⁸"Have any of the rulers or Pharisees believed in Him? ⁴⁹But this crowd that does not know the Law, they are under a curse." ⁵⁰Nicodemus, who had gone to Jesus earlier, and who himself was one of them, asked, ⁵¹"Does our law convict a man without first hearing from him to determine what he has done?" ⁵²"Aren't you also from Galilee?" they replied. "Look into it, and you will see that no prophet comes out of Galilee." ⁵³Then each went to his own home.

John 8

The Woman Caught in Adultery

¹But Jesus went to the Mount of Olives. ²Early in the morning He went back into the temple courts. All the people came to Him, and He sat down to teach them. ³The scribes and Pharisees, however, brought to Him a woman caught in adultery. They made her stand before them ⁴and said, "Teacher, this woman was caught in the act of adultery. ⁵In the Law Moses commanded us to stone such a woman. So what do You say?" ⁶They said this to test Him, in order to have a basis for accusing Him. But Jesus bent down and began to write on the ground with His finger. ⁷When they continued to question Him, He straightened up and said to them, "Let him who is without sin among you be the first to cast a stone at her." ⁸And again He bent down and wrote on the ground. ⁹When they heard this, a they began to go away one by one, beginning with the older ones, until only Jesus was left, with the woman standing there. ¹⁰Then Jesus straightened up b and asked her, "Woman, where are your accusers? Has no one condemned you?" ¹¹"No one, Lord," she answered. "Then neither do I condemn you," Jesus declared. "Now go and sin no more."

Jesus the Light of the World (1John 1:5-10)

¹²Once again, Jesus spoke to the people and said, "I am the light of the world. Whoever follows Me will never walk in the darkness, but will have the light of life." ¹³So the Pharisees said to Him, "You are testifying about Yourself; Your testimony is not valid." ¹⁴Jesus replied, "Even if I testify about Myself, My testimony is valid, because I know where I came from and where I am going. But you do not know where I came from or where I am going. ¹⁵You judge according to the flesh; I judge no one. ¹⁶But even if I do judge, My judgment is true, because I am not alone when I judge; I am with the Father, who sent Me. ¹⁷Even in your own Law it is written that the testimony of two men is valid. ¹⁸I am One who testifies about Myself, and the Father, who sent Me, also testifies about Me." ¹⁹"Where is Your Father?" they asked Him. "You do not know Me or My Father," Jesus answered. "If you knew Me, you would know My Father as well." ²⁰He spoke these words while teaching in the temple courts, near the treasury. Yet no one seized Him, because His hour had not yet come. ²¹Again He said to them, "I am going away, and you will look for Me, but you will die in your sin. Where I am going, you cannot come." ²²So the Jews began to ask, "Will He kill Himself, since He says, 'Where I am going, you cannot come'?" ²³Then He told them, "You are from below; I am from above. You are of this world; I am not of this world. ²⁴That is why I told you that you would die in your sins. For unless you believe that I am He, you will die in your sins." ²⁵"Who are You?" they asked. "Just what I have been telling you from the beginning," Jesus replied. ²⁶"I have much to say about you and much to judge. But the One who sent Me is truthful, and what I have heard from Him, I tell the world." ²⁷They did not understand that He was telling them about the Father. ²⁸So Jesus said, "When you have lifted up the Son of Man, then you will know that I am He, and that I do nothing on My own, but speak exactly what the Father has taught Me. ²⁹He who sent Me is with Me. He has not left Me alone, because I always do what pleases Him."

The Truth will Set You Free (2John 1:4-6)

³⁰As Jesus spoke these things, many believed in Him. ³¹So He said to the Jews who had believed Him, "If you continue in My word, you are truly My disciples. ³²Then you will know the truth, and the truth will set you free." ³³"We

are Abraham's descendants," they answered. "We have never been slaves to anyone. How can You say we will be set free?" ³⁴Jesus replied, "Truly, truly, I tell you, everyone who sins is a slave to sin. ³⁵A slave is not a permanent member of the family, but a son belongs to it forever. ³⁶So if the Son sets you free, you will be free indeed.

The Children of the Devil

³⁷I know you are Abraham's descendants, but you are trying to kill Me because My word has no place within you. ³⁸I speak of what I have seen in the presence of the Father, and you do what you have heard from your father." ³⁹"Abraham is our father," they replied. "If you were children of Abraham," said Jesus, "you would do the works of Abraham. ⁴⁰But now you are trying to kill Me, a man who has told you the truth that I heard from God. Abraham never did such a thing. ⁴¹You are doing the works of your father." "We are not illegitimate children," they declared. "Our only Father is God Himself." ⁴²Jesus said to them, "If God were your Father, you would love Me, for I have come here from God. I have not come on My own, but He sent Me. ⁴³Why do you not understand what I am saying? It is because you are unable to accept My message. ⁴⁴You belong to your father, the devil, and you want to carry out his desires. He was a murderer from the beginning, refusing to uphold the truth, because there is no truth in him. When he lies, he speaks his native language, because he is a liar and the father of lies. ⁴⁵But because I speak the truth, you do not believe Me! ⁴⁶Which of you can prove Me guilty of sin? If I speak the truth, why do you not believe Me? ⁴⁷Whoever belongs to God hears the words of God. The reason you do not hear is that you do not belong to God."

Before Abraham was Born, I Am

⁴⁸The Jews answered Him, "Are we not right to say that You are a Samaritan and You have a demon?" ⁴⁹"I do not have a demon," Jesus replied, "but I honor My Father, and you dishonor Me. ⁵⁰I do not seek My own glory. There is One who seeks it, and He is the Judge. ⁵¹Truly, truly, I tell you, if anyone keeps My word, he will never see death." ⁵²"Now we know that You have a demon!" declared the Jews. "Abraham died, and so did the prophets, yet You say that anyone who keeps Your word will never taste death. ⁵³Are You greater

than our father Abraham? He died, as did the prophets. Who do You claim to be?" ⁵⁴Jesus answered, "If I glorify Myself, My glory means nothing. The One who glorifies Me is My Father, of whom you say 'He is our God.' ⁵⁵You do not know Him, but I know Him. If I said I did not know Him, I would be a liar like you. But I do know Him, and I keep His word. ⁵⁶Your father Abraham was overjoyed to see My day. He saw it and was glad." ⁵⁷Then the Jews said to Him, "You are not yet fifty years old, and You have seen Abraham?" ⁵⁸"Truly, truly, I tell you," Jesus declared, "before Abraham was born, I am!" ⁵⁹At this, they picked up stones to throw at Him. But Jesus was hidden and went out of the temple area.

John 9

Jesus Heals the Man Born Blind

¹Now as Jesus was passing by, He saw a man blind from birth, ²and His disciples asked Him, "Rabbi, who sinned, this man or his parents, that he was born blind?" ³Jesus answered, "Neither this man nor his parents sinned, but this happened so that the works of God would be displayed in him. ⁴While it is daytime, we must do the works of Him who sent Me. Night is coming, when no one can work. ⁵While I am in the world, I am the light of the world." ⁶When Jesus had said this, He spat on the ground, made some mud, and applied it to the man's eyes. ⁷Then He told him, "Go, wash in the pool of Siloam" (which means Sent). So the man went and washed, and came back seeing. ⁸At this, his neighbors and those who had formerly seen him begging began to ask, "Isn't this the man who used to sit and beg?" ⁹Some claimed that he was, but others said, "No, he just looks like him." But the man kept saying, "I am the one." ¹⁰"How then were your eyes opened?" they asked. ¹¹He answered, "The man they call Jesus made some mud and anointed my eyes, and He told me to go to Siloam and wash. So I went and washed and received my sight." ¹²"Where is He?" they asked. "I do not know," he answered.

The Pharisees Investigate the Healing

¹³They brought to the Pharisees the man who had been blind. ¹⁴Now the day on which Jesus had made the mud and opened his eyes was a Sabbath. ¹⁵So the Pharisees also asked him how he had received his sight. The man

answered, "He put mud on my eyes, and I washed, and now I can see." ¹⁶Because of this, some of the Pharisees said, "This man is not from God, for He does not keep the Sabbath." But others said, "How can a sinful man perform such signs?" And there was division among them. ¹⁷So once again they asked the man who had been blind, "What do you say about Him, since it was your eyes He opened?" "He is a prophet," the man replied. ¹⁸The Jews still did not believe that the man had been blind and had received his sight until they summoned his parents ¹⁹and asked, "Is this your son, the one you say was born blind? So how is it that he can now see?" ²⁰His parents answered, "We know he is our son, and we know he was born blind. ²¹But how he can now see or who opened his eyes, we do not know. Ask him. He is old enough to speak for himself." ²²His parents said this because they were afraid of the Jews. For the Jews had already determined that anyone who confessed Jesus as the Christ would be put out of the synagogue. ²³That was why his parents said, "He is old enough. Ask him." ²⁴So a second time they called for the man who had been blind and said, "Give glory to God! We know that this man is a sinner." ²⁵He answered, "Whether He is a sinner I do not know. There is one thing I do know: I was blind, but now I see!" ²⁶"What did He do to you?" they asked. "How did He open your eyes?" ²⁷He replied, "I already told you and you did not listen. Why do you want to hear it again? Do you also want to become His disciples?" ²⁸Then they heaped insults on him and said, "You are His disciple; we are disciples of Moses. ²⁹We know that God spoke to Moses, but we do not know where this man is from." ³⁰"That is remarkable indeed!" the man said. "You do not know where He is from, and yet He opened my eyes. ³¹We know that God does not listen to sinners, but He does listen to the one who worships Him and does His will. ³²Never before has anyone heard of opening the eyes of a man born blind. ³³If this man were not from God, He could do no such thing." ³⁴They replied, "You were born in utter sin, and you are instructing us?" And they threw him out.

Spiritual Blindness

³⁵When Jesus heard that they had thrown him out, He found the man and said, "Do you believe in the Son of Man?" ³⁶"Who is He, Sir?" he replied. "Tell me so that I may believe in Him." ³⁷"You have already seen Him,"

Jesus answered. "He is the One speaking with you." ³⁸"Lord, I believe," he said. And he worshiped Jesus. ³⁹Then Jesus declared, "For judgment I have come into this world, so that the blind may see and those who see may become blind." ⁴⁰Some of the Pharisees who were with Him heard this, and they asked Him, "Are we blind too?" ⁴¹"If you were blind," Jesus replied, "you would not be guilty of sin. But since you claim you can see, your guilt remains."

John 10

Jesus the Good Shepherd (Psalm 23:1-6; Ezekiel 34:11-24)

¹"Truly, truly, I tell you, whoever does not enter the sheepfold by the gate, but climbs in some other way, is a thief and a robber. ²But the one who enters by the gate is the shepherd of the sheep. ³The gatekeeper opens the gate for him, and the sheep listen for his voice. He calls his own sheep by name and leads them out. ⁴When he has brought out all his own, he goes on ahead of them, and his sheep follow him because they know his voice. ⁵But they will never follow a stranger; in fact, they will flee from him because they do not recognize his voice." ⁶Jesus spoke to them using this illustration, but they did not understand what He was telling them. ⁷So He said to them again, "Truly, truly, I tell you, I am the gate for the sheep. ⁸All who came before Me were thieves and robbers, but the sheep did not listen to them. ⁹I am the gate. If anyone enters through Me, he will be saved. He will come in and go out and find pasture. ¹⁰The thief comes only to steal and kill and destroy. I have come that they may have life, and have it in all its fullness.

¹¹I am the good shepherd. The good shepherd lays down His life for the sheep. ¹²The hired hand is not the shepherd, and the sheep are not his own. When he sees the wolf coming, he abandons the sheep and runs away. Then the wolf pounces on them and scatters the flock. ¹³The man runs away because he is a hired servant and is unconcerned for the sheep. ¹⁴I am the good shepherd. I know My sheep and My sheep know Me, ¹⁵just as the Father knows Me and I know the Father. And I lay down My life for the sheep. ¹⁶I have other sheep that are not of this fold. I must bring them in as well, and they will listen to

My voice. Then there will be one flock and one shepherd. ¹⁷The reason the Father loves Me is that I lay down My life in order to take it up again. ¹⁸No one takes it from Me, but I lay it down of My own accord. I have authority to lay it down and authority to take it up again. This charge I have received from My Father." ¹⁹Again there was division among the Jews because of Jesus' message. ²⁰Many of them said, "He is demon-possessed and insane. Why would you listen to Him?" ²¹But others replied, "These are not the words of a man possessed by a demon. Can a demon open the eyes of the blind?"

The Unbelief of the Jews
²²At that time the Feast of Dedication took place in Jerusalem. It was winter, ²³and Jesus was walking in the temple courts in Solomon's Colonnade. ²⁴So the Jews gathered around Him and demanded, "How long will You keep us in suspense? If You are the Christ, tell us plainly." ²⁵"I already told you," Jesus replied, "but you did not believe. The works I do in My Father's name testify on My behalf. ²⁶But because you are not My sheep, you refuse to believe. ²⁷My sheep listen to My voice; I know them, and they follow Me. ²⁸I give them eternal life, and they will never perish. No one can snatch them out of My hand. ²⁹My Father who has given them to Me is greater than all. No one can snatch them out of My Father's hand. ³⁰I and the Father are one." ³¹At this, the Jews again picked up stones to stone Him. ³²But Jesus responded, "I have shown you many good works from the Father. For which of these do you stone Me?" ³³"We are not stoning You for any good work," said the Jews, "but for blasphemy, because You, who are a man, declare Yourself to be God." ³⁴Jesus replied, "Is it not written in your Law: 'I have said you are gods'? ³⁵If he called them gods to whom the word of God came—and the Scripture cannot be broken—³⁶then what about the One whom the Father sanctified and sent into the world? How then can you accuse Me of blasphemy for stating that I am the Son of God? ³⁷If I am not doing the works of My Father, then do not believe Me. ³⁸But if I am doing them, even though you do not believe Me, believe the works themselves, so that you may know and understand that the Father is in Me, and I am in the Father." ³⁹At this, they tried again to seize Him, but He escaped their grasp.

John's Testimony Confirmed

⁴⁰Then Jesus went back across the Jordan to the place where John had first been baptizing, and He stayed there. ⁴¹Many came to Him and said, "Although John never performed a sign, everything he said about this man was true." ⁴²And many in that place believed in Jesus.

John 11

The Death of Lazarus

¹At this time a man named Lazarus was sick. He lived in Bethany, the village of Mary and her sister Martha. ²(Mary, whose brother Lazarus was sick, would later anoint the Lord with perfume and wipe His feet with her hair.) ³So the sisters sent word to Jesus, "Lord, the one You love is sick." ⁴When Jesus heard this, He said, "This sickness will not end in death. No, it is for the glory of God, so that the Son of God may be glorified through it." ⁵Now Jesus loved Martha and her sister and Lazarus. ⁶So on hearing that Lazarus was sick, He stayed where He was for two days, ⁷and then He said to the disciples, "Let us go back to Judea." ⁸"Rabbi," they replied, "the Jews just tried to stone You, and You are going back there?" ⁹Jesus answered, "Are there not twelve hours of daylight? If anyone walks in the daytime, he will not stumble, because he sees by the light of this world. ¹⁰But if anyone walks at night, he will stumble, because he has no light." ¹¹After He had said this, He told them, "Our friend Lazarus has fallen asleep, but I am going there to wake him up." ¹²His disciples replied, "Lord, if he is sleeping, he will get better." ¹³They thought that Jesus was talking about actual sleep, but He was speaking about the death of Lazarus. ¹⁴So Jesus told them plainly, "Lazarus is dead, ¹⁵and for your sake I am glad I was not there, so that you may believe. But let us go to him." ¹⁶Then Thomas called Didymus said to his fellow disciples, "Let us also go, so that we may die with Him."

Jesus Comforts Martha and Mary

¹⁷When Jesus arrived, He found that Lazarus had already spent four days in the tomb. ¹⁸Now Bethany was near Jerusalem, a little less than two miles a away, ¹⁹and many of the Jews had come to Martha and Mary to console

them in the loss of their brother. ²⁰So when Martha heard that Jesus was coming, she went out to meet Him; but Mary stayed at home. ²¹Martha said to Jesus, "Lord, if You had been here, my brother would not have died. ²²But even now I know that God will give You whatever You ask Him." ²³"Your brother will rise again," Jesus told her. ²⁴Martha replied, "I know that he will rise again in the resurrection at the last day." ²⁵Jesus said to her, "I am the resurrection and the life. He who believes in Me will live, even though he dies. ²⁶And everyone who lives and believes in Me will never die. Do you believe this?" ²⁷"Yes, Lord," she answered, "I believe that You are the Christ, the Son of God, who was to come into the world." ²⁸After Martha had said this, she went back and called her sister Mary aside to tell her, "The Teacher is here and is asking for you." ²⁹And when Mary heard this, she got up quickly and went to Him. ³⁰Now Jesus had not yet entered the village, but was still at the place where Martha had met Him. ³¹When the Jews who were in the house consoling Mary saw how quickly she got up and went out, they followed her, supposing she was going to the tomb to mourn there. ³²When Mary came to Jesus and saw Him, she fell at His feet and said, "Lord, if You had been here, my brother would not have died." ³³When Jesus saw her weeping, and the Jews who had come with her also weeping, He was deeply moved in spirit and troubled. ³⁴"Where have you laid him?" He asked. "Come and see, Lord," they answered. ³⁵Jesus wept. ³⁶Then the Jews said, "See how He loved him!" ³⁷But some of them asked, "Could not this man who opened the eyes of the blind also have kept Lazarus from dying?"

Jesus Raises Lazarus (Acts 20:7-12)
³⁸Jesus, once again deeply moved, came to the tomb. It was a cave with a stone laid across the entrance. ³⁹"Take away the stone," Jesus said. "Lord, by now he stinks," said Martha, the sister of the dead man. "It has already been four days." ⁴⁰Jesus replied, "Did I not tell you that if you believed, you would see the glory of God?" ⁴¹So they took away the stone. Then Jesus lifted His eyes upward and said, "Father, I thank You that You have heard Me. ⁴²I knew that You always hear Me, but I say this for the benefit of the people standing here, so they may believe that You sent Me." ⁴³After Jesus had said this, He called out in a loud voice, "Lazarus, come out!" ⁴⁴The man who had been dead came

out with his hands and feet bound in strips of linen, and his face wrapped in a headcloth. "Unwrap him and let him go," Jesus told them.

The Plot to Kill Jesus (Matthew 26:1-5; Mark 14:1-2; Luke 22:1-6)
⁴⁵Therefore many of the Jews who had come to Mary, and had seen what Jesus did, believed in Him. ⁴⁶But some of them went to the Pharisees and told them what Jesus had done. ⁴⁷Then the chief priests and Pharisees convened the Sanhedrin and said, "What are we to do? This man is performing many signs. ⁴⁸If we let Him go on like this, everyone will believe in Him, and then the Romans will come and take away both our place and our nation." ⁴⁹But one of them, named Caiaphas, who was high priest that year, said to them, "You know nothing at all! ⁵⁰You do not realize that it is better for you that one man die for the people than that the whole nation perish." ⁵¹Caiaphas did not say this on his own. Instead, as high priest that year, he was prophesying that Jesus would die for the nation, ⁵²and not only for the nation, but also for the scattered children of God, to gather them together into one. ⁵³So from that day on they plotted to kill Him. ⁵⁴As a result, Jesus no longer went about publicly among the Jews, but He withdrew to a town called Ephraim in an area near the wilderness. And He stayed there with the disciples. ⁵⁵Now the Jewish Passover was near, and many people went up from the country to Jerusalem to purify themselves before the Passover. ⁵⁶They kept looking for Jesus and asking one another as they stood in the temple courts, "What do you think? Will He come to the feast at all?" ⁵⁷But the chief priests and Pharisees had given orders that anyone who knew where He was must report it, so that they could arrest Him.

John 12

Mary Anoints Jesus (Matthew 26:6-13; Mark 14:3-9)
¹Six days before the Passover, Jesus came to Bethany, the hometown of Lazarus, whom He had raised from the dead. ²So they hosted a dinner for Jesus there. Martha served, and Lazarus was among those reclining at the table with Him. ³Then Mary took about a pint of expensive perfume, made of pure nard, and she anointed Jesus' feet and wiped them with her hair. And the house was filled with the fragrance of the perfume. ⁴But one of His disci-

ples, Judas Iscariot, who was going to betray Him, asked, ⁵"Why wasn't this perfume sold for three hundred denarii and the money given to the poor?" ⁶Judas did not say this because he cared about the poor, but because he was a thief. As keeper of the money bag, he used to take from what was put into it. ⁷"Leave her alone," Jesus replied. "She was intended to keep this perfume to prepare for the day of My burial. ⁸The poor you will always have with you, but you will not always have Me."

The Plot to Kill Lazarus

⁹Meanwhile a large crowd of Jews learned that Jesus was there. And they came not only because of Him, but also to see Lazarus, whom He had raised from the dead. ¹⁰So the chief priests made plans to kill Lazarus as well, ¹¹for on account of him many of the Jews were deserting them and believing in Jesus.

The Triumphal Entry (Zechariah 9:9-13; Matthew 21:1-11; Mark 11:1-11; Luke 19:28-40)

¹²The next day the great crowd that had come to the feast heard that Jesus was coming to Jerusalem. ¹³They took palm branches and went out to meet Him, shouting: "Hosanna!" "Blessed is He who comes in the name of the Lord!" "Blessed is the King of Israel!" ¹⁴Finding a young donkey, Jesus sat on it, as it is written: ¹⁵"Do not be afraid, O daughter of Zion. See, your King is coming, seated on the colt of a donkey."

¹⁶At first His disciples did not understand these things, but after Jesus was glorified they remembered what had been done to Him, and they realized that these very things had also been written about Him. ¹⁷Meanwhile, many people continued to testify that they had been with Jesus when He called Lazarus from the tomb and raised him from the dead. ¹⁸That is also why the crowd went out to meet Him, because they heard that He had performed this sign. ¹⁹Then the Pharisees said to one another, "You can see that this is doing you no good. Look how the whole world has gone after Him!"

Jesus Predicts His Death

²⁰Now there were some Greeks among those who went up to worship at the feast. ²¹They came to Philip, who was from Bethsaida in Galilee, and requested of him, "Sir, we want to see Jesus." ²²Philip relayed this appeal to

Andrew, and both of them went and told Jesus. ²³But Jesus replied, "The hour has come for the Son of Man to be glorified. ²⁴Truly, truly, I tell you, unless a kernel of wheat falls to the ground and dies, it remains only a seed; but if it dies, it bears much fruit. ²⁵Whoever loves his life will lose it, but whoever hates his life in this world will keep it for eternal life. ²⁶If anyone serves Me, he must follow Me; and where I am, My servant will be as well. If anyone serves Me, the Father will honor him. ²⁷Now My soul is troubled, and what shall I say? 'Father, save Me from this hour'? No, it is for this purpose that I have come to this hour. ²⁸Father, glorify Your name!" Then a voice came from heaven: "I have glorified it, and I will glorify it again." ²⁹The crowd standing there heard it and said that it had thundered. Others said that an angel had spoken to Him. ³⁰In response, Jesus said, "This voice was not for My benefit, but yours. ³¹Now judgment is upon this world; now the prince of this world will be cast out. ³²And I, when I am lifted up from the earth, will draw all men to Myself." ³³He said this to indicate the kind of death He was going to die. ³⁴The crowd replied, "We have heard from the Law that the Christ will remain forever. So how can you say that the Son of Man must be lifted up? Who is this Son of Man?" ³⁵Then Jesus told them, "For a little while longer, the Light will be among you. Walk while you have the Light, so that darkness will not overtake you. The one who walks in the darkness does not know where he is going. ³⁶While you have the Light, believe in the Light, so that you may become sons of light." After Jesus had spoken these things, He went away and was hidden from them.

Belief and Unbelief

³⁷Although Jesus had performed so many signs in their presence, they still did not believe in Him. ³⁸This was to fulfill the word of Isaiah the prophet: "Lord, who has believed our message? And to whom has the arm of the Lord been revealed?" ³⁹For this reason they were unable to believe. For again, Isaiah says: ⁴⁰"He has blinded their eyes and hardened their hearts, so that they cannot see with their eyes, and understand with their hearts, and turn, and I would heal them." ⁴¹Isaiah said these things because he saw Jesus' glory and spoke about Him. ⁴²Nevertheless, many of the leaders believed in Him; but because of the Pharisees they did not confess Him, for fear that they

would be put out of the synagogue. ⁴³For they loved praise from men more than praise from God. ⁴⁴Then Jesus cried out, "Whoever believes in Me does not believe in Me alone, but in the One who sent Me. ⁴⁵And whoever sees Me sees the One who sent Me. ⁴⁶I have come into the world as a light, so that no one who believes in Me should remain in darkness. ⁴⁷As for anyone who hears My words and does not keep them, I do not judge him. For I have not come to judge the world, but to save the world. ⁴⁸There is a judge for the one who rejects Me and does not receive My words: The word that I have spoken will judge him on the last day. ⁴⁹I have not spoken on My own, but the Father who sent Me has commanded Me what to say and how to say it. ⁵⁰And I know that His command leads to eternal life. So I speak exactly what the Father has told Me to say."

John 13

Jesus Washes His Disciples' Feet
¹It was now just before the Passover Feast, and Jesus knew that His hour had come to leave this world and return to the Father. Having loved His own who were in the world, He loved them to the very end. ²The evening meal was underway, and the devil had already put into the heart of Judas, the son of Simon Iscariot, to betray Jesus. ³Jesus knew that the Father had delivered all things into His hands, and that He had come from God and was returning to God. ⁴So He got up from the supper, laid aside His outer garments, and wrapped a towel around His waist. ⁵After that, He poured water into a basin and began to wash the disciples' feet and dry them with the towel that was around Him. ⁶He came to Simon Peter, who asked Him, "Lord, are You going to wash my feet?" ⁷Jesus replied, "You do not realize now what I am doing, but later you will understand." ⁸"Never shall You wash my feet!" Peter told Him. Jesus answered, "Unless I wash you, you have no part with Me." ⁹"Then, Lord," Simon Peter replied, "not only my feet, but my hands and my head as well!" ¹⁰Jesus told him, "Whoever has already bathed needs only to wash his feet, and he will be completely clean. And you are clean, though not all of you." ¹¹For He knew who would betray Him. That is why He said, "Not all of you are clean." ¹²When Jesus had washed their feet and put on His outer

garments, He reclined with them again and asked, "Do you know what I have done for you? [13]You call Me Teacher and Lord, and rightly so, because I am. [14]So if I, your Lord and Teacher, have washed your feet, you also should wash one another's feet. [15]I have set you an example so that you should do as I have done for you. [16]Truly, truly, I tell you, no servant is greater than his master, nor is a messenger greater than the one who sent him. [17]If you know these things, you will be blessed if you do them.

Jesus Predicts His Betrayal (Psalm 41:1-13; Matthew 26:17-25; Mark 14:12-21; Luke 22:7-13)
[18]I am not speaking about all of you; I know whom I have chosen. But this is to fulfill the Scripture: 'The one who eats bread with Me has lifted up his heel against Me.' [19]I am telling you now before it happens, so that when it comes to pass, you will believe that I am He. [20]Truly, truly, I tell you, whoever receives the one I send receives Me, and whoever receives Me receives the One who sent Me." [21]After Jesus had said this, He became troubled in spirit and testified, "Truly, truly, I tell you, one of you will betray Me." [22]The disciples began to look at one another, perplexed as to which of them He meant. [23]One of His disciples, the one whom Jesus loved, was reclining at His side. [24]So Simon Peter motioned to him to ask Jesus which one He was talking about. [25]Leaning back against Jesus, he asked, "Lord, who is it?" [26]Jesus answered, "It is the one to whom I give this piece of bread after I have dipped it." Then He dipped the piece of bread and gave it to Judas son of Simon Iscariot. [27]And when Judas had taken the piece of bread, Satan entered into him. Then Jesus said to Judas, "What you are about to do, do quickly." [28]But no one at the table knew why Jesus had said this to him. [29]Since Judas kept the money bag, some thought that Jesus was telling him to buy what was needed for the feast, or to give something to the poor. [30]As soon as he had received the piece of bread, Judas went out into the night.

Love One another (Romans 12:9-13; 1 John 3:11-24)
[31]When Judas had gone out, Jesus said, "Now the Son of Man is glorified, and God is glorified in Him. [32]If God is glorified in Him, God will also glorify the Son in Himself—and will glorify Him at once. [33]Little children, I am

with you only a little while longer. You will look for Me, and as I said to the Jews, so now I say to you: 'Where I am going, you cannot come.' ³⁴A new commandment I give you: Love one another. As I have loved you, so also you must love one another. ³⁵By this all men will know that you are My disciples, if you love one another."

Jesus Predicts Peter's Denial (Matthew 26:31-35; Mark 14:27-31; Luke 22:31-38)
³⁶"Lord, where are You going?" Simon Peter asked. Jesus answered, "Where I am going, you cannot follow Me now, but you will follow later." ³⁷"Lord," said Peter, "why can't I follow You now? I will lay down my life for You." ³⁸"Will you lay down your life for Me?" Jesus replied. "Truly, truly, I tell you, before the rooster crows, you will deny Me three times.

John 14

In My Father's House are Many Rooms
¹Do not let your hearts be troubled. You believe in God; a believe in Me as well. ²In My Father's house are many rooms. If it were not so, would I have told you that I am going there to prepare a place for you? ³And if I go and prepare a place for you, I will come back and welcome you into My presence, so that you also may be where I am. ⁴You know the way to the place where I am going."

The Way, the Truth, and the Life
⁵"Lord," said Thomas, "we do not know where You are going, so how can we know the way?" ⁶Jesus answered, "I am the way, the truth, and the life. No one comes to the Father except through Me. ⁷If you had known Me, you would know My Father as well. From now on you do know Him and have seen Him." ⁸Philip said to Him, "Lord, show us the Father, and that will be enough for us." ⁹Jesus replied, "Philip, I have been with you all this time, and still you do not know Me? Anyone who has seen Me has seen the Father. How can you say, 'Show us the Father'? ¹⁰Do you not believe that I am in the Father and the Father is in Me? The words I say to you, I do not speak on My own. Instead, it is the Father dwelling in Me, performing His works. ¹¹Believe

Me that I am in the Father and the Father is in Me—or at least believe on account of the works themselves. ¹²Truly, truly, I tell you, whoever believes in Me will also do the works that I am doing. He will do even greater things than these, because I am going to the Father. ¹³And I will do whatever you ask in My name, so that the Father may be glorified in the Son. ¹⁴If you ask Me anything in My name, I will do it.

Jesus Promises the Holy Spirit (Joel 2:28-32; John 16:5-16; Acts 2:1-13; Acts 10:44-48; Acts 19:1-7)

¹⁵If you love Me, you will keep My commandments. ¹⁶And I will ask the Father, and He will give you another Advocate to be with you forever—¹⁷the Spirit of truth. The world cannot receive Him, because it neither sees Him nor knows Him. But you do know Him, for He abides with you and will be in you. ¹⁸I will not leave you as orphans; I will come to you. ¹⁹In a little while, the world will see Me no more, but you will see Me. Because I live, you also will live. ²⁰On that day you will know that I am in My Father, and you are in Me, and I am in you. ²¹Whoever has My commandments and keeps them is the one who loves Me. The one who loves Me will be loved by My Father, and I will love him and reveal Myself to him." ²²Judas (not Iscariot) asked Him, "Lord, why are You going to reveal Yourself to us and not to the world?" ²³Jesus replied, "If anyone loves Me, he will keep My word. My Father will love him, and we will come to him and make Our home with him. ²⁴Whoever does not love Me does not keep My words. The word that you hear is not My own, but it is from the Father who sent Me. ²⁵All this I have spoken to you while I am still with you. ²⁶But the Advocate, the Holy Spirit, whom the Father will send in My name, will teach you all things and will remind you of everything I have told you.

Peace I Leave with You (Romans 5:1-5)

²⁷Peace I leave with you; My peace I give to you. I do not give to you as the world gives. Do not let your hearts be troubled; do not be afraid. ²⁸You heard Me say, 'I am going away, and I am coming back to you.' If you loved Me, you would rejoice that I am going to the Father, because the Father is greater than I. ²⁹And now I have told you before it happens, so that when it does happen, you will believe. ³⁰I will not speak with you much longer, for the prince of

this world is coming, and he has no claim on Me. ³¹But I do exactly what the Father has commanded Me, so that the world may know that I love the Father. Get up! Let us go on from here.

John 15

Jesus the True Vine

¹I am the true vine, and My Father is the keeper of the vineyard. ²He cuts off every branch in Me that bears no fruit, and every branch that does bear fruit, He prunes to make it even more fruitful. ³You are already clean because of the word I have spoken to you. ⁴Remain in Me, and I will remain in you. Just as no branch can bear fruit by itself unless it remains in the vine, neither can you bear fruit unless you remain in Me. ⁵I am the vine and you are the branches. The one who remains in Me, and I in him, will bear much fruit. For apart from Me you can do nothing. ⁶If anyone does not remain in Me, he is like a branch that is thrown away and withers. Such branches are gathered up, thrown into the fire, and burned. ⁷If you remain in Me and My words remain in you, ask whatever you wish, and it will be done for you. ⁸This is to My Father's glory, that you bear much fruit, proving yourselves to be My disciples.

No Greater Love

⁹As the Father has loved Me, so have I loved you. Remain in My love. ¹⁰If you keep My commandments, you will remain in My love, just as I have kept My Father's commandments and remain in His love. ¹¹I have told you these things so that My joy may be in you and your joy may be complete. ¹²This is My commandment, that you love one another as I have loved you. ¹³Greater love has no one than this, that he lay down his life for his friends. ¹⁴You are My friends if you do what I command you. ¹⁵No longer do I call you servants, for a servant does not understand what his master is doing. But I have called you friends, because everything I have learned from My Father I have made known to you. ¹⁶You did not choose Me, but I chose you. And I appointed you to go and bear fruit—fruit that will remain—so that whatever you ask the Father in My name, He will give you. ¹⁷This is My command to you: Love one another.

The Hatred of the World

[18] If the world hates you, understand that it hated Me first. [19] If you were of the world, it would love you as its own. Instead, the world hates you, because you are not of the world, but I have chosen you out of the world. [20] Remember the word that I spoke to you: 'No servant is greater than his master.' If they persecuted Me, they will persecute you as well; if they kept My word, they will keep yours as well. [21] But they will treat you like this on account of My name, because they do not know the One who sent Me. [22] If I had not come and spoken to them, they would not be guilty of sin. Now, however, they have no excuse for their sin. [23] Whoever hates Me hates My Father as well. [24] If I had not done among them the works that no one else did, they would not be guilty of sin; but now they have seen and hated both Me and My Father. [25] But this is to fulfill what is written in their Law: 'They hated Me without reason.' [26] When the Advocate comes, whom I will send to you from the Father—the Spirit of truth who goes out from the Father—He will testify about Me. [27] And you also must testify, because you have been with Me from the beginning.

John 16

Persecution Foretold (Acts 23:12-22)

[1] I have told you these things so that you will not fall away. [2] They will put you out of the synagogues. In fact, a time is coming when anyone who kills you will think he is offering a service to God. [3] They will do these things because they have not known the Father or Me. [4] But I have told you these things so that when their hour comes, you will remember that I told you about them. I did not tell you these things from the beginning, because I was with you.

The Promise of the Holy Spirit (Joel 2:28-32; John 14:15-26; Acts 2:1-13; Acts 10:44-48; Acts 19:1-7)

[5] Now, however, I am going to Him who sent Me; yet none of you asks Me, 'Where are You going?' [6] Instead, your hearts are filled with sorrow because I have told you these things. [7] But I tell you the truth, it is for your benefit that I am going away. Unless I go away, the Advocate will not come to you; but if I

go, I will send Him to you. ⁸And when He comes, He will convict the world in regard to sin and righteousness and judgment: ⁹in regard to sin, because they do not believe in Me; ¹⁰in regard to righteousness, because I am going to the Father and you will no longer see Me; ¹¹and in regard to judgment, because the prince of this world has been condemned. ¹²I still have much to tell you, but you cannot yet bear to hear it. ¹³However, when the Spirit of truth comes, He will guide you into all truth. For He will not speak on His own, but He will speak what He hears, and He will declare to you what is to come. ¹⁴He will glorify Me by taking from what is Mine and disclosing it to you. ¹⁵Everything that belongs to the Father is Mine. That is why I said that the Spirit will take from what is Mine and disclose it to you. ¹⁶In a little while you will see Me no more, and then after a little while you will see Me."

Grief to Joy
¹⁷Then some of His disciples asked one another, "Why is He telling us, 'In a little while you will not see Me, and then after a little while you will see Me' and 'Because I am going to the Father'?" ¹⁸They kept asking, "Why is He saying, 'a little while'? We do not understand what He is saying." ¹⁹Aware that they wanted to question Him, Jesus said to them, "Are you asking one another why I said, 'In a little while you will not see Me, and then after a little while you will see Me'? ²⁰Truly, truly, I tell you, you will weep and wail while the world rejoices. You will grieve, but your grief will turn to joy. ²¹A woman has pain in childbirth because her time has come; but when she brings forth her child, she forgets her anguish because of her joy that a child has been born into the world. ²²So also you have sorrow now, but I will see you again and your hearts will rejoice, and no one will take away your joy.

Ask and You will Receive
²³In that day you will no longer ask Me anything. Truly, truly, I tell you, whatever you ask the Father in My name, He will give you. ²⁴Until now you have not asked for anything in My name. Ask and you will receive, so that your joy may be complete. ²⁵I have spoken these things to you in figures of speech. A time is coming when I will no longer speak to you this way, but will tell you plainly about the Father. ²⁶In that day you will ask in My name. I am

not saying that I will ask the Father on your behalf. ²⁷For the Father Himself loves you, because you have loved Me and have believed that I came from God. ²⁸I came from the Father and entered the world. In turn, I will leave the world and go to the Father." ²⁹His disciples said, "See, now You are speaking plainly and without figures of speech. ³⁰Now we understand that You know all things and that You have no need for anyone to question You. Because of this, we believe that You came from God." ³¹"Do you finally believe?" Jesus replied. ³²"Look, an hour is coming and has already come when you will be scattered, each to his own home, and you will leave Me all alone. Yet I am not alone, because the Father is with Me. ³³I have told you these things so that in Me you may have peace. In the world you will have tribulation. But take courage; I have overcome the world!"

John 17

Prayer for the Son
¹When Jesus had spoken these things, He lifted up His eyes to heaven and said, "Father, the hour has come. Glorify Your Son, that Your Son may glorify You. ²For You granted Him authority over all humanity, so that He may give eternal life to all those You have given Him. ³Now this is eternal life, that they may know You, the only true God, and Jesus Christ, whom You have sent. ⁴I have glorified You on earth by accomplishing the work You gave Me to do. ⁵And now, Father, glorify Me in Your presence with the glory I had with You before the world existed.

Prayer for the Disciples
⁶I have revealed Your name to those You have given Me out of the world. They were Yours; You gave them to Me, and they have kept Your word. ⁷Now they know that everything You have given Me comes from You. ⁸For I have given them the words You gave Me, and they have received them. They knew with certainty that I came from You, and they believed that You sent Me. ⁹I ask on their behalf. I do not ask on behalf of the world, but on behalf of those You have given Me; for they are Yours. ¹⁰All I have is Yours, and all You have is Mine; and in them I have been glorified. ¹¹I will no longer be in the world, but they are in the world, and I am coming to You. Holy Father,

protect them by Your name, the name You gave Me, so that they may be one as We are one. ¹²While I was with them, I protected and preserved them by Your name, the name You gave Me. Not one of them has been lost, except the son of destruction, so that the Scripture would be fulfilled. ¹³But now I am coming to You, and I am saying these things while I am in the world, so that they may have My joy fulfilled within them. ¹⁴I have given them Your word and the world has hated them; for they are not of the world, just as I am not of the world. ¹⁵I am not asking that You take them out of the world, but that You keep them from the evil one. ¹⁶They are not of the world, just as I am not of the world. ¹⁷Sanctify them by the truth; Your word is truth. ¹⁸As You sent Me into the world, I have also sent them into the world. ¹⁹For them I sanctify Myself, so that they too may be sanctified by the truth.

Prayer for all Believers
²⁰I am not asking on behalf of them alone, but also on behalf of those who will believe in Me through their message, ²¹that all of them may be one, as You, Father, are in Me, and I am in You. May they also be in Us, so that the world may believe that You sent Me. ²²I have given them the glory You gave Me, so that they may be one as We are one—²³I in them and You in Me—that they may be perfectly united, so that the world may know that You sent Me and have loved them just as You have loved Me. ²⁴Father, I want those You have given Me to be with Me where I am, that they may see the glory You gave Me because You loved Me before the foundation of the world. ²⁵Righteous Father, although the world has not known You, I know You, and they know that You sent Me. ²⁶And I have made Your name known to them and will continue to make it known, so that the love You have for Me may be in them, and I in them."

John 18

The Betrayal of Jesus (Matthew 26:47-56; Mark 14:43-52; Luke 22:47-53)
¹When Jesus had spoken these words, He went out with His disciples across the Kidron Valley, where they entered a garden. ²Now Judas, His betrayer, also knew the place, because Jesus had often met there with His disciples.

³So Judas brought a band of soldiers and officers from the chief priests and Pharisees. They arrived at the garden carrying lanterns, torches, and weapons. ⁴Jesus, knowing all that was coming upon Him, stepped forward and asked them, "Whom are you seeking?" ⁵"Jesus of Nazareth," they answered. Jesus said, "I am He." And Judas, His betrayer, was standing there with them. ⁶When Jesus said, "I am He," they drew back and fell to the ground. ⁷So He asked them again, "Whom are you seeking?" "Jesus of Nazareth," they answered. ⁸ "I told you that I am He," Jesus replied. "So if you are looking for Me, let these men go." ⁹This was to fulfill the word He had spoken: "I have not lost one of those You have given Me." ¹⁰Then Simon Peter drew his sword and struck the servant of the high priest, cutting off his right ear. The servant's name was Malchus. ¹¹"Put your sword back in its sheath!" Jesus said to Peter. "Shall I not drink the cup the Father has given Me?" ¹²Then the band of soldiers, with its commander and the officers of the Jews, arrested Jesus and bound Him. ¹³They brought Him first to Annas, who was the father-in-law of Caiaphas, the high priest that year. ¹⁴Caiaphas was the one who had advised the Jews that it would be better if one man died for the people.

Peter's First Denial (Matthew 26:69-71; Mark 14:66-67; Luke 22:54-57)
¹⁵Now Simon Peter and another disciple were following Jesus. Since that disciple was known to the high priest, he also went with Jesus into the courtyard of the high priest. ¹⁶But Peter stood outside at the door. Then the disciple who was known to the high priest went out and spoke to the doorkeeper, and brought Peter in. ¹⁷At this, the servant girl watching the door said to Peter, "Aren't you also one of this man's disciples?" "I am not," he answered. ¹⁸Because it was cold, the servants and officers were standing around a charcoal fire they had made to keep warm. And Peter was also standing with them, warming himself.

Jesus Before the High Priest (Isaiah 53:1-8; Matthew 26:57-68; Mark 14:53-65; 1Peter 2:21-25)
¹⁹Meanwhile, the high priest questioned Jesus about His disciples and His teaching. ²⁰"I have spoken openly to the world," Jesus answered. "I always taught in the synagogues and at the temple, where all the Jews come together.

I said nothing in secret. ²¹Why are you asking Me? Ask those who heard My message. Surely they know what I said." ²²When Jesus had said this, one of the officers standing nearby slapped Him in the face and said, "Is this how You answer the high priest?" ²³Jesus replied, "If I said something wrong, testify to what was wrong. But if I spoke correctly, why did you strike Me?" ²⁴Then Annas sent Him, still bound, to Caiaphas the high priest.

Peter's Second and Third Denials (Matthew 26:71-75; Mark 14:68-72; Luke 22:58-62)
²⁵Simon Peter was still standing and warming himself. So they asked him, "Aren't you also one of His disciples?" He denied it and said, "I am not." ²⁶One of the high priest's servants, a relative of the man whose ear Peter had cut off, asked, "Didn't I see you with Him in the garden?" ²⁷Peter denied it once more, and immediately a rooster crowed.

Jesus Before Pilate (Matthew 27:11-14; Luke 23:1-6)
²⁸Then they led Jesus away from Caiaphas into the Praetorium. By now it was early morning, and the Jews did not enter the Praetorium to avoid being defiled and unable to eat the Passover. ²⁹So Pilate went out to them and asked, "What accusation are you bringing against this man?" ³⁰"If He were not a criminal," they replied, "we would not have handed Him over to you." ³¹"You take Him and judge Him by your own law," Pilate told them. "We are not permitted to execute anyone," the Jews replied. ³²This was to fulfill the word that Jesus had spoken to indicate the kind of death He was going to die. ³³Pilate went back into the Praetorium, summoned Jesus, and asked Him, "Are You the King of the Jews?" ³⁴"Are you saying this on your own," Jesus asked, "or did others tell you about Me?" ³⁵"Am I a Jew?" Pilate replied. "Your own people and chief priests handed You over to me. What have You done?" ³⁶Jesus answered, "My kingdom is not of this world; if it were, My servants would fight to prevent My arrest by the Jews. But now, My kingdom is not of this realm." ³⁷"Then You are a king!" Pilate said. "You say that I am a king," Jesus answered. "For this reason I was born and have come into the world, to testify to the truth. Everyone who belongs to the truth listens to My voice." ³⁸"What is truth?" Pilate asked. And having said this, he went out

again to the Jews and told them, "I find no basis for a charge against Him. ³⁹But it is your custom that I release to you one prisoner at the Passover. So then, do you want me to release to you the King of the Jews?" ⁴⁰"Not this man," they shouted, "but Barabbas!" (Now Barabbas was an insurrectionist.)

John 19

The Soldiers Mock Jesus (Isaiah 50:4-11; Matthew 27:27-31; Mark 15:16-20; Luke 22:63-65)

¹Then Pilate took Jesus and had Him flogged. ²The soldiers twisted together a crown of thorns, put it on His head, and dressed Him in a purple robe. ³And they went up to Him again and again, saying, "Hail, King of the Jews!" and slapping Him in the face. ⁴Once again Pilate came out and said to the Jews, "Look, I am bringing Him out to you to let you know that I find no basis for a charge against Him." ⁵When Jesus came out wearing the crown of thorns and the purple robe, Pilate said to them, "Here is the man!" ⁶As soon as the chief priests and officers saw Him, they shouted, "Crucify Him! Crucify Him!" "You take Him and crucify Him," Pilate replied, "for I find no basis for a charge against Him." ⁷"We have a law," answered the Jews, "and according to that law He must die, because He declared Himself to be the Son of God." ⁸When Pilate heard this statement, he was even more afraid, ⁹and he went back into the Praetorium. "Where are You from?" he asked. But Jesus gave no answer. ¹⁰So Pilate said to Him, "Do You refuse to speak to me? Do You not know that I have authority to release You and authority to crucify You?" ¹¹Jesus answered, "You would have no authority over Me if it were not given to you from above. Therefore the one who handed Me over to you is guilty of greater sin."

¹²From then on, Pilate tried to release Him, but the Jews kept shouting, "If you release this man, you are no friend of Caesar. Anyone who declares himself a king is defying Caesar." ¹³When Pilate heard these words, he brought Jesus out and sat on the judgment seat at a place called the Stone Pavement, which in Aramaic is Gabbatha. ¹⁴It was the day of Preparation for the Passover, about the sixth hour. And Pilate said to the Jews, "Here is your King!" ¹⁵At this, they shouted, "Away with Him! Away with Him! Crucify Him!"

"Shall I crucify your King?" Pilate asked. "We have no king but Caesar," replied the chief priests.

The Crucifixion (Psalms 22:1-31; 69:1-36; Matthew 27:32-44; Mark 15:21-32; Luke 23:26-43)

[16]Then Pilate handed Jesus over to be crucified, and the soldiers took Him away. [17]Carrying His own cross, He went out to The Place of the Skull, which in Aramaic is called Golgotha. [18]There they crucified Him, and with Him two others, one on each side, with Jesus in the middle. [19]Pilate also had a notice posted on the cross. It read:

JESUS OF NAZARETH, THE KING OF THE JEWS.

[20]Many of the Jews read this sign, because the place where Jesus was crucified was near the city, and it was written in Aramaic, Latin, and Greek. [21]So the chief priests of the Jews said to Pilate, "Do not write, 'The King of the Jews,' but only that He said, 'I am the King of the Jews.'" [22]Pilate answered, "What I have written, I have written." [23]When the soldiers had crucified Jesus, they divided His garments into four parts, one for each soldier, with the tunic remaining. It was seamless, woven in one piece from top to bottom. [24]So they said to one another, "Let us not tear it. Instead, let us cast lots to see who will get it." This was to fulfill the Scripture: "They divided My garments among them, and cast lots for My clothing." So that is what the soldiers did. [25]Near the cross of Jesus stood His mother and her sister, as well as Mary the wife of Clopas and Mary Magdalene. [26]When Jesus saw His mother and the disciple whom He loved standing nearby, He said to His mother, "Woman, here is your son." [27]Then He said to the disciple, "Here is your mother." So from that hour, this disciple took her into his home.

The Death of Jesus (Psalm 22:1-31; Matthew 27:45-56; Mark 15:33-41; Luke 23:44-49)

[28]After this, knowing that everything had now been accomplished, and to fulfill the Scripture, Jesus said, "I am thirsty." [29]A jar of sour wine was sitting there. So they soaked a sponge in the wine, put it on a stalk of hyssop, and lifted it to His mouth. [30]When Jesus had received the sour wine, He said, "It is finished." And bowing His head, He yielded up His spirit.

Jesus' Side is Pierced (Zechariah 12:10-14)

³¹It was the day of Preparation, and the next day was a High Sabbath. In order that the bodies would not remain on the cross during the Sabbath, the Jews asked Pilate to have the legs broken and the bodies removed. ³²So the soldiers came and broke the legs of the first man who had been crucified with Jesus, and those of the other. ³³But when they came to Jesus and saw that He was already dead, they did not break His legs. ³⁴Instead, one of the soldiers pierced His side with a spear, and immediately blood and water flowed out. ³⁵The one who saw it has testified to this, and his testimony is true. He knows that he is telling the truth, so that you also may believe. ³⁶Now these things happened so that the Scripture would be fulfilled: "Not one of His bones will be broken." ³⁷And, as another Scripture says: "They will look on the One they have pierced."

The Burial of Jesus (Isaiah 53:9-12; Matthew 27:57-61; Mark 15:42-47; Luke 23:50-56)

³⁸Afterward, Joseph of Arimathea, who was a disciple of Jesus (but secretly for fear of the Jews), asked Pilate to let him remove the body of Jesus. Pilate gave him permission, so he came and removed His body. ³⁹ Nicodemus, who had previously come to Jesus at night, also brought a mixture of myrrh and aloes, about seventy-five pounds. ⁴⁰So they took the body of Jesus and wrapped it in linen cloths with the spices, according to the Jewish burial custom.

⁴¹Now there was a garden in the place where Jesus was crucified, and in the garden a new tomb in which no one had yet been laid. ⁴²And because it was the Jewish day of Preparation and the tomb was nearby, they laid Jesus there.

John 20

The Resurrection (Psalm 16:1-11; Psalm 49:1-20; Matthew 28:1-10; Mark 16:1-8; Luke 24:1-12)

¹Early on the first day of the week, while it was still dark, Mary Magdalene went to the tomb and saw that the stone had been removed from the entrance. ²So she came running to Simon Peter and the other disciple, the one

whom Jesus loved. "They have taken the Lord out of the tomb," she said, "and we do not know where they have put Him!" ³Then Peter and the other disciple set out for the tomb. ⁴The two were running together, but the other disciple outran Peter and reached the tomb first. ⁵He bent down and looked in at the linen cloths lying there, but he did not go in. ⁶Simon Peter arrived just after him. He entered the tomb and saw the linen cloths lying there. ⁷ The face cloth that had been around Jesus' head was rolled up, lying separate from the linen cloths. ⁸Then the other disciple, who had reached the tomb first, also went in. And he saw and believed. ⁹For they still did not understand from the Scripture that Jesus had to rise from the dead.

Jesus Appears to Mary Magdalene (Mark 16:9-11)
¹⁰Then the disciples returned to their homes. ¹¹ But Mary stood outside the tomb weeping. And as she wept, she bent down to look into the tomb, ¹²and she saw two angels in white sitting where the body of Jesus had lain, one at the head and the other at the feet. ¹³"Woman, why are you weeping?" they asked. "Because they have taken my Lord away," she said, "and I do not know where they have put Him." ¹⁴ When she had said this, she turned around and saw Jesus standing there; but she did not recognize that it was Jesus. ¹⁵"Woman, why are you weeping?" Jesus asked. "Whom are you seeking?" Thinking He was the gardener, she said, "Sir, if you have carried Him off, tell me where you have put Him, and I will get Him." ¹⁶Jesus said to her, "Mary." She turned and said to Him in Aramaic, "Rabboni!" (which means Teacher). ¹⁷"Do not cling to Me," Jesus said, "for I have not yet ascended to the Father. But go and tell My brothers, 'I am ascending to My Father and your Father, to My God and your God.'" ¹⁸Mary Magdalene went and announced to the disciples, "I have seen the Lord!" And she told them what He had said to her.

Jesus Appears to the Disciples (Luke 24:36-43; 1John 1:1-4)
¹⁹It was the first day of the week, and that very evening, while the disciples were together with the doors locked for fear of the Jews, Jesus came and stood among them. "Peace be with you!" He said to them. ²⁰After He had said this, He showed them His hands and His side. The disciples rejoiced when they saw the Lord. ²¹ Again Jesus said to them, "Peace be with you. As the Father

has sent Me, so also I am sending you." ²²When He had said this, He breathed on them and said, "Receive the Holy Spirit. ²³If you forgive anyone his sins, they are forgiven; if you withhold forgiveness from anyone, it is withheld."

Jesus Appears to Thomas

²⁴Now Thomas called Didymus, one of the Twelve, was not with the disciples when Jesus came. ²⁵So the other disciples told him, "We have seen the Lord!" But he replied, "Unless I see the nail marks in His hands, and put my finger where the nails have been, and put my hand into His side, I will never believe." ²⁶Eight days later, His disciples were once again inside with the doors locked, and Thomas was with them. Jesus came and stood among them and said, "Peace be with you." ²⁷Then Jesus said to Thomas, "Put your finger here and look at My hands. Reach out your hand and put it into My side. Stop doubting and believe." ²⁸Thomas replied, "My Lord and my God!" ²⁹Jesus said to him, "Because you have seen Me, you have believed; blessed are those who have not seen and yet have believed."

The Purpose of John's Book

³⁰Jesus performed many other signs in the presence of His disciples, which are not written in this book. ³¹But these are written so that you may believe that Jesus is the Christ, the Son of God, and that by believing you may have life in His name.

John 21

Jesus Appears by the Sea of Tiberias

¹Later, by the Sea of Tiberias, Jesus again revealed Himself to the disciples. He made Himself known in this way: ²Simon Peter, Thomas called Didymus, Nathanael from Cana in Galilee, the sons of Zebedee, and two other disciples were together. ³Simon Peter told them, "I am going fishing." "We will go with you," they said. So they went out and got into the boat, but caught nothing that night. ⁴Early in the morning, Jesus stood on the shore, but the disciples did not recognize that it was Jesus. ⁵So He called out to them, "Children, do you have any fish?" "No," they answered. ⁶He told them, "Cast the net on the right side of the boat, and you will find some." So they cast it there, and

they were unable to haul it in because of the great number of fish. ⁷Then the disciple whom Jesus loved said to Peter, "It is the Lord!" As soon as Simon Peter heard that it was the Lord, he put on his outer garment (for he had removed it) and jumped into the sea. ⁸The other disciples came ashore in the boat. They dragged in the net full of fish, for they were not far from land, only about a hundred yards. ⁹When they landed, they saw a charcoal fire there with fish on it, and some bread. ¹⁰Jesus told them, "Bring some of the fish you have just caught." ¹¹So Simon Peter went aboard and dragged the net ashore. It was full of large fish,¹⁵³, but even with so many, the net was not torn. ¹²"Come, have breakfast," Jesus said to them. None of the disciples dared to ask Him, "Who are You?" They knew it was the Lord. ¹³Jesus came and took the bread and gave it to them, and He did the same with the fish. ¹⁴This was now the third time Jesus appeared to the disciples after He was raised from the dead.

Jesus Reinstates Peter

¹⁵When they had finished eating, Jesus asked Simon Peter, "Simon son of John, do you love Me more than these?" "Yes, Lord," he answered, "You know I love You." Jesus replied, "Feed My lambs." ¹⁶Jesus asked a second time, "Simon son of John, do you love Me?" "Yes, Lord," he answered, "You know I love You." Jesus told him, "Shepherd My sheep." ¹⁷Jesus asked a third time, "Simon son of John, do you love Me?" Peter was deeply hurt that Jesus had asked him a third time, "Do you love Me?" "Lord, You know all things," he replied. "You know I love You." Jesus said to him, "Feed My sheep. ¹⁸Truly, truly, I tell you, when you were young, you dressed yourself and walked where you wanted; but when you are old, you will stretch out your hands, and someone else will dress you and lead you where you do not want to go." ¹⁹Jesus said this to indicate the kind of death by which Peter would glorify God. And after He had said this, He told him, "Follow Me."

Jesus and the Beloved Apostle

²⁰Peter turned and saw the disciple whom Jesus loved following them. He was the one who had leaned back against Jesus at the supper to ask, "Lord, who is going to betray You?" ²¹When Peter saw him, he asked, "Lord, what

about him?" ²²Jesus answered, "If I want him to remain until I return, what is that to you? You follow Me!" ²³Because of this, the rumor spread among the brothers that this disciple would not die. However, Jesus did not say that he would not die, but only, "If I want him to remain until I return, what is that to you?" ²⁴This is the disciple who testifies to these things and who has written them down. And we know that his testimony is true. ²⁵There are many more things that Jesus did. If all of them were written down, I suppose that not even the world itself would have space for the books that would be written.

Please contact us at **lastchancemusic1@aol.com** *if you need a Bible and we will send you one at no cost. The price has been paid in full.*

Made in the USA
Monee, IL
31 July 2023

cb4259df-9899-4002-ba34-81754cf1d97bR01